POETRY AFTER MODERNISM

POETRY AFTER MODERNISM

EDITED BY

ROBERT McDOWELL

STORY LINE PRESS

1991

Library of Congress Catalog Card Number:
90-52850

ISBN: 0-934257-36-1 cloth
ISBN: 0-934257-35-3 paper

Book design by Lysa McDowell

Published by Story Press, Inc.
d.b.a. Story Line Press
Three Oaks Farm
Brownsville, OR
97327-9718

TABLE OF CONTENTS

INTRODUCTION

Most of the essays collected here were commissioned specifically for this book, which I first thought of producing four years ago. I intended to select essayists whose seminal critical work have changed the course of American poetry. Particularly in the eighties, these writers have consistently blasted stale rhetoric and forced the status quo back on its heels, creating in the process a small, select body of work that makes sense, finally, of Modernism and its aftermath.

In agreeing to write for this book, the authors accepted broad suggestions on topics, then followed their individual, aggressive instincts. We agreed that we did not aim to provide strict overviews of Modernism or polemical calls-to-arms, though elements of both appear in many of the essays. Rather, we sought to construct a definitive record of the opinions, analyses, and predictions of a new generation of American poet-critics, whose work in both forms will bridge the twentieth and twenty-first centuries.

Though many of these writers recently have been identified with the New Formalism and the New Narrative (referred to as the Expansive Movement in contemporary poetry), collectively they do not represent any group or movement here. On many points they strongly disagree, but arising out of this document of their discord and harmony is a shared conviction that the great forward sweep of Modernism ended long ago. As poetry in our time is threatened by cynical commercialization, illiteracy, institutionalization, and indifference, they share the belief that poetry must reject the recent decades of imitation and revaluation, and expand, both in subject and style, to create the most meaningful utterances of our national community.

Their work here represents a profound departure from the solipsism and small ambitions that characterize the grim bulk of most poetry in the latter half of the twentieth century. But their statements are not simply rebellious historical summations; they are forecasts, too, of the growing maturity and relevance of our first national art.

Robert McDowell
Brownsville, Oregon
March, 1990

POETRY AND POLITICS

By Frederick Pollack

1. IDEOLOGIES

With the advent of Fordist production, mass media and modern advertising, the assumptions and imaginative limits of all public discourse in America became those of the "middle class." The term notoriously designates a psychological rather than an economic order. The fact that almost everyone claims to belong to this order testifies to the triumph of words over facts. Among the deepest assumptions of this class are the following:

1) Individuality cannot be "reduced" to its social and economic determinants. If all of these could be listed, a core or essence of personality would remain. Personality as the middle class conceives it is oddly impersonal: each personality is equally unique and precious, each equally ineffable.

2) This timeless, hallowed core or essence is more important than any of the merely external factors that create empirical selves. Liberals admit the existence of these factors, in hopes of aiding the "better" self against them. Conservatives ascribe destiny to choice. For both, the ultimate unit of reality is the individual—not the economic system, class, race, sex, or their specific conjunctures.

3) Though in one respect it is absolute and ahistorical, personality is always in process. It can never be fully realized; realization, fulfillment, cannot even be

defined, yet one must always seek it. Conversely, fulfillment is what one seeks, whether the vehicle is a buying spree, cultism, a hard-won promotion, motherhood or "creativity."

4) In the search for fulfillment, feeling and intuition are surer guides than reason. The less articulable the emotion, the more poignant, and the more seriously it is to be taken. When the dichotomy between reason and feeling is denied (and the commonest gesture of middle-class thought is to triumph on paper over some dualism or other), it is denied at the expense of reason, not feeling.

5) It follows that what matters about a person is not the struggle he or she undertakes or is born into or implicated by, but a worldless subjectivity that can be only negatively defined. The self as it has made its way through our century is like a Third World economy, subject to endless exploitation and inflation. Moral terms for moral choices are replaced by psychologizing. Action is subsumed in "experience," experience in mood. Finally one cannot tell how passive one has become, since one's only measure is feeling rather than effect. And where all is feeling, where one's responsibility is to feel, feeling itself becomes wearisome.

> There's no way out.
> You were born to waste your life.
> You were born to this middleclass life
>
> As others before you
> Were born to walk in procession
> To the temple, singing.
>
> (Louis Simpson, "In the Suburbs")

Modern poetry, which is still almost exclusively a

lyric poetry, is the discourse in which these assumptions are most powerful. The result is that poetry seems not to be a *public* discourse at all, or to be only incidentally or vestigially public. It has become awkward to describe poetry as addressing anyone or addressing itself to anything. Current theory devaluates the idea of communication and that of mimesis: the reflection of reality a given communication communicates. Language is not predicated on communication; language is self-contained. Since it cannot demonstrate a world external to itself, it cannot build a bridge to that world. For the so-called Language poets, poetry is a non-discourse that neither reflects nor communicates anything, since both reflection and communication are illusions of language. The paradox we must confront is that the theoretical anti-subjectivism of much contemporary poetry, and its attendant critical visions of the self-created word, embody bourgeois subjectivism rather than negate it.

Literature necessarily communicates, though just as necessarily its communications are delayed, misperceived and unintended. If a poet abdicates conscious control over his words (like Jackson Mac Low in his chance-generated word-series, or various Beats or Surrealists playing with automatic writing), history will still force meaning upon them, and the responsibility for that meaning onto the poet. "Language" is as thin a disguise for a poet's ego as were the Freudian unconscious of the Surrealists and the Jungian unconscious of Bly.

To understand poetry politically, one must recognize that the poetry of a given era, like the individual poem, is about something. American poetry has been about private travail and private epiphany, and has defended bourgeois privilege by ignoring it. One ignores privilege by presenting it unproblematically. Privilege becomes the condition of one's consciousness, invisible because there is nothing to view it against; as in the poem quoted above, it becomes "life."

In their theoretical writings, American poets have attacked the subjectivism we are attacking. Hardly anyone in the poetic controversies of the last forty years has questioned the need for poetry to become more "accessible," less "elitist." But the cures poets attempt are new forms of the disease. Some poets reject theory as itself elitist, thereby relegating one of the most intellectually demanding human activities to the realm of hunch and dream. Other poets rationalize what they intend to write anyway. Language poets, using arguments similar to Robbe-Grillet's defense of the *nouveau roman*, pretend that their work expresses a popular "understanding," though few real people care to understand it. The apology for poetry in this century has resembled Lukacs' defense of Leninism: first the Symbol, then the Image, then the surreal image, then the spontaneous association, then the deliberately alogical association were supposed to correspond to the real need of the historic Reader—however faint the interest of merely empirical readers. In this way poetry has avoided, under the guise of pursuing, a reexamination of its social role.

In *From Modern to Contemporary: American Poetry 1945–1965*, James E. B. Breslin discusses five schools: the Beat Generation of Ginsberg, Lowell's Confessionalism, Olson's "Black Mountain," the "Deep Image" of Bly and Wright, and O'Hara's whimsical "Personism" (which set the tone and standards for the "New York School"). Two decades after the period Breslin describes, differences once thought substantive appear superficial, and as masks of a profound ideological consensus.

Olson advocated spontaneous linkage of perceptions, breaking free of received rhythms and received rationality. The "projective" poet is a technician of nerve-impulses. He may look outward, at "place" or history, but it is *his* history, and if "breath," Olson's divine afflatus, blows that way, the associations will be entirely and obscurely personal. The technique is supposed to circumvent the ego, which is conceived as a little bourgeois in the soul. One might ask, if ego is evaded, what does the associating.

Ginsberg's poet is a possessed bard, who alone can vouch for his possession. When he is possessed, anything he sings is important—transcendently true and honest, revolutionary by definition. (Until recently, Ginsberg never admitted the extensive editing that went into "Howl" and "Kaddish." Olson too was a careful editor, which would seem to contradict his theory.)

O'Hara insists that there are as many selves as there are perceptions, moods and situations. This blow against the supposedly rigid, work-bound bourgeois self would seem to imply an *oeuvre* like that of Fernando Pessoa, who became three different poets and two politically opposed journalists. But the values and sensibility that make up O'Hara are instantly recognizable in his work, and are its subject.

Of the poets Breslin discusses, only Lowell sought a public voice commensurate with political subject-matter. Though reluctant to theorize, Lowell understood that no story, especially one's own, is complete of itself. The better it is told the more it connects to other stories. Lowell's work is a record of oblique, hesitant approaches to a political stance and withdrawals from it.

In the 1980s, however, only the movement associated with Robert Bly, the late James Wright, and W. S.

Merwin retains an extensive following.

Bly did not invent and has often repudiated the phrase "Deep Image." He is stuck with it, however—and not unfairly: it is an adequate label for his poetics. Breslin summarizes a large number of Bly's lectures and essays:

[The theory] continually endorses inwardness and solitude, a descent to the unconscious which makes possible imaginative leaps, metaphoric transformations, images that arise from the depths of the psyche ... Arbitrary, private associations and ultimately solipsism constitute the dangers for poems evolved in accordance with this program ... but Bly actually makes the unconscious the basis for community. At the prelogical and primordial levels of his psyche the poet experiences ... an energy he shares with the natural world, with other human beings, and thus with readers.[1]

Regrettable as solipsism may be in the abstract, how does it endanger poetry?

Once Bly has turned his back on the ego and begun his dive into the psychic depths, he has left behind him all the mental gear that would allow him to judge particular images as good or bad ... The result is that, in theory at least, Bly has no alternative but to accept all images granted by the unconscious as sacred truths. This dilemma helps explain, in turn, Bly's wrathful impatience with writers who profess any interest in craft ... He really *does* mean it—he *has* to mean it—when he says that 'great poets merely are sensitive.'[2]

This criticism has political implications. Despite its apparent anarchism, Bly's theory is manipulative if not coercive. If the truth that is vital for everyone lives in the depths of dream and emotion rather than in observable social interaction, people, not just readers, need a guru to guide them to it. A reality conceived as physi-

cal, political and historical may be subject to obfusca-
tion and hard to understand; it is also homogeneous,
partly visible to everyone and in principle understandable. But a collective unconscious must ultimately be
taken on faith. Its supposed images never seem as universal as its partisans maintain, nor their significance
as clear, nor their usefulness as a guide to living as
self-evident.

A poetics, of course, is not poetry. The poems Bly
wrote against the Vietnam War are passionate and
memorable; his personal opposition was courageous.
The political and ecological poems of Merwin's *The Lice*
(1968) successfully combine protest with metaphysics.
Neither reader nor poet may count, however, on the
work being wiser than the theory, and the theory behind Deep Image poetry epitomizes the ideology we
have been discussing.

Detached from their original rationales (and, usually,
from any other), techniques and echoes from all five
schools make up the usual poetry-magazine offering,
the dull epiphany Donald Hall calls a "McPoem." Reality in this poem is seen as residing within the individual soul. No attempt need be made, therefore, to
make personal experience representative. Rather, the
fragmentariness of a reminiscence suggests its universality, just as the murky illogic of the symbols reveals
the depth from which they came.

The conventions of magazine verse have been ade-
quately described in Breslin's book and in Robert Pinsky's
The Situation of Poetry. The specifically political incom-
prehensions of some widely-followed poets are well
analyzed in Eliot Weinberger's recent essay collection,
Works on Paper. I have written elsewhere about the
Language school and its politics, and this essay will
not discuss in detail either Deep Image or Language

poets. The poets of the present decade whom I consider more important have resisted the formlessness, symbolism for symbolism's sake, Jungian mysticism and anti-intellectualism that have made the Deep Image so widely followed. At the same time they have rejected the opposite but equal self-indulgence sanctioned by Language theory: a hermetic academicism in leftist dress. There are other ways, however, to exclude political reality from one's work. This section will discuss the ideological stances of *Ashbery* and of several poets associated with the *New Formalism*. We shall see how these styles represent the breakdown of the middle-class consensus into more desperate and more nakedly class-bound ideologies. The next section will celebrate poetry that struggles in various ways against ideology and injustice. The contemporary poetry I feel is most vital—*Neo-Narrative* poetry—will be discussed in the next section.

Ashbery, the Language poets, some New Formalists and even a Neo-Narrative poet like Mark Jarman refer back to a common revered ancestor. During his lifetime, Wallace Stevens held an uneasy place apart in American poetry. ("Better than us; less wide," said Berryman.) Today in the universities, Stevens' work has replaced Eliot's as what Harold Bloom calls a "Chinese Wall of verse." Poetry in this position is only judged on its own terms. Eliot, unlike Stevens, helped to make himself impregnable by putting forth his terms in voluminous criticism. Such poetry is less a fact to be studied than a shibboleth to be invoked. Genuinely critical readings of it are discouraged; political readings especially are dismissed as "reductive." Only if the wall is breached, however, can we understand the poetry of its era.

Stevens' unique perspective, and the energy with which he applied it, derived from his position in the older, Eastern Establishment of the corporate-executive class. He was a singer of this class, not a propagandist: his anti-communist *Owl's Clover* was a failure, and suppressed; his support for Mussolini[3] —an attitude widespread among executives in the early '30s—went unproclaimed in his verse. His usual case against revolution is that it is an "affair of logical lunatics": the "grubby faith" of Marxism ignores the vital particulars that shatter any system (except one's own, which is, of course, not a system). The tenor of his work is overwhelmingly positive. Despair itself appears, in "The Auroras of Autumn," as a modulation into the minor of his main theme. One statement of this theme is that "The greatest poverty is not to live / In a physical world"; but to believe that empirical poverty determines imaginative poverty demonstrates the latter. Stevens expresses a sense of unlimited potency, a confidence in Imagination's ability to assimilate everything, a will to realize spirit in (commodified) matter. For Imagination read capitalism. I do not claim that Stevens intended this reading—only that his poetic ideology was the most refined form of the faith, almost forgotten now, that fueled the Detroit and Pittsburgh of his time. Roosevelt shared this faith; the Depression could not shake it; the War and Marshall Plan justified it. The poems in *Transport to Summer* allude to the uses of that war:

> At dawn
> The paratroopers fall and as they fall
> They mow the lawn.

("Esthetique du Mal")

We drank Meursault, ate lobster Bombay with mango
Chutney.

("Notes Towards a Supreme Fiction")

"Imagination" has to do with advertising. Managers
needed power and technological sophistication to control fantasy; but once they had that power, and could
coordinate work, fantasy and consumption, they could
define if not create selves. Stevens felt the pathos of
this process; it moved him more than particular selves
and fantasies, including his own. (His recent biogra-
phers err in assuming that petty-bourgeois assumptions
about the self, happiness, and the priority of inner over
outer apply to everyone.) Predictably, however, he placed
responsibility for self-construction back on the individual. He did so under the guise of praising "the Imagination" or "the mind." In his poems, people like the
Polacks in the park or the figures around the Emperor
of Ice Cream come in for harsh satire; their vulgarity
seems to consist of generating their own selves / fantasies, which are, in several senses, cheap. The "impersonality" of Stevens, his Olympian quality, does not
derive from avoidance of the personal, but from describing the process that *defines* the individual as if it
were a process *of* the individual—and the faculty that
permits, or invites, manipulation as if it were freedom
itself. Impersonality, however, is the after-image, not
the experience, of reading Stevens. If he is lovable as a
poet, it is precisely for the intimacy of his relation to
the reader. Any neurotic can bawl out on paper his
ugly pain or insipid guilt, and oppress by parading
weakness; but only Stevens can invite one, as it were,
up to his office in Hartford. His relation to the reader
is that of a fiduciary: Imagination is capital he can help
one to invest. "Money is a kind of poetry," he said;[4]

he could just as well have said the reverse.

Old money, heavy industry, and managers like Stevens led America through her brief Golden Age. This could be seen to have ended in April, 1975, and the clout and priorities of the "Eastern Establishment" did not long survive it. Military Keynesianism has replaced social investment. Finance, to a greater extent than in the '20s, floats free of production. Top executives demand ever more privilege, and more limits on other people's "entitlements"; middle ranks, increasingly insecure in their jobs, compete desperately; the corporate atmosphere combines pessimism and buccaneering. From the Reagan-Sunbelt stratum, of course, no kind of art can be expected. But the grim self-consciousness of today's managers is reflected in the work of Dana Gioia, a top executive with a major Eastern corporation.

"The Man in the Open Doorway"

This is the world in which he lives:
Four walls, a desk, a swivel chair,
A doorway with no door to close,
Vents to bring in air.

There are two well-marked calendars,
Some pencils, and a telephone
The women at the front desk answer
Leaving him alone.

There is a clock he hardly sees
Beside the window on the wall.
It moves in only one direction,
Never stops at all.

Outside the February wind
Scrapes up against the windowpane,

And a blue-green land is fading,
Scarred by streaks of rain.

The phones go off. The files are locked.
But the doorway still is lit at night
Like the tall window of a church
Bleached in winter light.

Sometimes the shadow of his hand
Falls from his desk onto the wall
And is the only thing that moves
Anywhere at all.

Or else he will drive back at night
To walk along the corridor
And, thinking of the day's success,
Trace his steps once more,

Then pause in a darkened stairway
Until the sounds of his steps have ceased
And stroke the wall as if it were
Some attendant beast.

Two sets of values contend for this poem, whose quiet tension and precise images point up the conflict. In one, the protagonist is an icy, power-hungry narcissist. He likes having "the women" as a buffer between him and the world and he likes being their superior. His love for himself drives him back to the office to listen to his footsteps and to stroke the wall; his shadow on it was not enough. Winter outside matches rigidity within, while the blue-green land of the affective self fades, and time, unregarded, works even more inexorably than the protagonist.

This reading can take us no further. It cannot account for the "church window" comparison. While the clock only moves in one direction, the hand "is the only thing that moves / Anywhere at all," i.e. purposefully. The landscape, scarred by spring, may be read as less coherent, less reflective of human will (this human will) than the office. The protagonist is perhaps narcissistic but he has a right to be: "success" is not mocked. In the last stanza the hero is a barbarian or feudal lord. His gesture shows an amoral delight in power which a middle-class reader might find hard to accept, unconsciously knowing that it comes at his expense. It is a feeling a poet ideologically close to the middle class would not have imagined.

In moving from Stevens to a newcomer and neoformalist like Gioia, on what is apparently the sole shared ground of corporate status, I could be accused of a literary Stalinism like Christopher Caudwell's. The comparison, however, is neither forced nor unfair. Stevens' and Gioia's class did not write their poetry, any more than the world of small and ever-failing business writes David Ignatow's. Social classes produce an indefinite number of talents who could write many different types of poetry, or none. But—deliberately and / or otherwise, and whether one describes the connection as one of "reflection" or "trace"—all poems embody the conditions of their production. Stevens expressed the confidence of managerial capitalism at the height of its power. His abstractness and grand manner suited that power. His class can no longer afford his vision. From the perspective of that class, explorations of the new, harsh, corporatist spirit like "The Man in the Open Doorway" are now more meaningful, and the old-world clang of rhyme sounds more valuable, than blank-verse metaphysics. Gioia's implied reader may also find poignancy in elegies for the older "humanist" values held by managers as individuals, elegies like Gioia's sad and lovely "In Cheever Country":

But splendor in ruins is splendor still,
even glimpsed from a passing train,
and it is wonderful to imagine standing
in the balustraded gardens above the river
where barges still ply their distant commerce.

Gioia is among the most talented of the younger New Formalists. Just as a taste for rhyme and meter has not prevented some of these poets from doing capable work in free verse, formalism alone implies no particular ideology. The traditional avant-garde prejudice that a received form is, in some innate sense, politically reactionary has been discredited—not least by Language poets' chronic dismissal of all forms but their own as both reactionary and received. Probably the most effective leftist poems now being written in English—within the confines of the lyric—are the highly-wrought sonnets of Tony Harrison.

The exemplars of American formalism, however, are not politically outspoken poets like Harrison (or, on the other side, Hill and Sisson), but Richard Wilbur, Anthony Hecht and James Merrill. The deep conservatism of their work is not a matter of explicit commitment but of class assumption. Hecht mourns, Merrill celebrates the isolation that comes with wealth and leisure; but for both, a refined delectation is the point of things. When this poetry looks at other classes it is unconsciously but painfully condescending. The reminiscences of Shirley Carson, fat drunk amidst whoopee cushions in Hecht's "The Short End," exist only to prove that one can be utterly prole and still feel the same cosmic loneliness as Hecht. In "House Sparrows," "pictures of Biafra and Auschwitz" are compared to the frail bones of the birds (who end the poem by singing "'Summers, Summers, Summers'"). The character-

istic gesture of this poetry is to replace the social /
historical fact with an art work, or with an artifact or
natural object treated like an art work. The risk of this
gesture is that, rather than elucidating reality, the metaphor diminishes it, evades the threat it poses, and dif-
fuses the emotion it evokes. Both Hecht and Wilbur
are aware of substituting art for fact. Hecht, in such
poems as "Still Life" and the elegy for Santayana, portrays the gesture as unsatisfying, immoral or destruc-
tive; "The Deodand" terrifyingly demonstrates that
"Exactions shall be made, an expiation, / A forfeiture."
Yet Hecht can find no other posture to adopt toward
experience. Wilbur meanwhile sees aestheticization as
a necessary, even a praiseworthy, aspect of his understanding:

"Looking Into History"

Five soldiers fixed by Mathew Brady's eye
Stand in a land subdued beyond belief.
Belief might lend them life again. I try
Like orphaned Hamlet working up his grief

To see my spellbound fathers in these men
Who, breathless in their amber atmosphere,
Show but the postures men affected then
And the hermit faces of a finished year.

The guns and gear and all are strange until
Beyond the tents I glimpse a file of trees
Verging a road that struggles up a hill.
They're sycamores.
                              The long-abated breeze

Flares in those boughs I know, and hauls the sound
Of guns and a great forest in distress.
Fathers, I know my cause, and we are bound
Beyond that hill to fight at Wilderness.

What is lost is not the sense of other people—they are there insofar as they can be observed—but any hope of a relationship that would go beyond observation and an occasional *egoisme a deux*. This kind of poetry works (most effectively, I think, in Hecht's longer narratives like "The Venetian Vespers") when one feels the private horror lurking behind the aestheticism and demanding it. Otherwise, a privileged and narrow sensibility is passed off as universal. A pall of good taste descends; neither outrage nor generous pity seem appropriate in the poem—or anywhere. It is in terms of this limited social and emotional horizon that the current American formalism may be said to derive from Wallace Stevens; but where Stevens was a confident manager, these poets are wistful coupon-clippers. Only a few poets whose names may be associated with this movement (the gnomic, historically perceptive Turner Cassity, the caustic Southern satirist R. S. Gwynn), have tried in any way to dramatize political conflict. To date, however, the most famous New Formalist attempt at a social vision has been Frederick Turner's.

In a recent interview in the *Southwest Review*, Turner, doyen of the formalist "Expansive Movement," defended his epic *The New World*, bestowed laurels upon Merrill, Gioia and others, and upheld "tonality, the figurative, the representational in the visual arts, and meter and the great poetic genres, and plot in the novel"[5] on neurological, cultural and ethical grounds. In the interview the word "we" is used continually, yet without hint of qualification or self-questioning. "We" are by turns Expansive poets, poets, the West, and all mankind. Turner does not dwell on which modernists, postmodernists, cultural pessimists etc. he opposes; he specifies only friends' viewpoints. "The new poet," he states, "has to be able to take in our whole mass of science, politics, philosophies, and conflicting religious and ideological systems" in order to become "a clear and beautiful voice of action for the whole culture."[6] He neglects to say where poets should position themselves in this mass, or what the voice should say. One gathers it should defend "excellence," which seems to mean whatever executives mean when they invoke the word before layoffs. To the question, "When was it that poets combined all of the disciplines of wisdom to make poetry?" Turner replies:

> ... we have managed, at times, through some kind of great summative effort of economic cleverness, of real economic genius ... A lot of this is a matter of the creation of wealth, which is, perhaps, in its lower levels, pretty crass—but you have to have that—and out of that comes the flower of technology, and out of that comes the flower of science, and out of that comes the flower of art...[All] of the requirements...are present right now here in America.[7]

Many of Turner's points are well taken: the need for poets to respect science, the decadence of the modern lyric, the potential vitality of a revived epic and the realization that "All of this is a matter of economics." The meanings he gives his terms are typically Neo-conservative: evasive, sentimental and self-serving.

Even a traditionalist should try to "make it new," and this Turner fails to do in *The New World*. His impulse was sound; science fiction offers the epic poet new plots, new approaches to character, more broadly integrative perspectives—new myths, in short. The poem uses none of them. Turner justly complains that the *New York Times* and other reviewers were hostile to the poem because it was science fiction. Unfortunately, he has followed the worst of the genre. *The New World* is a romance, with horses and knights in armor, transposed to 2376. The horses and knights are eugenically improved, the swords have microprocessors and the armor is laserproof ceramic, but it makes no difference: the relationships are feudal, the emotions courtly-love. The book does not so much extrapolate as stylize the present, weighting conflicts and values the poet considers real. What is good in post-petroleum "Ahiah" are small Jeffersonian city-states, whose people are happy, intelligent, energetic, devoted to small business and to a religion for which great claims are made but which seems to be a cross between Episcopalianism and yoga. Predictably, questions such as what keeps the businesses small are lost in a golden haze. Multinational corporations also exist: they dot the landscape with benign, clever small peddlers and franchisers. The Ahians have been at war for centuries with the "Mad Counties," fundamentalist Christians of the sort you love to hate. In Ahiah all this testing has led to the natural selection of "The Hero" (labeled as such), James George Quincy, and "The Heroine," Ruth McCloud. (I should point out that the whole scene is *very* Wasp. Turner, like Robert Heinlein, believes in breeding; in his forthcoming epic, he has announced, one noble line is entrusted with the terraforming of Mars.) The remaining social groups of *The New World* are the Burbs and the Riots. The Riots are the former cities, inhabited by crazy violent matriarchal anarchists. You just know what color these are, but wait!—The Hero is counseled by wise old Kingfish, who lives in the sewers beneath Hattan Riot and talks like ... Kingfish. The Burbs are the former suburbs. Their relation to the Riots is summed up by a Sears rep; the poem gives us no reason to doubt that his analysis represents the author's:

No Rioter works, as you know; work
infringes their freedom; the world owes them a living.
But Burbians work, to pay the Rioters' levies,

and sometimes keep something by between burnings and
taxes.
Burbians (pardon me, Ma'am) have no balls to speak of
and Rioters scare them shitless. The Burbian Government
(which used to be called the Uess Federal Government)
is controlled by the Riots.

Frankly I find this despicable: a projection by the
suburban bourgeoisie onto the people who clean its
toilets. In Frederick Turner the ethos of Reaganism has
found its poetic voice.

The poet most often cited as Stevens' successor is
John Ashbery. The critic who has been the most powerful champion of both poets has phrased their relation in terms of the Romantic Imagination. This is a
kind of minor *Weltgeist* or demiurge which transmi-
grates from poet to poet and whose sole task is to proclaim or to despair of (or to proclaim and then despair
of) its abilities. Originally revolutionary, the Romantic
Imagination is now, at best, vaguely liberal. It can afford to be indifferent to politics or, in the case of Yeats
or Stevens, to permit reprehensible politics, because
politics are merely a crude image of itself. With each
incarnation, the Romantic Imagination finds it harder
and harder to believe in itself, i.e. to believe that the
mind creates rather than reflects reality. The cycle from
self-faith to self-despair and back begins closer to the
despair pole in Ashbery than in Stevens, and Ashbery's
language is correspondingly jazzier, more disorderly.
But the struggle the two oeuvres enact is the same: a
struggle for faith in itself, and in the self of the poet
who writes it.

Ashbery's real relation to Stevens cannot be perceived
in these terms. As we have seen, "Imagination" in Stevens involves the creation of valued commodities. The

reader is not an equal, but a close subordinate being trained to handle mediated reality and manipulable desire. Narrative stance in Stevens must be coherent, even where narration and persona are most at issue; it is the line of command. Ashbery's narration is incoherent. "The personal pronouns in my work," he says:

"very often seem to be like variables in an equation. 'You' can be myself or it can be another person ... and so can 'he' and 'she' for that matter and 'we' ... my point is also that it doesn't really matter very much, that we are some-how all aspects of a consciousness giving rise to the poem and the fact of addressing someone, myself or someone else, is what's the important thing at that particular mo-ment rather than the particular person involved. I guess I don't have a very strong sense of my own identity and I find it very easy to move from one person in the sense of a pronoun to another ...which I again feel is a means to-ward a greater naturalism."[8]

For the word "poem" substitute "society" or "com-modity"; the sense of the statement will be the same. The voice is that of a masterless subordinate, unable to see how things work. If Stevens was an investment broker, Ashbery is a consumer. He sees the same proc-esses as Stevens (except that "The system was break-ing down": *Three Poems*, 1972). But he has no power over these processes. Reluctant even to conceive of such power, he decides that "we" have it. He is on the re-ceiving end. Militant consumption has little to do with hedonism—like Faust, the consumer is damned if he cries "Stay!" to the moment—and is actively opposed to "taste." Or rather, in an economy of accelerated and manipulated fads, taste is anti-taste. Endlessly eclec-tic, it thrives on attempts to anticipate it, and creates an atmosphere of unfocused irony which dissolves sat-ire and corrodes values. It destroys the past by sentimentalizing it until memory itself becomes first questionable, then laughable. Finally, when there is no value, anything can be equated with (sold for) anything. I am describing, among other things, a poetic.

The above may sound harsh; if Ashbery is about shopping, one of his grander efforts like "Self-Portrait in a Convex Mirror" is like a really great mall: the Beverly Center in Los Angeles, where there are Italian fashions, art movies, and bookstores with books that defend or attack malls. The "Self-Portrait" is generally a defense:

> We don't need paintings or
> Doggerel written by mature poets when
> The explosion is so precise, so fine.
> Is there any point even in acknowledging
> The existence of all that? Does it
> Exist? Certainly the leisure to
> Indulge stately pastimes doesn't,
> Any more. Today has no margins, the event arrives
> Flush with its edges, is of the same substance,
> Indistinguishable. "Play" is something else;
> It exists, in a society specifically
> Organized as a demonstration of itself.
> There is no other way, and those assholes
> Who would confuse everything with their mirror games
> Which seem to multiply stakes and possibilities, or
> At least confuse issues by means of an investing
> Aura that would corrode the architecture
> Of the whole in a haze of suppressed mockery,
> Are beside the point. They are out of the game,
> Which doesn't exist until they are out of it.
> It seems like a very hostile universe
> But as the principle of each individual thing is
> Hostile to, exists at the expense of all the others
> As philosophers have often pointed out, at least
> *This* thing, the mute, undivided present
> Has the justification of logic...

Marjorie Perloff and Robert van Hallberg are critics whose models of literature admit more heteronomy than Harold Bloom's, though they dislike political concerns as much as he. Ashbery's style invites any number of equally confident readings—and in English departments nowadays his coattails are wide. Perloff and van Hallberg place him against the widest horizon they can imagine, that of systems theory. Perloff quotes a description of Ashbery's "'mental space humming with signal and noise, focus and blur'," and speaks of "a litany for the computer age."[9] For her, such lines as "Today has no margins, the event arrives / Flush with its edges" link Ashberian discourse to the overtoneless, value-free, purely tactical style of computer "messages." Why is this a good thing, or sufficient reason for me to like Ashbery? Perloff never says. Van Hallberg does:

> "The optimism of systems analysis derives from a belief that much of what appears disordered is in fact complexly ordered, and that the conflicts inherent in economic, political, and social activity can be reduced by the proper coordination of competing factors. This kind of optimism is characteristically American in seeing a way around political and ideological confrontation. When Ashbery and Creeley engage the figures of systems analysis, they are testing this strain of American social thought and, it must be admitted, suggesting how the easily parodied American trust in understanding, planning, and ingenuity provides terms and figures sufficiently rich to illuminate our experiences of loneliness, maturation, love, and the coming of spring."[10]

Whatever else may be said about it, this claim is at odds with the sharply confrontational, even Hobbesian passage we have quoted. In that passage, "assholes," I think, refers to Marxists ("aura" may allude to Walter

Benjamin), and to other readers who believe poetry should "mirror" reality or that it does so whether it wants to or not. These tedious people do not realize that even what they call "mature" discourse is "doggerel." Their "games" speciously "multiply stakes and possibilities" in a life and a society that otherwise could be taken merely as a "game." In fact, American society must be seen as "'play'"; that is its "logic," the "principle" by which it "exists at the expense of all the others." To demand referential (i.e. critical) meaning here is as outmoded as to expect poetry to be "stately" (a set of opinions, perhaps, on the coming of spring). Such a demand corrodes "the architecture / of the whole" with "mockery."

Ashbery seems to be projecting here; one wonders whom he is assuring that "There is no other way." But one needn't worry: the mall would not be great if it did not also sell tasteful, assimilated criticism of itself. "Description of a Masque" (in the recent *A Wave*) is full of this, though characteristically deflected toward easy targets: the "Goddess Mania," who seems to be the Self (poet's or reader's), blames the poet for not being lyrical enough, not writing about *her*:

"I'm used to not blending in with the environment—it's my business not to. But I thought you were going to take me away from all that, to some place where scenery made no difference any more... "

What follows, however, is a remarkable *ars poetica*:

Then we all realized what should have been obvious from the start: that the setting would go on evolving eternally, rolling its waves across our vision like an ocean, each one new yet recognizably a part of the same series, which was creation itself. Scenes from movies, plays, operas, televi-

sion; decisive or little-known episodes from history; pre-
natal and other early memories from our own solitary,
separate pasts; events yet to come from life or art; calami-
ties or moments of relaxation; universal or personal tragedies; or little vignettes from daily life that you just had to
stop and laugh at, they were so funny, like the dog chas-
ing its tail on the living-room rug ... And the corollary of
all this was that we would go on witnessing these tableaux, not that anything prevented us from leaving the
theater, but there was no alternative to our interest in finding out what would happen next. This was the only thing
that mattered for us, so we stayed on although we could
have stood up and walked away in disgust at any moment.

Ascribing creativity to the stream of life or to what
"evolves," equating life with society, society with media,
and art with entertainment, and insisting on his role
as epicure spectator, Ashbery justifies his claim to "a
greater naturalism." This in turn invites an eventual
shrug from readers who may find his work amusing,
but to whom what's on next is not the only thing that
matters, nor acceptance the only course.

2. STRUGGLE

Poetry a reader can admire may not be poetry a poet
can emulate. Critics avoid this distinction by leaving
it implicit. Marxist critics also avoid it, but at greater
cost than their colleagues. For the circumstances in which
the most effective political poetry is written are very
different from those of any North American poet. They
are circumstances of collective struggle.

Under total censorship, to circulate an illicit love-
poem is an act of rebellion. Under partial censorship,

people read with passionate interest between the lines. Poetry need not be great to arouse this interest: in 1956, Yevtushenko was all his people legally had and he filled stadia. The political content of poetry may be especially hard to translate. In Poland, the cool aphorisms of "Mr. Cogito," Zbigniew Herbert's longtime persona, have a resonance his American admirers can only imagine. It would require study for me to understand what Wole Soyinka's fellow-countrymen think, reading the lyrics he wrote in darkness, on the insides of cigarette packages, while in prison protesting the massacre of Biafra. Political poetry that is unequivocal in its times may have different uses to posterity. Marti is quoted both by Radio Havana and by the Miami radio station that bears his name. One hopes that the poems Yannis Ritsos wrote in the prisons of three fascist dictatorships will never again be banned in Greece, yet there are circumstances where he would want them banned. And one wonders if the mimeographed sonnets of the exiled George Faludy, which now pass from hand to hand in Hungary, will be given elegant editions centuries hence. Faludy himself has no doubts:

> "To a Friend on His Acceptance of
> Hungary's Chief Literary Award"
>
> They'll never give me such a medal,
> Not in a thousand years they won't!
> Not me, because of what I write;
> But you, because of what you don't.

Finally, one cannot assume that good poetry is all on one side. Cuban poetry includes that of Heberto Padilla, imprisoned by the Revolution, and that of the young poets of the Saiz Brothers Brigade whom the Revolution taught to write. Some poets, like MacDiarmid apotheosizing Stalin, lie to themselves at the cost of intellect and integrity. Others, like Yeats, Pound, Gottfried Benn in 1933 and Takamura Kotaro in 1942, serve evil.

We might be satisfied to say that history is what makes poetry political, depoliticizes it, or repoliticizes it in new positions, and that any poem may be politically rationalized. Some poets, however, are not satisfied, either with "revolutionary tourism" or the eventual luck of the draw. They seek a form that is immediately, unequivocally and inherently revolutionary, and they seek to write good poetry in that form. Poetry that seeks this goal may be called poetry in struggle. The examples we shall discuss are based on different standards than any we have yet considered, imply different relations between poet and audience, and impose different distinctions between the admirable and the useful.

> I was walking on the shore and they took me in the ship
> And they throw me overboard
> And I swam right out of the belly of the whale
> And I never get weary yet
> They put me in jail and I did not do no wrong
> And I never get weary yet
> Say they put me in jail and I didn't get no bail
> And I never get weary yet
> Never get weary yet
>> I know I was from before
>> Christopher Columbus
>> And I was born before
>> The Arawak Indians
>> Trod in creation
>> Before this nation
>> I'll always remember
>> I can't forget
>> Never get weary yet

> (F. "Toots" Hibbert, Jamaican reggae poet;
> from "Never Get Weary")

Listening to recorded performances of Hibbert, Onuora,
Linton Kwesi Johnson, then reading their words in Paula
Burnett's Penguin anthology of Caribbean poetry, an
American poet envies the reciprocity between singer
and audience. The verse traditions associated with reg-
gae and calypso facilitate the transmission of news,
political analysis and propaganda, and a high degree
of community involvement. Since Independence, the
folk poetries of Jamaica, Trinidad / Tobago and other
new nations of the region have been as critical of home-
grown injustices as of neocolonialism. Literary poets
like Derek Walcott, Edward Braithwaite and James Berry
have drawn on these traditions and on the experience
of the Caribbean diaspora. Their work continues to speak
for and to a community, as in Walcott's great elegy
for a calypsonian:

> All those who promise free and just debate,
> then blow up radicals to save the state,
> who allow, in democracy's defense,
> a parliament of spiked heads on a fence,
> all you go bawl out, "Spoils, things ain't so bad."
> is human nature, Spoiler, after all,
> it ain't big genocide, it just bohbohl;
> safe and conservative, 'fraid to take side,
> they say that Rodney commit suicide,
> is the same voices that, in the slave ship,
> smile at their brothers, "Boy, is just the whip,"
> I free and easy, you see me have chain?
> A little censorship can't cause no pain,
> a little graft can't rot the human mind,
> what sweet in goat-mouth sour in his behind.
> So I sing with Attila, I sing with Commander,
> what right in Guyana, right in Uganda.
> The time could come, it can't be very long
> when they will jail calypso for picong,

for first comes television, then the press,
all in the name of Civic Righteousness;
it has been done before, all Power has
made the sky shit and maggots of the stars ...

(from "The Spoiler's Return")

To live, said Gramsci, is to take sides. What distinguishes the poetry of collective struggle is its ability to escape the unconscious conventions limiting what people of a dominant class, nation or culture feel, see and say. Poets of a group in struggle, if they have talent as well as commitment, can say "I" without narcissism and "we" without forcing, while the oppressive "they" becomes, however implicitly, a "you" addressed from strength. The characteristic note of such work is therefore one of confidence. To the outsider such confidence seems heroic and paradoxical, like religious faith. One hears it in some Chicano poetry, in Jimmy Santiago Baca and Gary Soto. It also exists in some Black poetry: in Hughes and Brooks and in a poet shamefully ignored by whites, Henry Dumas:

"Kef 106"

The Mosaics are a people filled with color.
They are a people born because
God is just and loves the just.
The Mosaics sing, dance, and pray in color.

"Kef 107"

The holidays of the Mosaics are legends of color.
Number one
is the Holy Day of Red.
Number two
is the Holy Day of Black.

Number three is the Holy Day of Green
Number four is the Holy Day of Blue.
Number five is the Holy Day of Yellow.
Number six is the Holy Day of Blindness.

But this quality, which we are inadequately calling confidence, appears only intermittently in any American poetry. The phrase "collective struggle" cannot apply in the same way to a minority in the metropole as to the majority population of a former colony. American racial minorities are subject to the atomization of experience that besets all social classes, and whose effects are amplified by the ghetto. (Dumas was shot to death at 34.) "We" for a minority poet is an abstraction, though less of one than for a white. It implies a shared history and a shared victimization. It does not mean a Sartrean group-in-fusion engaged in organized resistance. The word "we" can be used with complete honesty only where one needn't watch one's back. To pretend otherwise is sentimentalism, of the political sort that in America is called "rhetoric." Militant statements, and poems, of racial and other minorities are often sentimental in this sense.

Black poets facing this quandary have responded in several ways. The career of Amiri Baraka has been a series of attempts to quantify "we." From the Beat Generation to Black Nationalism to Marxism-Leninism he has sought the true, representative vanguard. (Critics who mock this pursuit are generally comfortable in their own contexts.) In the course of his search, Baraka has had repeatedly and painfully to ask whether the black cause can be separately won.

Other poets refuse to be "black poets"—refuse, as they see it, to limit themselves. This decision is understandable but it has its risks; they are posed by the first person plural. All the available forms of this pronoun—the phenomenological "we" of Stevens, Ashbery's decentered performative, the "we" that sometimes issues from the Deep Image, the bland caress of magazine verse, and the "we" of newscasters and politicians—ignore real contradictions, and exclude through false universality. They are discriminatory in themselves, and remain so when a minority poet uses them.

The third way in which black and other minority poets try to speak collectively but unrhetorically is to insist, within the lyric, on the real circumstances of their lives. Poetic diction today is a set of props, the "moon, snow, light" etc. Pinsky has satirized. The landscape of Wanda Coleman's work, and its concerns, are real:

"Murder"

by arson. the yente landlady
who keeps calling me up to tell me how much
she hates to evict us
for blacks, we're nice people

by mass gassing in ovens. the automobile
manufacturers of america who mated
the car to planned obsolescence

by hanging. my employer
who's figured out
how badly i need this shit job

by bullet. my lover and my girlfriend
who slept together over my dead body
then resurrected me for
parasexual trial

by starvation. my ex-husband
who never has a card or kind word
for his children

by poison. the me
who has faith in people

Coleman is a poet I admire; no one poem I wanted
to include was fully representative. She is capable of
great economy:

"On Green Money Street"

unable to buy things
he moves away
sheets cold white still avenues
i wait, anxious beneath the solitary lamp
listen for the echo of his steps

he never shows

at sunrise
i move on with the traffic

This style can be described as a lyrical naturalism,
and as such it faces two sets of problems. The stylistic
burden of all naturalism is specialized vocabulary, which
includes vernacular speech as well as jargon. Both carry
their own contexts into the text:

it's done by computer. no mirrors here
this strange magic of certification / proof
of existence (we do not live until our papers
are stored, our numbers assigned)

(from "At Vital Statistics")

Here metaphor is defeated by the language, and the
reality, of bureaucratic procedure. The conflict would
make the passage weak, even if the metaphors were
stronger; no "magic" can survive "certification." The

point is of wider relevance, for the bathos of Sixties (and later) "political" poetry—Denise Levertov's, Carolyn Forché's—results from this conflict of vocabularies. Poets like Robert Duncan, who inflate metaphor into "vision" (during one demonstration, a university official turned into a dragon even as Duncan watched), fare even worse. A poetry whose sole aim is metaphor, whether or not it views metaphor as man's link to the collective unconscious, must write itself into a ghetto of poetic diction. Coleman, whose goal is a portrait of one woman in her times, uses the language of those times. To avoid being used by it, she employs guerrilla tactics: careful selection, sudden assaults, ambiguous messages. Even in the above passage, one notices the biblical resonance of "our numbers assigned." Putting multiple overtones in an apparently deadpan last line, unifying the poem's languages, is a technique she uses to better effect elsewhere.

The other danger of naturalistic lyric is that it will be read as the record of one person's adventures. Coleman invites this when she describes her readings; Bukowski is unconvincing as a voice from the underclass when he dwells on the recognition writing has brought him. But the problem lies primarily with the audience. A willingness to compare experience and draw social conclusions must be brought to any work. No one work can create it. As it retreats into solipsism, the bourgeois sensibility loses the capacity to identify with characters it cannot perceive as bourgeois: whose problems are more than mere "problems." The protagonists of both art and entertainment (if the distinction remains) have become as atomized as readers and viewers; "minimalist" novels, like movies or sitcoms, are "about this guy who... "

The primacy of the lyric in the poetry of the last

century has been a response to capitalism's integration of the self into increasingly heteronomous structures, and like every aspect of individualist ideology it serves what it tries to oppose. Naturalistic lyric may perhaps sustain the subtlety of analysis and the war of vocabularies modern political poetry requires. It fails, however, on grounds where lyricism as a whole is inadequate. These are: 1) Beyond a certain point, one cannot assume that one's feelings and experiences are representative. 2) Nor can one assume that what one feels about another's experience is important with respect to that experience. 3) Nor can one assume that the subjective component of a situation is the most meaningful.

The *Neo-Narrative* current in contemporary poetry consists of young and not-so-young poets who have drawn these conclusions, and have identified the central weakness of modern poetry as the "lyrical imperative" followed by all its schools. They believe that a poetry reoriented towards story-telling and authorial impersonality may regain, and may deserve to regain, a reputation for wisdom. Only a few neo-narrativists, however, accept the primacy of political forces over the experience they seek to reflect. One of them is the young Detroit poet Jim Daniels. The theme of Daniels' first book, *Places /Everyone*[11], is capitalism's betrayal of its most loyal workers, the betrayal known as "deindustrialization."

It is instructive to compare Daniels' work with that of another Detroit native, Phil Levine. In the early '70s, Levine was widely regarded as the long-awaited Lefty of poetry. No reader can mistake this poet's identification with working people, his sense of struggles past and elsewhere, or the cumulative power of his long, short-lined stanza. These strengths are vitiated by received ideas of how a poet signifies Significance. Complex social and family situations are presented as tableaux rather than as stories. Feelings and private associations of characters are emphasized though the characters are barely distinct. The main character is "I." And even the moving "On the Murder of Lieutenant Jose del Castillo by the Fascist Bravo Martinez, July 12, 1936" is marred by generalizing mannerisms reminiscent of the Deep Image. The fact that the murder is political, and the specific politics involved, are revealed only by the title. Without the title the situation is vague and the rhetoric of the poem seems inflated. There is a discrepancy between the passive figure, shot four times and falling toward the pavement, and the symbol he is made into: "he knew only / that he would not die ... ," "heaven was nowhere and in his eyes / slowly filling with their own light ... " The unstated message of the poem is entrusted to a highly abstract Nature, as if the poet expected no real response to it:

> There is more
to be said, but by someone who has suffered
and died for his sister the earth
and his brothers the beasts and the trees.
The Lieutenant can hear it, the prayer
that comes on the voices of water, today
or yesterday, from Chicago or Valladolid...

Jim Daniels has rid his work of this kind of gesturing. Precise, circumstantial, his lines both expect and command attention. For the most part he straightforwardly tells stories. Even when these are in the first person and involve the poet's family, the self is not their subject. The stories are parts of a larger story, which is also present in the two "Still Lives":

"#2, Parking Lot, Ford Sterling Plant"

Empty pallets stacked against the fence,
a few cars scattered across the blacktop,
a barren landscape decaying under grey sky.

167 days since the last work-loss accident
This lot under closed-circuit surveillance
Authorized personnel only

An empty bag blown flush against the fence.
A set of keys in the middle of an aisle.
A flattened oil can, a lottery ticket,
a paperback with no cover.

There's a man in this picture.
No one can find him.

Part Two of Daniels' book concerns—literally addresses—a man named Digger, a middle-aged Detroit
auto worker with a wife, a son and two daughters. At
one point Digger and "the girls" go on vacation:

At the beach
your foot in the sand
outlines the part
you weld onto axles.

"What's that, Daddy?"
You kick sand
over the drawing.
"Nothin'."
But no matter how many times
you kick the sand
it still looks like
something.

And eventually we see "Digger Laid Off":

Tonight you beat up four little kids
to get a baseball at Tiger Stadium.
After the game you sit in a bar
watching fat naked women
rub mud over their bodies.
You throw your ball in the mud pit
and a dancer picks it up
rubs it over her muddy crotch
and throws it back to you.
In the parking lot
you throw the ball against a windshield
but it will not crack.

It is possible that poets will escape the "lyrical imperative" through genres other than narrative; what matters is that they escape. The late-Romantic lyric— which remains, variously disguised, the prevalent genre of our poetry—ignores, distorts or de-emphasizes conflict. It imposes a synchronic vision or pretense of vision on diachronic reality. History, that is, becomes a series of snapshots, with the poet in every scene. Since "narrative" became a buzzword, many mainstream poets, making no serious attempt at plot, character, dialogue, drama or authorial distance, have pretended that albums or collages of such snapshots are new narrative forms. The poet who wishes to write genuine narrative, with original plots and convincing characters, must 1) respect time, 2) locate elements of struggle in apparently inert situations, and 3) observe without sentiment. These are basic requirements of political consciousness, which is why narrative poetry especially may reflect and further it.

Our critique of bourgeois poetry, our goal of poetry in struggle, and the poems we have cited as examples of the latter may all be deemed inadequate on various grounds. One is that the poetry of the printed page,

whether lyric or narrative, "experimental" or traditionalist, is obsolete; struggle must now be waged by other
means. This is the position of Anthony Easthope in
his *Poetry as Discourse*:

> Lucien Goldmann writes that 'The most important conse-
> quence of the development of a market economy is that
> the individual... becomes... an independent element, a sort
> of monad, a *point of departure*.' In underwriting this view
> the present study has sought to analyse bourgeois poetic
> discourse as producing ... a position for the supposedly
> unified 'individual' as 'point of departure' for discourse
> rather than its effect. The term 'bourgeois' describes such
> a discourse as characterizing not just a period but an ep-
> och of history. But if this epoch is over—or if not over, at
> least since 1848 in its terminal crisis—what happens to the
> poetic discourse appropriate to it? It can hardly be denied
> that the canonical tradition, the poetry of the 'single voice',
> is now dying both from inward exhaustion and external
> erosion. Since the work of the great Modernists sixty years
> ago—work whose project anyway was to subvert the in-
> herited discourse—where has that tradition shown unmis-
> takable signs of its continuing vitality? Charles Olson, for
> example, asserts that poetry can only move forward 'by
> getting rid of the lyrical interference of the individual as
> ego, of the "subject" and his soul,' a principle which dis-
> misses all the tradition stands for. Bourgeois poetic dis-
> course now has no real audience. It is kept alive only in a
> tainted and complicit form. The state promotes it in sec-
> ondary and higher education ... Meanwhile, people are much
> more interested in such genuinely contemporary media as
> cinema, television and popular song in its many varieties
> ... Most poetry in most epochs has been linked intimately
> with music and dancing, and so with a range of social
> institutions ... There seems no reason to believe that the
> canonical tradition will continue and no particular reason
> to regret [this]. There seem good grounds to suppose that
> poetic discourse will live on, especially if it is reunited
> with music and even with dancing as well.[12]

Easthope has useful things to say about the social conjunctures behind the rise of iambic pentameter, the consecutive English styles, and the "supposedly unified 'individual'," but his conclusion is overstated. What is the difference between a bourgeois poet and a poet? Has the latter no future if unwilling to learn rock guitar? A certain professorial nearsightedness is evident, not only in dating the *terminal* crisis of capitalism to the publication of the *Communist Manifesto*, but in the evaluation of Olson. We have seen how ostensibly radical critiques of lyrical subjectivism, Olson's included, have only provided it with new metaphors. Olson's work, though only recently accepted by English departments, was always fully canonical in Easthope's sense. More important, it is very much a poetry of the "single voice." So are most rock lyrics. Masses of adolescents hearing their own unexamined rage blaring back at them experience a collective smugness and a collective self-pity. These reactions have nothing to do with either revolutionary action or self-understanding; many of the young suicides of this decade died to music. The biases of "genuinely contemporary media" are scarcely *less* bourgeois than poetry's. These media are simply more accessible to people who have, with their help, grown up passive, confused and illiterate.

Easthope's populism is extended, however, by Roger Taylor of Sussex University, author of *Art: an Enemy of the People* and *Beyond Art*. Borrowing a label, Taylor introduces his own category of the "as if." Modern mass entertainment allows people to feel, and even to behave, as if they were free—i.e. participating in, even somehow creating, "independent worlds" of power and pleasure. This state can result from passive activities like watching television or from active ones like slam-dancing. Cultural elitists may call it an illusion of freedom, but a feeling cannot be illusory; Taylor equates the feeling of freedom with freedom. The feeling occurs, as yet, within certain limits. Pleasure, however, is explosive, and pushes those limits outward. Some "entertainment objects" may be abstractly admirable, on moral, formal, or political grounds. This fact does not make of them a separate realm, "higher" than other entertainment. Given economic progress, the demand for which it excites, the "as if" state entertainment induces may lead to the defeat of the reality principle and of all other repressive fetishes, and to a world in which "the possibilties of life become the possibilities of mixed media."[13] For Roger Taylor, then, both poetry and struggle are obsolete.

Beyond Art, though vilely written, is worth considering: it is a naive and comprehensive expression of the ideology of "Post-Modernism." This term, if it has meant anything for art, has meant suicide: voluntary absorption into entertainment. The Marxist element in Taylor is vestigial. "Talk of the dulling and escapist character of the mass of popular culture" is dismissed as "quite without evidence."[14] Alienation is seen as "a progressive feature ... [the] very gradual emergence of a desocialised, self-sufficient man ... The life imaged [sic] becomes a series of roles, where role-playing has reverted to its theatrical context or origins."[15] This distracted creature is then identified with the skilled postrevolutionary generalist Marx imagined. Laurie Anderson's view, expressed recently on PBS, was more cogent: she called electronic media simply "the environment" and smiled at artists who "will not come to terms with it." Like network and other corporate executives, and all media ideologues since McLuhan, Taylor inverts capitalism's causes and effects: it is the public that chooses, that imposes, that demands, that creates—

not advertisers or stockholders. If there is manipulation, we manipulate ourselves. This is true, but only partly true.

Political post-modernism represents the collapse of radical thinking beneath a widespread radical pressure: the need to avoid, at any cost, even the appearance of elitism. The less political leverage one has, the more one needs to believe in popular virtue; the less one is in a position to teach the people, the more one wants to feel they already know. Both poets and activists tend to seek these consolations; both tend to hate and to defeat themselves when their enemy appears impregnable. In Thatcher's England as in Reagan's America, leftists are weak, isolated, and fearful of impending fascism. Some adopt a populism of despair, in which media take the place of the vanguard party.

Conceptually, at least, this impasse can be broken by anyone willing to make unpleasant distinctions. Capitalism has no right to the word "popular"; the correct term is "mass." Mutabaruka's "Free Up de Lan, White Man" is popular music. So is a Robert Johnson blues, or Billie Holliday singing "God Bless the Child." Michael Jackson's "Beat It" is a legal drug, harmless in itself, less so at high volume, still less when repeated. A stoned illiterate teenager mellowing out with it after watching five straight hours of soap operas is participating in nothing. Certainly there is a grey area, where "pop" forms have been used to express a rebellious populism, or for art of some complexity. Some protest singers have avoided cooptation; some lyrics of David Byrne and Randy Newman are creditable poems. Rock music, however, is itself a signifier, stronger than any lyric; what it signifies is freedom in Taylor's sense. The distinction between art and entertainment is no less clear for being quantitative: art demands thought.

Entertainment doesn't. Thinking is hard, especially in Laurie Anderson's "environment"; art attempts to teach it by example. To state, finally, that the masses are confused is not elitist. It is elitist to believe that they must be.

Since the early '50s, the English socialist poet Adrian Mitchell has invaded the grey area. His work has no analogue in contemporary American poetry. He uses every resource of Anglo-American pop—blues form, rock beat, dance rhythms, light verse, Steadman's drawings, slang, ads and profanity. Among artifacts valued in the academy he has been choosier, accepting delicate symbolism, wild but brief surrealist flights, precise verbal collages, but not portentousness, obscurity or posturing. His humor and humanity are his own. He has even written the obligatory poem about "The Swan":

> The beauty of the swan
> Is the sermon
> Preached between battles.

What is perhaps most impressive in Mitchell is his access to folk idioms that still exist alongside commercial forms. These include blues, Burns-like ballads, and "New Skipping Rhymes":

> Good little Georgie
> Worked like a madman
> Three years at Oxford
> Five years an adman
> Went on Mastermind
> Did so well on that show
> Now he's the host
> Of a TV Chat Show (...)

Pretty little Pam
Passed her exam
What shall we give her?
Doughnuts with jam

Stupid little Sam
Failed his exam
What shall we give him?
Who gives a damn?

Like the greatest political poets—Brecht, MacDiarmid,
Nazim Hikmet—Mitchell strives for absolute accessibility. In one sense he achieves it. We must remember,
however, that ideology is only secondarily doctrine,
or any kind of coherent idea. Primarily it is the replacement of thought by custom. People do not read
poetry, for example, because people do not read poetry; it does not matter how clear that poetry is. Or
rather, clarity and accessibility are a function of context; and because few institutions in our society offer
them, few clients of those institutions will recognize
or value them. "It was not that they didn't understand
what he was telling them," wrote Enzensberger in *The
Sinking of the Titanic.* "They didn't understand him."
Mitchell's "A Prayer for the Rulers of This World" begins:

God bless their suits
God bless their ties
God bless their grubby
Little alibis

God bless their firm
Commanding jaws
God bless their thumbs
God bless their claws

There is no chance the rulers of this world will ever read this, and if they did they would not recognize themselves. If informed, they would neither be alarmed that someone hates them this much, nor wonder why. A middle-class person, if shown the poem, would not feel he had the right to understand it. Digger might shrug. So Adrian Mitchell, like Carolyn Forché, preaches to the converted. But to be roused to action is intolerable where action is impossible. This fact of itself tends to depoliticize art. It is unlikely that a "popular" poet, if thoughtful and critical, will be popular in American society.

The goal of poetry in struggle, however, may be pursued in the opposite direction: instead of seeking an accommodation with entertainment one may reject it totally. Within Marxism, the aesthetic of T. W. Adorno is the most rigorously predicated on opposition to what he and Horkheimer called "the culture industry." In Adorno's view, all social reality is now "administered." Socialist revolutions have resulted in societies more oppressive, and requiring at least as many lies, as those of the West. The philosopher without options, if he cannot hope to change the world, must go on interpreting it. No viewpoint, however, may think itself uncompromised, and with relentless skepticism Adorno attacks not only the fetishes of liberalism and technocracy but his own positions as they emerge. The *Negative Dialectics* outlines and demonstrates his method. The unfinished *Aesthetic Theory* claims art as its ally. Not all art, however; only a critical art can carry "criticism" forward. Such art is formally experimental, self-conscious and demanding—not as a game, but as the negation of illusion. Schoenberg, Kafka and Beckett are its paradigms. "Beckett views his task as moving in an infinitely small space, ultimately a one-dimensional point

...The only *telos* towards which the dynamic of the immutable moves is perennial disaster. Beckett's writings face this unpleasant truth squarely." In his next paragraph, however, Adorno characteristically raises strong counter-arguments similar to Easthope's:

> Consciousness exposes the infinity of self-congratulatory progress as an illusion dished up by the absolute subject. Social labour defies aesthetically the bourgeois pathos of subjectivity, because the abolition of labour is within reach of being realized...[However,] Since the potential of freedom is scuttled by social conditions, it cannot come to the fore in art either. This accounts for the ambivalence of aesthetic construction [i.e. "difficult," self-conscious form— FP.]. Construction...can codify the resignation of the emaciated subject, and promote absolute estrangement by incorporating it in art; or it can project the image of a reconciled future... There are many linkages between the principle of construction and technocracy, linkages that reinforce the suspicion that construction belongs inevitably to the administered, bureaucratized world. Yet it may also terminate in an as yet unknown aesthetic form, the rational organization of which might point to the abolition of all notions of administrative control and their reflexes in art.[16]

Adorno is perhaps most famous for his remark that poetry is impossible after Auschwitz. He made an exception for Paul Celan, and it is possible that he would have liked George Oppen. Oppen wrote no poetry between 1934 and 1959; he was busy as a machinist, Communist labor organizer, soldier, then in Mexico as a refugee from McCarthy. He said later that he gave up poetry during this time because he didn't believe it was politically efficacious. But the first poem in his last book is entitled:

"A Political Poem"

for sometimes over the fields astride
of love? begin with

nothing or

everything   the nerve

the thread
reverberates
in the unfinished

voyage loneliness

of becalmed ships and the violent men

and women of the cities'
doorsteps unexpected

this sad and hungry

wolf walks in my footprints fear fear
birds stones, and the sun-lit

earth turning, that great

loneliness all

or nothing
confronts us
the image

the day

dawns on the doorsteps its sharpness
dazes and nearly blinds us

To understand this poem, the reader must read backwards and forwards and be open to the many meanings of simple words. In the process, these words become no longer simple but very valuable—which is what the words are saying about people. The poem describes a vision or recognition that comes only "sometimes"; one may seek it "astride / of love" or be chased into it by a "sad and hungry / wolf [of] fear" who is oneself. It comes to someone who is waiting out an "unfinished / voyage," whose special "voyage loneliness" is that "of becalmed ships." "Loneliness" may refer to political despair, but the syntax indicates that it is shared by the "violent men / and women" who occasion it. They are creatures of thresholds, "doorsteps"; they and their capacities are "unexpected." So is the fear that, if unrestrained, can become a fear of "birds, stones, and the sun-lit / earth"; administered reality shares the loneliness it causes. The "nothing or / everything" one confronts becomes the "all or / nothing" one must accept: a slogan without a movement, yet a precondition of movement.

The poem has other riches to yield, and its effect on the attentive reader is to move him or her, along with whatever shadows, into the radiance it mentions. Here surely is a forerunner of an "aesthetic form, the rational organization of which might point to the abolition of ... administrative control." The attention the poem requires is a kind of participation the ideologues of post-modernism have forgotten: not only co-creating the work, but creating with its help a tiny liberated zone within language. And the pronoun that ends the poem is one that has been fought for. However—and I do not think Oppen would have denied this—the poem also embodies the "absolute estrangement" it opposes. For whether or not we suspect, with Adorno, that the complexity of such poetry mimics that of technical systems, we know that few people are capable of the attention it demands. Hence the paradox of "A Political Poem," and a socialist poetry, composed for a small elite—an elite that neither wants this status nor benefits from it.

3. THE POET AS INTELLECTUAL

If art for its subject
will have a broken jar
a small broken soul
with great self-pity

what will remain after us
will be like lovers weeping
in a small dirty hotel
when wallpaper dawns

(Zbigniew Herbert, "Why the Classics")

1. Two decades ago it was a cliche that man had within his grasp the possibility of a life of security and plenty. For many in the West this prospect was a source of unadmitted terror. Who after all is "man"? The ultimate answer can only be that I am. What must man do to realize the potential of technology? He need only act rationally and collectively. How rationally have I ever acted? What experience do I have of collective action? The lowered expectations of the '70s and '80s have been for many people a source of relief as much as of fear, for they return us to *life*. "Life" is the familiar realm of fate and chaos, and of that disaster which, as long as it only strikes others, we can call "risk" and "challenge." Life, however, has lost respectability; even

the dimmest mind now senses there was an alternative.

2. Not only another way of life but another definition of life is called for, one that emphasizes planning, collective action, the collective triumph over cruelty and insecurity.—Who "calls" for it, however? Masses of Chinese happily reverting to sweatshop family enterprise? Millions of ordinary Russians nursing nationalism and anti-Semitism? The American workers who, as plants closed, voted for Reagan?—People who are oppressed and tortured will dream of a better life, but to them this probably means peace, an end to torture, and a plot of land, and implies nothing about the system that is to provide them. The conditions of struggle in a given country may create, in its people, an equation between socialism and their needs. But it is only intellectuals who need socialism.

3. Many factors make that last sentence painful or even unthinkable for many leftists. These factors include: fear of Leninism. Of fascism. Of agreeing with bigots who say the same thing. Of finding oneself in a cul-de-sac of elitist disdain. The image of Allende in his last hour, armed and nearsighted, saying "It is the people who make history." Lingering allegiance to the "scientific" pretensions of Marxism. Fear of losing any sense of a historical continuum that explains and supports one's struggle. Disgust for post-modernists who have abandoned that continuum, and for Neoconservatives who have replaced it with "tradition." Reluctance to identify oneself as a member of yet another suspect minority. (Poets also are subject to this fear; it accounts for a certain regular-guy, baseball-fan stance in both groups.) Finally, leftists tend to dislike psychology except as theory, and not to want to connect their ideas with their needs.

4. What a modern intellectual learns is that his feelings and values are received, malleable, *a posteriori*. Determinism is not one intellectual possibility among others; determinism, with whatever dialectical auxiliaries and "structural" qualifications, is what one knows. Only fools, and a few honest mystics like Weil and Shestov, equate freedom with rejection of determinism. Left intellectuals get their vision of freedom from reading the masters of economic and psychological determinism inversely, as Blake read Milton—continually detaching ideas from their institutional expressions. Freud tells the story of the childhood we should have had; Marx, that of the world we should have grown up in. If we relinquish either of these two stories we relinquish hope, for hope at its most intimate is the hope for another childhood, a second chance, a new life. On balance the twentieth century has been one of stagnation, not only because the ideals of its master thinkers have not been realized, but because its only convincing models of happiness and maturity are those ideals.

5. If modern thought, like modern art, has been an "indirect communication," it remains for both artist and thinker to tell its stories more directly—There exists a ghost realm that favors cooperation over competition; that wagers immense energies on collectively planned goals, and is thus both secure and adventurous; that welcomes rather than insults intelligence; that sets real challenges we could respect, rather than challenges we only respect because they are real; that assumes complete racial and sexual equality; and where we could talk to anyone without distrust or evasion or the self-hatred entrenched stupidity evokes in the intelligent. The self I would be, had I been born in that world, would be happier and more coherent than the one I

am. There is no sense in which that alternate self is my "real" one, but it is preferable; my tastes, reading, politics, and art are dedicated to its articulation. This ghost-world or ghost-self has haunted the intellectuals of this century, and for all of them it is both a promise and a threat. For in that society we would no longer be alone, and would thus have no further excuse for arrogance; if we failed there our failure would be real, not the usual moral victory. Socialism is a humiliating perspective, a superego-function; or else, in Alexander Mitscherlich's formula, it is the slow, painful extension of ego into the void superego left. One's politics and much else will depend on whether one accepts its judgment cheerfully or angrily or whether one rejects it.

6. Some poets have begun to appropriate this alternate (or "critical," or "utopian") self. The idea becomes clearer as the possibility recedes; it lives in faith, since both capitalism and communism have decided it cannot be realized. Few poets would describe the new intuition in these terms; they only feel there must be something better to write about than the usual ragbag of moods and memories. They want to use their minds rather than to go out of them, to be honest intellectuals rather than pro forma visionaries. But to be an intellectual is to see the self from outside. The self is a specific relation to power. Its own powers are limited. It can either express itself in the terms power has given it or strive to see how power gave it those terms. The role of imagination is either to conceal impotence or to outline new relations to (distributions of) power. The poetic ideologies we have touched on in this essay are for the most part compensatory fairy-tales.

7. The equation of poetry with lyric poetry, which has prevailed during the two centuries of bourgeois

rule, assumes that every important fact appears in the world as a feeling. It doesn't matter whether the etiology of feeling is ascribed to memory, the archetypes, or an actual Goddess; whether the poet's or the reader's feeling is the poem's focus; whether the Symbol or some inscrutable non-sequitur is supposed to evoke it; whether its metaphors are derived from art-museums or from dreams. All of these currently competing models are models of lyricism and tied to a common error: they deny the collective nature of experience. Truth is not only what I feel but what we do. To convey this truth, genres larger than the lyric are needed.

---

1 James E. B. Breslin, From Modern to Contemporary: American Poetry, 1945—1965 (Chicago, Illinois: University of Chicago Press, 1984), pp. 178-179.

2 Ibid., pp. 180-181.

3 cf. John P. Diggins, Mussolini and Fascism: The View from America (Princeton, New Jersey: Princeton University Press, 1972), p. 245.

4 Wallace Stevens, Opus Posthumous, ed. Samuel F. B. Morse (New York: Alfred A. Knopf, 1966), p. 165.

5 Wade Newman, "An Interview with Frederick Turner," Southwest Review, Summer 1986, p. 337.

6 Ibid., p. 343.

7 Ibid., p. 356.

8 quoted in Marjorie Perloff, The Poetics of Indeterminacy (Princeton, New Jersey: Princeton University Press, 1981), p. 258.

9 Ibid., p. 287.

10 Robert van Hallberg, American Poetry and Culture, 1945—1980 (Cambridge, Mass.: Harvard University Press, 1985), p. 61.

11 Jim Daniels, Places/Everyone, University of Wisconsin Press (Madison, Wisconsin: 1985).

12 Anthony Easthope, Poetry as Discourse (New York: Methuen, Inc., 1983), pp. 160-162.

13 Roger Taylor, Beyond Art (Totowa, New Jersey: Barnes and Noble Books, 1981), p. 167.

14 Ibid., p. 164.

15 Ibid., pp. 168-9.

16 Theodor Adorno, Aesthetic Theory (New York: Rutledge and Kegan Paul, 1984), p. 319.

POETRY AND THE UNIVERSITY

By Bruce Bawer

We live in an era when the poetic act—in America, at least—is increasingly performed on assignment and negotiated in committee under the auspices of a bureaucracy. I am speaking, of course, of that unique contemporary phenomenon known as the university creative-writing program. A bizarre institution, it has, in the manner of a black hole, grown more ominous and powerful with every poet, big and small, that it has swallowed up. It is a venue in which, all too frequently, the quality of the verse that a contemporary poet has written seems a far less reliable index of his relative importance than the grants and fellowships he has received, the writing colonies he has attended, the universities at which he has studied, taught, or given readings, and the number of books he has published. A poem is, after all, a fragile thing, and its intrinsic worth, or lack thereof, is a frighteningly subjective consideration; but fellowships, grants, degrees, appointments, and publication credits are objective facts. They are quantifiable; they can be listed on a resume. Like any bureaucracy, the university creative writing program tends to be more comfortable with these kinds of concrete attainments than with artistic accomplishments whose actual value, if any, cannot be determined without the strenuous exercise of intelligent critical judgment.

Parts of this essay appeared originally in *The New Criterion* (December 1985) and in *The American Spectator* (December 1987).

Perhaps the most disturbing thing about this state of affairs is that increasing numbers of young people—like their counterparts in *1984*—seem not to realize that it was not ever thus. For their sakes, then, let us begin at the beginning.

Once upon a time, the university and the writing of poetry had little to do with each other. Plato—the very first academic—banned poetry from the perfect state that he imagined in the *Republic*. The first great poet in the English language, Geoffrey Chaucer, held in his sixty years (1340-1400) a wide variety of occupations—among them page, soldier, valet, diplomat, clerk, controller of customs, member of Parliament, and deputy forester—but never took a university degree, and never taught. To be sure, such was not the case with all of the early English poets. In the succeeding two centuries, a number of poets—notably Wyatt, Sidney, Spenser, Nashe, and Marlowe—attended either Cambridge or Oxford; it was at the former university that Spenser wrote (actually, translated) his first verses, and that Marlowe wrote his first plays. Both universities bestowed the title of "poet laureate" upon John Skelton (1460-1529). Among the most famous poets of the Renaissance period, moreover, were the "university wits"—Nashe, Marlowe, Greene, Peale.

For all this, however, the university was far from being the focus of Renaissance England's equivalent of the "poetry world." On the contrary, literary writing was generally centered at court, and it was felt by many readers that what poetry did come out of the university was inferior, corrupted by academic language as opposed to the purer, leaner language of court verse. It cannot be said, then, that the Renaissance university itself—where education consisted largely of theology and the classical languages—played a deliberate, systematic role in any English poet's development; rather, it simply happened to be the place where articulate young men met each other, translated the *Iliad* and the *Aeneid*, and found time to devote to the writing of verse in the vernacular.

Though Shakespeare, of course, never attended a university, most seventeenth-century poets were members of the upper classes, and thus many were the products of universities. Lovelace and Vaughan attended Oxford; Marvell, Milton, and Cleveland attended Cambridge; Donne attended both. In the eighteenth century, the center of the literary world shifted away from court—yet it shifted not to the university but to the city of London. Of the major poets of the day, Dryden and Smart attended Cambridge (where the latter won a literary prize), the Earl of Rochester and William Collins attended Oxford, Swift and Goldsmith attended Trinity College, Dublin, and Thomas Gray was a professor at Cambridge; but Pope and Gay and Prior did not attend university, and Dr. Johnson left Oxford without a degree. Doubtless the most important thing about the university for eighteenth-century poets was that it provided them with a background in the classics.

To the Romantic poets, the university seems to have meant next to nothing. Though Wordsworth and Byron both earned degrees at Cambridge, and Southey, Beddoes, and Landor went to Oxford, Shelley was expelled from Oxford after six months, Coleridge left Cambridge without a degree, Keats went straight from his father's stable to medical school, Burns was self-educated, and Blake attended art school. In America, Dickinson spent a year at Mount Holyoke and Whitman left school at age eleven (though he would go on to be a schoolteacher, among other things). As for the Victorians, Browning studied briefly at the University of

London, Tennyson was at Cambridge, and Arnold, Clough, and Swinburne were at Oxford. During all this time, naturally, the university curriculum underwent a gradual expansion. In the nineteenth century it was possible for a distinguished poet to become, as Arnold did at Oxford, a professor of poetry—a post that would have been well-nigh inconceivable in Chaucer's time. But of course professors of poetry did not teach the writing of poetry, and they almost never taught the work of living writers. This held true during most of the early part of this century, and did not change noticeably, in America, until mid-century, when a substantial number of universities began to offer courses and workshops in writing. One of the first of these workshops was the famous Iowa Writers' Workshop, where in the early postwar years many distinguished poets helped train many distinguished-poets-to-be. Out of these courses and workshops grew the almost ubiquitous system of creative-writing programs with which we are familiar today.

And why did these institutions develop in the first place? In a roundabout way, I think, they're a consequence of modernism—an unfortunate, unforeseen by-product of the modernist precept that poetry should be avant-garde and should *epater le bourgeoisie*, of T.S. Eliot's pronouncement that poetry must be difficult, of Ezra Pound's deliberate composition of poetry for an audience not of ordinary literate people but of poets. During the modern period, such attitudes as these, on the parts of poets, effectively alienated them from the general public; no longer "the unacknowledged legislators of the world," they became Talmudic scholars of a sort, communing with themselves and with one another in language that was often deliberately private, uninviting, exclusionary. Though, in the years since

World War Two, the language of a good many poets has become more comprehensible, this change has arrived too late; Americans have grown used to the notion—young Americans nowadays seem to be born with it—that poetry is confusing, and that to read it is a peculiar, idle, self-indulgent, and radical activity.

This is true even of literate young people—up to a point. They're not about to read Chaucer or Milton or Browning, say, on their own; they'll willingly read that sort of thing for a class, naturally, and maybe even learn to appreciate it, but they won't run across a copy of *The Ring and The Book* in bookstore (assuming it could indeed find its way into a contemporary bookstore) and say, "Hm, this looks interesting, let's try it out." What such literate young people *will* often do, however, is what literate young people throughout history have done, whatever the present literary situation might happen to be: they'll sit down and write poems of their own. Of course, like all young people who have never read enough good poems to know what a good poem looks like, they'll tend to write poems that are—well—peculiar, idle, self-indulgent, and/or radical. They'll write corny love poems; poems about their parents not understanding them; poems that romanticize their own self-destructive and narcissistic tendencies. They'll write clumsy formal poems with terrible rhymes and metronomic rhythms; or—far more commonly nowadays—they'll write clumsy formless poems that read as if they were ripped right off the tops of their heads ("Oh Jimmy doesn't love me / at least I *think* he doesn't / why did he look at me like that today?? / oh god love is *so* difficult!!!").

For the authors of clumsy formal poems, there may be a modicum of hope: these young people may labor under the delusion that poems have to rhyme, but at least they've recognized, somewhere along the way, that writing poetry involves some sort of discipline. If they can be made to read the great poetry of ages past, and if they have a natural poetic talent to begin with, they may yet develop into real poets. As for the other young would-be poets—those writers of clumsy form-less poems—they may turn out to be poets, too. But they need to learn discipline; they need a sense of lit-erary tradition, of form, of poetry as craft. They may not realize it, but they're the product of a sensibility that came into the ascendant, in postwar America, with the Beats, and has in one form or another remained in the ascendant ever since. This sensibility is diametri-cally opposed to that of the modernists—for if the modernists conspired to put some distance between poetry and the general public, the adherents of this post-Beat philosophy have conspired to make the gen-eral public—or whatever elements of it would bother to listen to them—believe that poetry is not only some-thing that anyone can read, but something that any-one can write. In a grotesque reaction to high modern-ism, post-Beat poets have encouraged young people to think of poetry as something that requires not craft or intelligence or talent so much as sincerity. Just write what you feel, the idea goes, and you have a poem. Many of the young people, then, who have turned to writing poetry in recent years have done so not out of a desire to express themselves in a more memorable, sophisticated, and intensely compressed manner than is ordinarily possible in prose—or, for that matter, to surmount the difficulties posed by one or another sys-tem of meter or rhyme—but to pour their guts out in whatever words happen to be nearest at hand. Pecu-liar, idle, self-indulgent, and radical indeed.

It is out of this bizarre conjunction of developments

that the creative-writing program was born. As a consequence of modernist elitism, poetry was deprived of a general audience and increasingly retreated to the only place that would have it—the university. And why would the university have it? Because, in the Beat-inspired atmosphere of postwar literary America, young people in growing numbers who really didn't want to *read* poetry, and who certainly didn't know the first thing about it, were eager as hell to write it.

And so the universities obliged them. They took these young people who were utterly innocent of prosody and *Literaturwissenschaft* and the history of English verse and put them in classrooms with Real Poets where they could read and discuss each other's poems. And the universities told these young people that after spending a couple of years doing this sort of thing, they'd be Real Poets themselves, and could then go on to other universities, to train other young people to become Real Poets too.

From a business point of view, the creative-writing racket has been one of the biggest success stories of the past generation. Creative-writing programs have provided more and more poets, over the past generation, with a wonderful way of supporting themselves. For the poets, then, and for the universities (many of which have instituted their programs in the last ten years, largely because they were having a hard time finding qualified students who were interested in *reading* literature at the graduate level), these programs have been a magnificent development. But as far as the welfare of American poetry itself is concerned, their influence has not been at all salutary. To be sure, many of the finer poets of our day are the products of poetry workshops; and many poets whom I respect are teachers of poetry workshops. But there are workshops

and there are workshops. A small number of genuinely promising poets meeting regularly with a dedicated, perceptive, selfless, and articulate teacher: certainly there can be some benefit in this sort of thing,
for some poets, anyway. But during the past several
years, the poetry workshop has become not just one
optional element of a young poet's education, but rather
the very center of most young poets' educations. In
the last decade or so, as a matter of fact, many people
in the poetry world have begun to take it for granted
that the only serious way of preparing for a career as
a poet is to enter a university creative-writing program.

Nowadays, therefore, the young college graduate who
wants to be a poet usually goes straight into a program. Getting into one is no great trick; the hard part
is paying the tuition. Indeed, because the tuition fees
are so high, the admissions standards so lax, and the
objective value of a master's or doctorate in creative
writing so questionable, many creative-writing programs—especially the most prestigious (i.e., the most
expensive) ones—have become, in large part, playgrounds
for the modestly talented children of the rich and the
well-to-do.

This would be perfectly understandable—so what if
a bunch of spoiled kids, who have nothing better to
do anyway, pay poets to read and comment on their
work?—if not for the fact that these programs have
become enormously important in the making of poetic
careers. For in return for their parents' cash, these kids
receive exactly what they need to make it as poets in
the 1980s. I'm not speaking of an education: many a
creative-writing student receives his degree without ever
having looked at a poem by Milton, say, or Wordsworth.
Nor are most of these students helped to "find their
own voices." *Au contraire.* Most of their teachers are

likely to be middling poets themselves, more interested in promoting their own careers and proselytizing for their own brand of poetry than in pursuing the painstaking task of helping someone else to discover himself as a writer. Besides, how can a teacher, even a well-meaning one, begin to have a clue of what most of his students' "own voices" might sound like, when the majority of them enter the program with only the crudest idea of what a poem is anyway, when he's exposed to them (typically) for a relatively brief period, and when he has ten or twenty or fifty of them to "teach" at any given time?

No, what these lucky students get out of the creative writing program is *connections.* That, in essence, is what makes the "better" creative-writing programs better: the profs have superior connections. Study with the right person at the right university, and you'll stand a much better chance of getting your poems into the best magazines and journals, of having a book published, of receiving invitations to read, and of winning grants and awards. After all, most of the periodicals that publish poems in the United States (and here I'm not counting those mimeographed, stapled-together "magazines" that thousands of individuals run off in their garages) are issued by university English or creative-writing departments; most of the poetry books bear the imprints of university presses. To be in a university creative-writing program is to study under poets who have graduated from *other* creative-writing programs, and who therefore know—or at least know people who know—many of the people that an ambitious young poet most needs to know.

The teachers often help their students to find jobs, too—as (what else?) creative-writing teachers. Many of them will be hired even though they're not particu-

larly good poets or teachers—for the main qualification to teach poetry-writing at most American universities is not that one's work be first-rate but that one
have a degree from a creative-writing program.

What can be said about the poetry written by these
program-bred poets? For one thing, they write it in
quantity. They've been trained to *crank it out*—whether
or not they feel like it, whether or not they're inspired,
whether or not they have a fresh and compelling topic.
When Eliot or Williams or Stevens didn't feel like writing a poem, they didn't—they had jobs. But these program poets *have* to write poems. When they're students,
they have to write them for homework; when they become teachers, they have to write them in order to
accumulate enough publications to secure tenure and
promotions. Like scholars, in other words, poets in the
academy are subject to that old academic dictum: publish or perish. And just as this dictum has led to the
writing of innumerable volumes of gratuitous scholarly prose, so it has led, in recent years, to the creation of countless expendable poems. As with those volumes of scholarship, the problem with these poems is
not that they're *terrible*, really; on the contrary, most
of them are quite competently written. The problem,
usually, is that they're *dead*—flat, arid, inert. And un-
distinctive, too: many a creative writing program poem
is virtually interchangeable with dozens of other poems
not only by its author but by any number of similar
program poets.

This is not to say that all poets who have come out
of programs sound alike. Some, of course, are highly
distinctive. But there are armies of successful program
poets out there who do sound almost like clones of
one another. They write dull, desultory free-verse poems
that often seem to be haphazardly lineated and pointlessly

descriptive or anecdotal. Frequently these poems concern personal topics—families, romances—but one
sometimes has the impression, nevertheless, that their
authors are trying desperately to avoid expressing a
recognizable human feeling. One reason why there are
so many poems of this sort in circulation is that creative-writing teachers, aware of their inability to help
most of their students "find their voices," or to turn
them into mature and original poets of a more formal
bent, opt instead for what they apparently consider to
be the next best thing: they teach their students to write
poems that *look profes sional*. Which means that these
teachers—acting on the (probably correct) assumption
that the primary inclination of most young amateurs
is to write nauseatingly sentimental and self-pitying
effusions on such themes as the torments of young love—
drill their students in the avoidance of bathos and the
accumulation of objective detail (e.g., obscure plant names
and odd place names). The result: armies of poets who
are, essentially, rank amateurs, but who—like art students who produce copies of great paintings, or like
many an athlete who has successfully made the transi-
tion to movie star—have learned to fake it. They've
learned, that is, to mimic many of the effects of real
free-verse poets in such a way that their lack of talent
or of anything to say is not immediately apparent. They're
poets who avoid attempting difficult forms or rendering complex emotions for fear of exposing their limitations, who avoid sensitivity itself for fear of crossing the line into sentimentality. Most creative-writing-
program poets learn how not to communicate the essential truths of their souls, then—or, for that matter,
how to work in form—but how to contrive verses that
are as cold and impassionate as a don. They learn to
aim not for excellence but for productivity and pub-

lishability; they learn to write poems, in other words, of a sort that they know will be acceptable to the editors of the magazines and poetry series in which they want to be published.

And the result is a stunning lack of variety in their productions. To glance through the pages of certain poetry magazines and anthologies is to learn a quick and sobering lesson in the monotony of creative-writing-program poetry. Read one poem after another in a recent *Pushcart Prize* volume, for instance, and the sameness of the voices will soon render you numb. Start with a few lines from "Without End" by Elizabeth Thomas:

> Now I think of a sleeper in my lap,
> your weight round as the slow nest
> of summer. Steady as sleep.
> My hands smell of feed, of manure,
> of everything rising around us.
> Do I call you daughter? Lover?
> We watch as two people watch nothing:
> the afternoon's marriage
> of lawn and maples, the grasses'
> under-water green, under, under
> maple shadow, your hidden face,
> your hair, rest.
> We keep five roosters, too few
> hens. Across the lawn they wake us.
> Bug-eyed they cackle and laugh at us.

Then there's some of "Chief" by Michael S. Harper:

> In the year of the blizzard
> in the month of February
> I have traipsed up the middle
> of Lexington Avenue, a spectacular
> middle passage in the snow

to my own poetry reading:
James Wright, Philip Levine,
each having written about a horse,
neither a hero of myth
nor witness to history alone,
nor a palomino looking for a drink.

—which is followed immediately by "And the Scream,"
by Stephen Berg:

The thirtyish, Irish, red-nosed carpenter
who works for Coonan—he rehabs houses up here—
is already half-stoned on beer
before eight and chases his son past my front window,
screaming at him, the kid's glasses
thick as my little finger,
bobbling on his nose.
Thin, steady, grayish drizzle, gray sky,
long smudges yellowing the sky,
clouds darkening the street abruptly,
Pat and Jack Laurent's house gloomy
across from mine (they're away), even the embroidery
of lace curtains, the high-
arched Victorian doors a failure.

And so on. I could keep quoting interminably, of
course: every year there are thousands of poems like
these, published by hundreds of poets in dozens of
magazines. And every year, in classrooms across the
country, students are being encouraged to write this
way. These are not, to be sure, very bad poems; they're
not very *anything* poems. What they are is safe, flat,
unimaginative. They're formulaic. Right now, poems
are being published, young poets taught, and poetry
teachers hired, by people to whom the above excerpts
represent some sort of ideal of contemporary poetry.
Show the average creative-writing student a poem by

Arnold or Keats or Sir Thomas Wyatt and he'll look at you strangely: why should he read this? Poems like this don't get published. There's no profit in his reading such things. Besides, even if he wanted to write like Arnold or Keats or Wyatt—or in a way that might owe something to their example—he knows in his heart of hearts that he doesn't have what it takes. But show him a poem by Michael S. Harper or Stephen Berg, and consciously or unconsciously, he'll think: Hm, that's not so hard. I can do that. And, hey, that's what gets published.

This is the sort of mentality that reigns in the creative-writing program. Poetry has become something you do to get a master's or a doctorate, to get a book published, to get a tenure-track teaching job, to get a name; poetry is, like investment banking or real estate, a rat race that one either wins or loses. Yes, poets of an earlier day were ambitious and competitive too; it was said of John Berryman that he watched the rise and fall of his contemporaries' reputations the way a broker watches the fluctuations of stock prices. But poets like Berryman wanted to succeed because they adored poetry itself. They lived to write poetry; to them, it was not a means to anything, but an end—a glorious end—in itself. None of them would ever have published a word in which he did not believe wholeheartedly; none of them would ever have manufactured a poem just to earn a degree, or adopted a style because of its acceptability in the magazines and publishing houses.

And though it's true that there has always been some degree of political gamesmanship operating in the poetry world, it is safe to say, I think, that now more than ever the poetry world is a buddy network in which poems and books are published, and awards and grants distributed, not on the basis of the quality of one's work but on the basis of one's connections; it is a bureaucracy increasingly dominated by minimally talented and maximally ambitious people who care little about the traditions and possibilities of poetry but who care everything about the poets who are their competitors in the all-important Reputation Game. It's a world whose rampant careerism, politicking, and log-rolling sometimes make one feel as if poetry itself has gotten lost in the shuffle. And the place where most of the shuffling is being done, the institution which is most responsible for the misbegotten mentality that dominates the scene, is the university creative-writing program.

THE EMPEROR'S NEW CLOTHES

By Dick Allen

Few anecdotes have been so damaging to attitudes toward modern poetry as one about W.H. Auden, approvingly related in John Ciardi's influential textbook, *How Does a Poem Mean*: "W. H. Auden was once asked what advice he would give a young man who wished to become a poet. Auden replied that he would ask the young man why he wanted to write poetry. If the answer was 'because I have something important to say,' Auden would conclude that there was no hope for that young man as a poet. If on the other hand the answer was something like 'because I like to hang around words and overhear them talking to one another,' then that young man was at least interested in a fundamental part of the poetic process and there was hope for him."

The implication is clear: poetry has nothing important to say or, as Auden himself put it in "In Memory of W.B. Yeats": "poetry makes nothing happen." It is "A way of happening, a mouth." Archibald MacLeish's equally influential "Ars Poetica" communicated a similar attitude: "A poem should be equal to: / Not true" and "A poem should not mean / But be."

Inherent contradictions should be self-evident. Both Auden and MacLeish have given us "meaning" statements to say poetry does not really "mean" anything. These statements, along with a multitude of others in countless New Critical works, have helped to convince several generations of poets that poetry should be its own excuse for being, not an art which can and does communicate denotatively as well as connotatively, intellectually as well as imagistically.

II

By "poetry," most modern American and British critics mean lyric poetry. In a process of synecdoche, lyric poetry had come by mid-century to stand for all verse. Forms other than the lyric continued to be written, but the criticism of the age—honed so finely to analyze lyric elements—has not encouraged them. And since the lyric lent itself so well to classroom teaching and poetry workshops, the lyric was perpetuated. Generations of beginning poets were encouraged to feel that if they mastered "how" a poem means, meaning would miraculously spring into being.

Poets do not usually call themselves "lyric poets," of course. The term carries with it a connotation of triviality. But if we remember that the lyric poet concentrates on the sound of the poem, writes from deep personal feeling, creates a relatively short and sustained composition in either open or closed form—and that these elements dominate whatever narrative and dramatic strains the poem may contain—it is evident the term applies. Here is Frost's "momentary stay against confusion" or Stevens' coloring of the gray rock.

Lyric dominance is primarily the result of Imagistic poetics. As William Pratt noted in his preface to *The Imagistic Poets*:

There is no need to argue for the historical importance of Imagist poetry. It was the beginning of what we now call "modern poetry" in English. It represented the first serious effort at reforming the diction of English poetry since Wordsworth and Coleridge, and it began as a reaction to the Romantic movement, just as the Romantics had begun by reacting against their predecessors, the Neo-Classical poets. But it went beyond simple reform and reaction to make the first concerted attempt since Elizabethan times at establishing a new English cadence, a "free verse" based on natural speech rhythm, to replace the blank verse, or iambic pentameter, line that had been the standard in English poetry since the Elizabethan period. It also experimented with the poetic symbol, striving to make it more visual, concrete, and concentrated in its effect, maintaining that "the natural symbol is always the *adequate* symbol," and that it should be presented without explicit moral interpretation, since the image itself was the means of verbal expression. All these efforts have received their fulfillment in the major achievements of modern English poetry.

Such a break with the past had strong support in fiction, notably with the reaction to World War I. In *A Farewell to Arms*, Frederick Henry thinks,

I was always embarrassed by the words sacred, glorious, and sacrifice and the expression in vain. We had heard them, sometimes standing in the rain almost out of earshot, so that only the shouted words came through, and had read them, on proclamations that were slapped by billposters over other proclamations, now for a long time, and I had seen nothing sacred, and the things that were glorious had no glory and the sacrifices were like the stockyards at Chicago if nothing was done with the meat except to bury it. There were many words that you could not stand to hear and finally only the names of places had dignity. Certain numbers were the same way and certain dates and these with the names of the places were all you could say and have them mean anything. Abstract words such as glory, honor, courage, or hallow were obscene beside the concrete names of villages, the numbers of roads, the names of rivers, the numbers of regiments and the dates.

Reactions against fatuous belief, messages, the morally uplifting painting, musical composition or story were primary elements of artistic expression. Most painting was to be looked at for its form rather than its content; most musical compositions were collections of startling moments. The bias was against certainty, and for ambiguity—for good reasons. In the 20th Century, those who were certain that they knew the right ways others should follow have endlessly encouraged military and economic wars that continue to lay waste to whole societies. Against such out-of-control power, supplemented by out-of-control technological innovations, the artist stubbornly maintained that any Truth could only be an individual's truth. If we can be led to see the thing itself, the red wheelbarrow, the butterfly sewed back on a branch, the pine trees of sea waves, we will perceive in sharper and clearer ways. Such perception will allow us to resist the dangerous abstractions that so blur the mass mind.

Concentration on the minute brought forth, almost inevitably, contemporary movements of poetry such as the Confessional, where the individual life became, in a sense, the only knowable "thing." In New Surrealism or Deep Image poetry there was an implicit joining of all images and things in the subconscious, as the underlying reality was a mystical Oneness which the image helped us uncover. Modern and contemporary art attempted to direct us, in Frost's wonderful

phrase, "Back out of all this now too much for us."
Beneath the surface, it assumed an archetypal ocean
of emotion and racial knowledge which could be felt
but seldom consciously known.

The result, for the state of poetry, was both good
and bad. Those English and American poets likely to
be notable centuries hence certainly include Yeats, Eliot,
Stevens, Williams, Frost. Most likely, survey anthologies will have poems by Wilbur, Lowell, Bishop, James
Wright, Plath; perhaps twenty other poets will be represented by a few of their finest lyrics. It has been an
extraordinarily rich time, a golden age of lyric poetry
such as we have never seen before and are not likely
to see again. Much of the poetry we have had is lovely
in its music. It is alternately complex, ironic, ambiguous, or hauntingly simple and pure. Yet since there is
a great burnished ocean of it, rather than a few high
waves, the reader's attention is naturally diffused. We
might even say that just as an abundance of bad at
least for a time forces out the good, so much "good"
makes it extremely difficult to pick out the finest. Responding to our age of planned obsolescence, fragmen-
tation, future shock, our lyric poets have created thousands of beautifully constructed artifacts, left to be found
when cheaply and hurriedly made walls crumble. The
presence of and fear of Death is so omniscient in our
century that many poets, most notably the Academic
formalists, were compelled to construct ornaments fashioned for immortality. For a time, high critical standards virtually eliminated the poem of mediocre thought
and uninspired feeling as well as the poorly made poem
from serious consideration. In the best of our poems,
sound and sight achieved small perfect harmonies.

Given such accomplishments, why then are we still
so uneasy about the state of late 20th Century poetry?

Perhaps the main answer to this is that poetry, like all literature, is able to communicate through more than the visual and the musical. We naturally look for ideas, for meaning, for more than feeling in it. When a poem says something to us, what it has to say should ultimately be more crucial for our lives than how this is said, even given that it could not "say" so well without the art bearing its meaning to us. It is only when the poem does not have much to say, does not have much meaning, that we adjust our sensibilities to refocus on *how* what meaning there is, is communicated.

Almost all modern and contemporary lyric poetry has played variations on the same theme, the theme of the overwhelmed self. This self, unable to achieve identity with forces outside it (and believing that such identity would be wrong and damaging) speaks from the "I." Express and feel individual perceptions strongly enough and the reader, so the implicit theory goes, will identify with the poet's "I" and be enriched by his enhanced ability to respond not only either to complexity or simplicity but to the present (the only thing knowable is the individual "now"). Moreover, he will take comfort in understanding that others feel isolation and longing to the same degree or deeper degree. Lyric poetry provides an understandable individualistic stance against change, society, and Death, even when it seems to accommodate them.

Such a stance is not inherently undesirable. Still, it was taken so often and so well that it came to seem the only one possible. If one wrote lyric poetry, one automatically must assume this stance. The poet is the one who defends, rather than one who imagines other ways for humans to be. The poet apologizes for the art: "I, too, dislike it." The craft becomes minor—beautiful, but minor. The poet is not considered—nor does he often so consider himself—as the prophet, seer, visionary, social critic, powerful rebel, satirist to be thrown in jail, but as the persistent artist, the Hugh Selwyn Mauberley safe "at last from the world's welter," who can take comfort in that the age, after all, will find he was right in refusing temptations to cheapen his art. He is neither the Bard nor the Fool.

At the present time, poets have reached a crossroads. If they work exclusively with formal lyric poetry it may have to be in the full knowledge that most beautifully rhymed and metered of its poems ultimately may seem to the future to lack in bursting emotion, idea and social content, thus being forever minor. If they work exclusively with free verse lyric poetry, they may have to admit that its lack of rhyme and regular meter almost automatically renders it forgettable unless it has the power of genius and long life of constructing what amounts to one book-length vision (Whitman, Williams, to some extent Stevens). A very few great lyric poets will still emerge—though the possibilities of lyricism seem more and more limited. Or poets such as those now being labeled the New Formalists and the New Narrative poets in the Expansive Movement can take a risk hitherto unthinkable in our age—dangerous in that it can let loose a flood of terrible junk—and turn a focus of their work more toward idea, subject, and society, letting verse be the vehicle rather than the thing itself.

An aspect of similar import has been attempted in our century—what we now call "Beat Poetry," principally represented by Allen Ginsberg's *Howl* and mainly important for that poem and the folk rock poetry of Bob Dylan it helped encourage—but its only lasting result (in combination with the Black Mountain School) was the breaking of Academic Poetry and New Criti-

cism strangleholds. Academic critics were right in one
thing—noted particularly at the launching of the Beat—
in observing that most of Beat poetry was crudely written, occasional poetry. Had that poetry been composed
in rhyme and meter—couplets, well-made ballads, even
blank verse—and had it become narrative and dramatic
rather than falling into the trap of an over-reliance on
word and form, it might have amounted to considerably more than it has.

Let me advance, then, a tentative hypothesis: if poetry is to become more than it is at the present, it will
need to be a narrative and dramatic poetry, stressing
meaning (social, political, scientific, philosophical, technological, etc.). The meaning shall be known by both
poet and reader to be of utmost importance, conveyed
by carefully constructed forms but ultimately transcending them.

III

How counter to modernist theories this hypothesis
is can be noted by remembering Imagist admonitions.
The three most famous, by Ezra Pound, were so accepted by modern and contemporary poets they seemed,
and still seem to many, to be common sense rather
than the formalization of a minor canon:

1) Direct treatment of the "thing" whether subjective or objective.
2) To use absolutely no word that does not contribute to the presentation.
3) As regarding rhythm: to compose in the sequence
of the musical phrase, not in sequence of a metronome.

The 1915 Preface to *Some Imagist Poets* amplified the
principles:

1) To use the language of common speech, but to employ always the *exact* word, not the nearly-exact, nor the merely decorative word.

2) To create new rhythm—as the expression of new moods—and not to copy old rhythms, which merely echo old moods. We do not insist upon "free-verse" as the only method of writing poetry. We fight for it as a principle of liberty. We believe that the individuality of a poet may often be better expressed in free-verse than in conventional form. In poetry, a new cadence means a new idea.

3) To allow absolute freedom in the choice of subject....

4) To present an image (hence the name: "Imagist"). We are not a school of painters, but we believe that poetry should render particulars exactly and not deal in vague generalities, however magnificent and sonorous. It is for this reason that we oppose the cosmic poet, who seems to us to shirk the real difficulties of his art.

5) To produce poetry that is hard and clear, never blurred and indefinite.

6) Finally, most of us believe that concentration is of the very essence of poetry.

These admonitions were, of course, not followed completely by any of our best poets and their original practitionners soon swerved from the ideals. Still, they provided the foundation of poetry in our age and clearly exclude types of poetry other than the lyric. Even though they have been questioned and attacked before, it is necessary—because their influence is still so pervasive—to indicate the limitations they impose on poetry, limitations which had as much to do with the lack of poetry's popularity in our century as they had with the excellence of lyric poetry resulting from their aesthetics.

We would not argue with the Preface's Principle 3.

Freedom in subject material is central to 20th Century art and—except in totalitarian regimes—taken for granted. Nor would we quibble much with using "the language of common speech"—still a necessary stricture to assure poetry speaks in the language of the century and does not use archaic and anachronistic expressions such as "o'er" and "twas" or awkward inversions for the sake of rhyme and meter. Yet we should note that by denying ourselves the use of such language we are accepting a *condition* which mitigates against exalted and elevated poetry, particularly dramatic poetry. Such language could conceivably be used if the poet were to write narrative and dramatic works with, say, science fiction or fantasy settings—after readers were convinced that characters actually spoke in this manner.

The concentration on the word itself is another matter. When the poet is admonished to make every single word count, he is being asked to place intense concentration on the *music* and *sound* and *imagery* of the poem; his concentration is on individual words and particular images rather than on entire lines, stanzas and episodes. He may, consequently, lose concentration on what the poem, overall, may be saying. A book-length poem written with such concentration is not only extraordinarily difficult to compose, it is finally quite unreadable—there being too little contrast. Imagine Chaucer, Shakespeare, even Milton written at such a pitch—or even seventy additional pages of *The Waste Land*. Ezra Pound's *Cantos*, to some extent *Patterson*, and some of the most unreadable Dylan Thomas and Robert Lowell show the results of over-concentration on word and image. To write in longer forms, the poet must be allowed some dull passages, fill-in words, mundane verse. I open, at random, *Paradise Lost*:

That day I oft remember, when from sleep
I first awakened, and found myself reposed
Under a shade on flowers, much wond'ring where
And what I was, whence thither brought, and how.

and

Let us descend now therefore from the top
Of speculation; for the hour precise
Enacts our party hence; and see the guards,
By me encamped on yonder hill....

and Byron's *Don Juan*:

His five brave boys no less the foe defied;
Whereon the Russian pathos grew less tender,
As being a virtue, like terrestrial patience,
Apt to wear out on trifling provocations.

No one would call these lines great poetry, yet only
contemporary critics, blind to how narrative functions—
with its intensity occuring in scenes and passages and
overall fictional construction, but not in *every* scene
and passage—would use them to dismiss *Paradise Lost*
and *Don Juan* as less than masterpieces. Those who
still doubt should reread *Paradise Lost*, *The Canterbury
Tales*, Shakespeare's Tragedies and Comedies, *The Divine Comedy*, the great epics of any language. Browning is particularly instructive, and Blake. Pope knew
enough to keep his long poems "short."

In the matter of rhythm, Pound's admonition helped
poets writing in fixed forms avoid singsong; free verse
loosened up the line to such an extent that the best
poets using fixed forms have learned to play marvelous variations on the basic iambic foot. But the Imagist
feeling that "old rhythms...merely echo old moods" is
patently false, like saying that Julius Irving could not

play a brilliant new mode of basketball inside the rules of the game or that Edward Hopper's paintings are not of this century because his figures are recognizable. Does "a new cadence" mean "a new idea"? Perhaps at the start of the century it did. At the century's end we have found that "the new cadence" is much more likely to express an old, trivial idea and feeling without even the grace of meter and pleasure of rhyme to enhance it.

The "direct treatment of the thing" and its many variations ("No ideas but in things"), the nominalist concentration on the specific, concrete image, "things as they are" was by far the most compelling and influential stricture of 20th Century poetry. It is almost impossible to imagine poetry in our time and future time without it.

Thus, when a 20th Century poet writes of an alarm clock, for instance, the clock must always first be the literal clock, on the literal dresser, despite what else it may stand for. "Time" is not on the dresser; the actual square white Timex with its black hands and its fluorescent second hand is there; the woman who turns in bed to read the clock is not some transcendent maiden but a real woman with a scratch on her nose, physically existing in what we might call the "real" time of the present. Imagism is a poetry of particulars. And there is little to be gained by letting down our guard against such abstractions as would blur our ability to see the actual clock and the actual woman (or, as Stevens asks, "O thin men of Haddam, / Why do you imagine golden birds? / Do you not see how the blackbird / Walks around the feet / Of the women about you?"). Where the problem arises is that the concentration upon particulars has been interpreted by poets to forbid such abstractions as the mind naturally makes following its concentration upon the literal. Abstractions have been made implicit rather than explicit: the reader is left to make them, or rather his subconscious is to make them, or his refined sensibility as he follows the logic of the imagination. Such a method and reliance makes a high art of poetry reading. It requires a flexible, alert, sensitive, highly trained and responsive reader.

It also makes poetry elitist, keeping those who have not been trained in the college classroom in the dark and damning them if their minds are not honed properly and they do not respond as it is assumed they should. Reading of much modern poetry becomes a process of translation where the reader learns that his hard-won paraphrase "is not it at all." Or it becomes a process of looking at things beautifully described (Elizabeth Bishop's "The Fish" is the favorite example). Thousands of poems in closed and open forms are perceived as mainly just good description. The main lesson for the novice to learn is how to note, grasp, and realize the reality of the specific. The assumption is that if we are trained to see actual things in the particular poem, not go immediately to abstractions, we will see through the obscenities of "glory, honor, courage, or hallow" and associated values. Ideally, this training (the poet may or may not be conscious of attempting its effect) would cause us to question all generalizations, all political and inter-personal cliches, helping us to combat mass media and soap opera conceptions of life that so dull the popular mind.

Moreover, New Criticism standards (in tandem with the influence of Imagist theory) admonish against the basic fallacies. If we take an interest in the relationship between the life of the poet and his poem and base some of our discussion and interpretation on such

a relationship, we may be committing "The Autobiographical Fallacy." If we listen too closely to what the
poet tells us were her intentions for the poem, we are
in danger of committing "The Intentional Fallacy." If
we speak of how the poem affects us, makes us want
to do this or that, we are engaged in "The Affective
Fallacy." We must approach the archetypal 20th Century poem as we would a time bomb. Even as we de-
fuse it, we learn it is likely to explode in our faces.

It is little wonder that many novice readers (including those in high school—where maimed English teachers have almost given up teaching poetry during the
past thirty years, except to advanced classes), seeing
how others in their classrooms have been wounded,
or hearing about such experiences, or being forced to
sit and watch as the super-trained poetry instructor
carefully dismantles the poem, simply keep well out
of the way of the dark street where the ticking poem
lies. The problem is compounded if the reader discovers that once the poem is defused, it lies there like
harmless debris. Certainly he does not wish to put it
together again. One should have more to gain after
going through such an adventure.

There is another interesting fallacy, "The Pathetic
Fallacy" also to be watched out for: inanimate objects
should not be given human attributes. Or, to put it
another way, the poet was advised to avoid personifi-
cation. Twentieth Century poets, however, found their
way around this stricture by use of surrealistic techniques. Anything in the subconscious could be mean-
ingfully personified; but doing this in a non-surrealist
poem was still taboo.

The Imagist-New Critical poem, then, kept the poet
rammed into a small space. The poet was advised not
to deal in "vague generalities" (surrealism has such,

but the application is to the Self). We were advised against the "cosmic poet." Poets were led to avoiding, or at least carefully tying to concrete particulars, such words as "God," "Soul," "Void," "World," "Hope," "Truth," "Beauty." Not many would wish a return to the overuse of such bald abstractions, but it is important to note that they are merely the opposite of previous centuries' feelings that poetry *does* deal with abstractions, vast inventions of the mind. From a quite different perspective, a poet of another time could reasonably argue that what we are writing is mainly good, untranscended description, not poetry at all.

It should by now be apparent that we have been extremely influenced by admonitions which led precisely to the characteristic poem of the age: the highly charged, small, concrete, personal, colloquial, descriptive, usually free verse lyric which does not deal directly with general matters. It is perhaps now interesting to remember stricture 3 ("To allow absolute freedom in the choice of subject....") and wonder if such allowance actually existed. The acceptable lyric form of the century precludes freedom, making many great subjects impossible to handle in a way meaningful and fulfilling to critics.

IV

But, one can object, the alternative to lyric poetry, the lengthy narrative and dramatic poem, has had its place usurped by the short story, the novel, television and movies. This might be true, except that these forms of fiction lack, at least generally, the intensity, the thoughts and feelings expressed in a memorable way, the elevations of which narrative and dramatic poetry are

capable.The very qualities which made our lyric poetry so fine—though these may be loosened or only
appear at intervals in the longer poem—are what make
the story-telling forms of poetry so ultimately satisfy-
ing and re-readable. All the best devices of lyric poetry can be used in the narrative and dramatic poem,
as long as they are not the only devices. The canvas is
that much bigger.

However, because the narrative and dramatic poem
does sacrifice some of the word-by-word intensity of
the lyric in favor of other kinds of intensity, it needs, I
believe, a relatively fixed form if it is not to be just
good prose chopped into lines. Open form imposes too
much musical difficulty on the story and tends to be
too self-delighting. There are possibilities of mixing open
and closed forms, just as there are possibilities of mixing prose or prose poetry and closed forms in a book-
length poem, as long as the narrative and dramatic
story threads hold the reader. More likely, the most
successful of these poems would be written in closed
form: blank verse, rhyming couplets, rhyme royale, or
other patterns—even linked sequences of dramatic lyrics can form a narrative.

But it is the subject matter which is most necessary
for poetry, if it is to be given the freedom of choice
that was only promised. In practice, our best-paying,
highest circulation magazines (*The New Yorker, The At-
lantic, Poetry, The American Poetry Review,* and most of
the distinguished literary quarterlies) publish mainly
short lyric poetry. The poet, if he or she is to have
books accepted, gain name recognition, win poetry
awards, is naturally encouraged to publish in these magazines. Earlier, the poet has had his poetry analyzed,
refined and directed in university poetry workshops
almost completely dominated by lyric poets—for the

writing of lyric poetry can be taught quite well. These magazines and workshops mainly discourage (outside of light verse) satirical poetry, poetry of statement, poetry in which the ideas or meaning are more important than the art, poetry with evident social content or criticism or suggestion, poetry of praise for social achievements, poetry which contains explicit sexual matter, overtly religious poetry. The much-heralded "freedom of subject material" turns out to be a freedom which says you may use it, but only in a few little or little-little magazines. The very elements which might do much for gaining poetry a somewhat increased audience, an audience of more than other poets, are virtually excluded. Poetry is a nice, safe art.

What is missing from our poetry, and what should be possible, is almost shocking to consider. Instead of satire (I think of Byron's *Don Juan*, and of Pope), we have the wit and irony of the academic formalist lyric, the bombast of the Beat, the mysticism of the New Surrealist. Yet America calls out for humor and satire: there is much that is ridiculous in our commercialized, mass media, mass technology society which could and should be ridiculed. Just one for instance: the discrepancy between what kinds of economic, social, and military reforms are needed today and the way citizens continue to go about their business as if nothing world-threatening was happening. A well-placed, quotable couplet could do more to illuminate this ridiculous contrast than a hundred novels.

And surely there are many important statements, judgments concerning society and its people that cry out to be made. Poetry, it must continually be stressed, is not the language of feeling and emotion alone. Where, except in the work of Frederick Turner and a too few others, is our poetry which helps translate philosophy to us and which—because poetry is also an analogy-making art—brings to the people new theories of science? Sociobiology and the new physics, to cite just two of many examples, have little reference in our poetry.

Does not poetry have a duty to society? *The Encyclopedia of Poetry and Poetics* notes several kinds of societies and responses of poets to them. There is the Unified Society, the Divided Society, the Threatened Society, and the Fragmented Society. Each of these have called forth various responses from their poets. In the Unified Society, or the society perceived as somewhat unified, patriotic poetry may be possible: "It is easy for moderns to forget how much of the world's great poetry is profoundly patriotic—Homer, Virgil, David, Dante, Shakespeare, Spenser, Corneille, Whitman, Wordsworth, as most important poets, have all written patriotic poetry." In the Threatened Society, "The close of Pope's *Dunciad* rises to pessimistic grandeur, telling and foretelling how men fall away from great norms of thought and content." The Fragmented Society, such as ours, has called forth the responses labeled as eclecticism, syncretism, mystical unity, marxist futurism, alienation of the individual (from society, himself, the past, and God), imaging the disorder by disorder, regionalism. Even if one accepts that these are the primary possible responses, one sees how the contemporary lyric poet has been mainly confined to the responses of alienation and regionalism. Surely other responses are possible. Certainly they are necessary. Alienation, especially, has deteriorated into a stance, and probably a false one at that. Most contemporary poets are relatively comfortable in a still-affluent America; they vote, watch TV, enjoy their teaching positions, drive their cars, eat their TV dinners. Yet they take the stance of the lonely, alienated individual in their poetry—chiefly, one suspects, because it is not fashionable and certainly is too Republican to praise their comfortable society. And although it is true that the well-off and physically unmarred may suffer, it is difficult to imagine a contemporary poet willing to trade his or her suffering for the kind undergone by the poor of underdeveloped countries, the politically repressed of totalitarian regimes, the war-ravaged of the Middle East.

These considerations lead inevitably to the problem of awareness itself. The contemporary poet in the technological society is offered such a sheer amount of constantly revised knowledge that he is overwhelmed. One understands Frost's cabin retreat and the retreat of many other poets to cultivating their own gardens. "The world is too much with us; late and soon, / Getting and spending, we lay waste our powers" has never been more true. We suspect we could write our lyric poetry better if we had no television, airplanes, telephones, vast highway system, shopping malls—oh, to live in a cabin in the dark woods and watch the butterflies in the morning and the moths at night. However, the technological-industrial society *does* exist, no matter how much we would will it away—and that our poetry has been inadequate to achieving major relevance in it is primarily attributable to our refusal or inability to deal with it in the lyrics to which we basically limit ourselves. A vast, changing world calls for a larger kind of poetry, a poetry calling us to much more than seeing specific objects. Going further, we should note that even the imagism which lyric poets have been trained to draw out of their personal experiences seems too individualized. Images and references to what is happening in other parts of the world on a national and international scale have become just as central to our lives as what is happening in our bedrooms and backyards.They appear on our television sets each evening. Do we ignore them? It would seem that in an expansive poem imagery might be drawn from many places at once. Eliot and Pound began to understand this and the new surrealists have an inkling of it, but most poets and poetry editors still distrust the poem too wide in its references. The single extended image is still primarily admired: the lyric poem which begins and ends with, say, pictures of sunlight on a house in the upper West Side of New York. We have sent too few adventurers wandering among the hemispheres. John Berryman in *The Dream Songs* and Robert Lowell, in *The Notebook*, did attempt some adventures, yet their visions were severely limited by emphasis on the "I." Most poets in a complex, fluctuating world create a poetry that retreats from instead of incorporates that world.

The lack of explicit sex in contemporary poetry seems, at first, understandable. The intense lyric, with its concentration upon specific words and music, cannot take four-letter words or explicit sexual description without their power to shock and arouse overwhelming other elements of the poem. Moreover, most of the major literary periodicals print a rather genteel poetry. One may describe almost anything but sex, and one is encouraged to, in very particular detail. However, this taboo against explicit sex does not really apply to the short stories many of these magazines publish, where the occasional sexually vernacular term or explicit scene (though generally brief) has won acceptance. An interesting double-standard—but again, sexuality is more apparent and shocking in the lyric poem.

Another reason for lack of sexuality in poetry is the

changing relationship of the sexes at the last part of the century. Both male and female poets often find it difficult to write when they are worried about offending and being labeled chauvinistic. But sex is endlessly fascinating, sexuality attracts readers, sexuality is, of course, an essence of human meaning. You would not guess this from our poetry. Whereas other forms of art, particularly fiction, have used the freer standards of the age, poetry remains relatively pure, the lyric poetry convention of dealing with sexuality close to that of previous centuries.

Or is it? Previous poets, working within the strictures of their societies, wrote and published some extraordinarily explicit poems even given these strictures. Going no farther in our age than they did in theirs, writing of sex in a muted and restrained way (not perceived of as restrained previously) we shock and arouse no one. The 20th Century has given us no major erotic poetry, when one would expect that erotic poetry is the least it might have provided. Such eroticism, four-letter words and explicit sexual scenes could well be handled in the narrative and dramatic poetry we have lacked. Chaucer, Shakespeare and Byron—to name only three of the great poets who come to mind—certainly had no reluctance to incorporate explicit sexuality, often bawdiness, into their work.

More important is the lack of overtly religious poetry. In a sense, this lack also has been understandable. Ours is neither an age of faith or belief. The characteristic stance is that of agnosticism and humanism, Wallace Stevens' "Sunday Morning" more influential on our poets' thinking and approach to religion than Eliot's *The Four Quartets*. What religious poetry we do have seems often to be a poet's afterthought or an instance of hedging the bets. Few poems are addressed to the monotheistic God and probably would not find a ready reception in the serious journals if they were. The main religious poetry we do have is found in New Surrealism, vaguely mystical, heavily influenced by Eastern religions, felt most deeply in the works of Robert Bly and James Wright.

The time's distrust of Ideology, or at least the western nations' distrust of Ideology, is to be expected after the two world wars, and the wars major powers have fought in colonies and protected nations. On the other hand, science—the new physics and cosmology, the exploration of space and the great N.A.S.A. picture of the Earth turning alone in the heavens, in addition to the continual increase in evidence that the "Big Bang" theory of the universe's origin is correct; the accompanying positings of black holes and white holes, matter continually vanishing and reappearing— has lent some credence to theories of a Prime Creator or creative force which we personify as the Creator. Add to this the speculations of "Life After Life" reports (despite the half mad, half desperate they seem to attract) and we have profound possibilities for renewed poetic exploration of the religious. Then, too, there is the overall realization that Earth is a single ecology, linked with the probability of men destroying all in the holocaust so convincingly pictured in Jonathan Schell's *The Fate of the Earth*. Many feel that only a religious vision of the present, of the future, of the human's responsibility for the planet and its past and future is likely to save us from destroying ourselves.

There is an old saw about avoiding mention of the three forbidden subjects—sex, politics, and religion— on social occasions. There is the usual rejoinder that sex, politics and religion are the supremely interesting things, often the only ones worth discussing. The vast majority of contemporary poetry avoids these three primary subjects, or treats them only in minor notes. It is no wonder contemporary poets have so few readers and are unlikely to have more until poetry has something to *say*, something that we must hear, something we will not be able to live reasonably full lives without encountering. Only the compelling book of poetry will compel readers.

That readers want, need, and read work which deals with religion, science, ideas—which tells stories and treats of wonder and awe—once a principle if not *the* principle province of poetry—is seen by the enormous hunger for science fiction felt worldwide. Here is another area—science fiction-oriented or based poetry— ripe for exploration. Many of the world's past great epics can, in fact, be considered as "science fiction." Unfortunately, most of those few poets attempting science fiction presently have tried to deal with it via imagistic lyrics. The lyric form is inadequate for the immensity of the subject.

If another type of poetry is to be written at the end of the century and into the next, a more universal, holistic, expansive poetry, it cannot flourish continually subjected to and judged solely by New Critical and Imagistic lyric poetry standards. Another set of criteria is necessary.

V

I have outlined what some of these criteria might be in a short essay, "The Forest for the Trees: Preliminary Thoughts on Evaluating the Long Poem," published in the Spring, 1983 issue of *The Kenyon Review*.

But in order to prepare for such evaluations, it seems to me that the modern critic's and poet's understanding of one more key term, *didacticism*, must be addressed.

The term is perjorative in our times. To write didactically is to intend that a work instruct; what follows is the connotation of teaching others too much, of lecturing, moralizing, preaching. Yet until our time, didacticism was a legitimate type of poetry, used by many to give information and instructions. It used the epistle, the verse essay, and the satire as its most important forms.

I would agree with most modern critics that almost all work which is *completely* didactic is best left to third-rate poets. However, two elements of didacticism, the informational element and the teaching element (this without overly moralizing or preaching), I would argue, are vital. I have already noted at length some of the informational aspects poetry can contain, particularly in longer narrative and dramatic forms. The teaching element, the meaning-bearing element, is a matter that requires further examination.

I think it can safely be said that almost all important poems, including lyric ones, contain a significant amount of didactic intent, and it is this didactic intent—so brushed aside by critics of our time—that makes them and their authors necessary to us. Forget Auden for a moment. Poets are not musicians and are not painters; the most important of them have important things to say as well as to imply, whether we regard their truths as pseudo-truths or not. To deny them ideas, philosophy, wisdom and vision is to limit and trivialize them and the capacity of their art.

The best example of didactic intent in a poem at hand is contained in one that many educated Americans consider the finest single American poem of the century, Wallace Stevens' "Sunday Morning." Despite its being presented as a woman's meditation on not attending church, her meditation counterpointed by a somewhat mysterious other voice, it is certainly a message-bearing poem, the strongest poetic argument for hedonism ever written. It is filled with what could certainly be termed didactic statements:

> Divinity must live within herself:
> Passions of rain, or moods in falling snow;
> Grievings in loneliness, or unsubdued
> Elations when the forest blooms; gusty
> Emotions on wet roads on autumn nights;
> All pleasures and all pains, remembering
> The bough of summer and the winter branch.
> These are the measures destined for her soul.

Stevens goes on to use a favorite device of modern poets who wish to make statements: asking rhetorical questions such as "And shall the earth / Seem all of paradise that we shall know?" knowing full well that a reader may be led to say, "Yes, the earth is the only paradise." Assuming agreement, he is free to write:

> The sky will be much friendlier then than now,
> A part of labor and a part of pain,
> And next in glory to enduring love,
> Not this dividing and indifferent blue.

He continues definitely to instruct us:

> There is not any haunt of prophecy,
> Nor any old chimera of the grave,
> Neither the golden underground, nor isle
> Melodious, where spirits gat them home,
> Nor visionary south, nor cloudy palm
> Remote on heaven's hill that has endured

As April's green endures; or will endure
Like her remembrance of awakened birds,
Or her desire for evening, tipped
By the consummation of the swallow's wings.

And he gives us, outright, the most famous statement, "Death is the mother of beauty" in the fifth stanza, repeating it in the sixth, and finally concluding with the magnificent closure continuing from "We live in an old chaos of the sun." Why we do not usually call this poem "didactic" is because Stevens has successfully directed the intent to instruct toward *one* person, rather than applying it to all people. Nonetheless, that one woman can obviously be taken to stand as our representative.

A second of our great moderns, Robert Frost, elevated much of his finest poetry with didactic intent: "Something there is that doesn't love a wall" and "Earth's the right place for love: / I don't know where it's likely to go better" and

My object in living is to unite
My avocation and my vocation
As my two eyes make one in sight.
Only where love and need are one,
And the work is play for mortal stakes,
Is the deed ever really done
For Heaven and the future's sakes.

Additionally, the didactic intentions of "Provide, Provide" and "Directive" should be recalled.

Stevens, Frost—what about Roethke? "Great nature has another thing to do..." and "In a dark time, the eye begins to see."

Williams? "I will teach you my townspeople / how to perform a funeral..."—surely a didactic poem through-

out. Or, from "At the Ball Game": "It is beauty itself /
that lives / // day by day in them / idly—."

Elizabeth Bishop: "The art of losing isn't hard to
master."

John Berryman: "Life, friends, is boring. We must
not say so."

In his later poetry, Robert Lowell often disguises his
didactic intent, his judgments, as parts of observation;
but they're present:

> The Aquarium is gone. Everywhere,
> giant finned cars nose forward like fish;
> a savage servility
> slides by on grease.

Sylvia Plath tells us outright: "Dying / Is an art,
like everything else."

And to return to W.H. Auden, we can remember the
last stanza of "Lullabye":

> Beauty, midnight, vision dies:
> Let the winds of dawn that blow
> Softly round your dreaming head
> Such a day of welcome show
> Eye and knocking heart may bless,
> Find our mortal world enough;
> Noons of dryness find you fed
> By the involuntary powers.
> Nights of insult let you pass
> Watched by every human love.

The "Emperor's New Clothes" point is that despite
all the attention given to "how a poem means" in modern times, poets, especially major poets, have something to say and in poem after poem have persisted in
saying it. We have so de-emphasized looking for
"meaning" in our poetry we have often come to ig-

nore or excuse its presence. The attention given to non-ideational aspects of poetry, much of it a result of New Critical practices and understandings, has continued beyond mid-century and become part of the lyric free verse confessional poetry basis, the poetry continuing to be written from a primarily imagistic conception. Thus, the *actual* poet himself or herself speaks the poem; yet this speaker, a product of our skeptical times, seldom cares or dares to teach, pronounce, moralize, or even judge. One's individual truth is not another's. The result is the characteristic neutral, descriptive, self-probing poem seldom expanding its attention beyond that which the particular "I" can know. I am not arguing against the principle of "show, don't tell." I'm saying that fiction writers (and poetry should best be understood, as it was until our time, as a fiction) have always understood that fiction is a *combination* of showing and telling; only the poets have come falsely to feel that showing without telling is all.

To reverse this situation, poets and critics will again have to bring back devices earlier 20th Century poets used to make their poetry carry an informational and teaching element. These devices include use of narrative and dramatic poetry elements, or narrative and dramatic poetry of almost any length in which the statements and judgments are not perceived as necessarily those of the author, but of the character—especially in the dramatic monologue—and the use of rhetorical questioning, such as practiced by Stevens. There will have to be reminders that didactic intent applied to the individual addressed in a poem (quite often the "you") is also quite often to be interpreted as applying to the general "you" (a disguise for the "we" poets are reluctant to use). There should be a renewed emphasis by teachers of poetry, poets and critics, on the use of the persona or mask—so mastered by W.B.Yeats—to re-move the burden of the poet's having to be "honest" all the time. Finally, younger critics might, by reading back more into past ages of poets, recall that the con-cept of the poet in the late 20th Century can be seen as a greatly diminished one when compared to the stat-ure poets have previously held in many countries and still hold in some others than the U.S. That concept sometimes allowed the poet, particularly the mature and proven poet, to take on the role of spokesman for his people, his country, his age. If he spoke sound words of wisdom; if he attempted to teach as well as sing; if he could translate major concepts, philosophy, under-standings of the hard and soft sciences into living, feel-ing language the layman could understand and be moved by; if he offered vision and perhaps even some proph-ecy; and if his art was equal to the task of all this *weight* in poetry, he might well be praised rather that scorned.

Something has obviously gone wrong in a nation which turns for its truths to psychologists, journalists and poli-ticians. The trivializing of poetry, the blind and too little questioning and untrue attitude that "A poem should not mean / But be" and that didactic intent or elements in a poem necessarily make it second rate have done great damage to our art. Until differing con-cepts of how poetry can be important in a way other than music or painting are important begin to be fully acknowledged again, our poets will be but small art-ists singing only in minor keys.

BUSINESS AND POETRY

By Dana Gioia

I. THE SITUATION

> if you demand on the one hand,
> the raw material of poetry in
> all its rawness and
> that which is on the other hand
> genuine, then you are interested in poetry.

(Marianne Moore, "Poetry")

"Money is a kind of poetry," wrote Wallace Stevens, a vice-president of Hartford Accident and Indemnity, a corporate lawyer, an expert on surety bonds, and, almost incidentally it might seem, one of America's greatest poets. It is a shame Stevens never expounded on this remark, for he certainly knew as much about both sides of the equation as any man of his time. But significantly Stevens, who spent most of his life working in a corporate office, never made the slightest mention of business or finance in all of his poetry and criticism.

That so prolific a writer would have maintained half a century of silence on the world of his daily life seems strange at first. His personality must be partially responsible. Few men and fewer writers have proven as reticent as Stevens about their private affairs. But personality is only part of it. Stevens' silence was hardly

---

"Reprinted by permission from *The Hudson Review*, Vol. XXXVI, No. 1 (Spring, 1983). Copyright 1983 by Dana Gioia

unusual when seen in the context of American poetry.

There have been many important American poets who supported themselves—either from necessity or choice—by working in business, but none of them has seen it as an experience fit to write about.

Another American poet, T. S. Eliot, spent the most productive decade of his life working in the international department of Lloyd's Bank of London, but the closest he ever came to writing about that milieu was in these lines from *The Waste Land*:

At the violet hour, when the eyes and back
Turn upward from the desk, when the human engine waits
Like a taxi throbbing waiting...

Hardly a major statement. But perhaps these lines summarize all that modern American poetry has had to say about the business world—its tedium, isolation, and impersonality.

American poetry has defined business mainly by excluding it. Business does not exist in the world of poetry, and therefore by implication, it has become everything that poetry is not—a world without imagination, enlightenment, or perception. It is the universe from which poetry is trying to escape.

Modern American poets have written superbly of bicycles, of groundhogs, of laundry left out to dry, of baseball cards and telephone poles. One of Randall Jarrell's best poems depicts a supermarket. Elizabeth Bishop has written movingly about an atlas, and Robert Lowell about breaking in a pair of contact lenses. James Dickey found a way to put animals in heaven, and Ezra Pound put many of his London literary acquaintances in hell. Sodomy, incest, and pedophilia have been domesticated by our domineering national Muse as readily as have skunks, armadillos, hop toads, and at least one wart hog. But somehow this same poetic tradition has never been able to look inside the walls of a corporate office and see with the same intensity what forty million Americans do during the working week. It often seems to be a poetry of the exception rather than the rule. Distant, visionary, refined, unreal and unrealistic. Our poetry, in short, seldom deals directly with the public institutions that dominate American life, or, with the situations that increasingly typify it. If our poetry recognizes business at all, it has reduced this enormous and diverse national enterprise into a few static images inherited from the movies—the factory smokestack belching fumes (circa 1870), the pot-bellied tycoon with the gold watch chain puffing his cigar (circa 1890), the Charlie Chaplin look-alike subverting the assembly line (circa 1920), and perhaps for the truly *au courant* the man in the gray flannel suit rushing to an expense account lunch on Madison Avenue (circa 1950). A few images of a world seen only from the outside. For American poetry what happens on Wall Street or Wilshire Boulevard seems, as remote as icebound Zembla. No, more remote, for even Zembla has had its recent admirers.

To say all this is not so much to criticize as to observe and, I believe, to observe fairly. The business world, including the huge corporate enterprises which for better and for worse have changed the structure of American life over the last fifty years, is generally and noticeably absent from the enormous body of poetry written in this century. While this omission is hardly a cause for alarm or even regret, it certainly deserves notice.

This exclusion is especially puzzling when one remembers that an important and recurring claim of contemporary American poetry has been its professed ability to deal with the full range of modern life. Everything, critics have insisted for decades, is the proper subject for modern poetry; unlike the art of the past, contemporary poetry excludes nothing. Likewise our poets have often announced their almost indiscriminate openness to experiencing and writing about everything America encompasses. One of the best and certainly the most succinct of these avowals appeared in Louis Simpson's Pulitzer Prize-winning volume, *At the End of the Open Road* (1963). Instructively the poem is entitled "American Poetry," and in it Simpson quickly summarizes the positions of both the formalist and experimental factions of modern verse. The entire poem runs:

> Whatever it is, it must have
> A stomach that can digest
> Rubber, coal, uranium, moons, poems.
>
> Like the shark, it contains a shoe.
> It must swim for miles through the desert
> Uttering cries that are almost human.

A brilliant short poem. One that almost rings authentic. But like most discussions of our native genius, it is prescriptive rather than descriptive. Like it or not, certain foods agree best with certain stomachs. American poetry has always had an easier time digesting other poems than rubber or coal, and it has found even the most seasoned executives unpalatable. Although American poetry sets out to talk about the world, it usually ends up talking mainly about itself.

II. A DILATION OF MONEY

Give money me, take friendship whoso list.

(Barnabe Googe)

Money and wealth are ancient subjects, as old as poetry. Although economic interpretations of culture mainly hit their vogue in the last century, philosophers, moralists, theologians, and historians have discussed the role of money since Xenophon. It has been from the beginning a constantly interesting and perplexing subject. The Bible is full of maxims and parables on earthly riches. Likewise the mythology and folklore of every Western culture contain cautionary tales on the pursuit and possession of wealth—from Midas to Dives and on to Rumpelstiltskin. Greed and parsimony have always stood as standard subjects for comedy. In our own tradition money has been a standard subject in poetry since Chaucer's pilgrims, and has continued to remain important not only in major poets like Ben Jonson and Alexander Pope but also in lesser ones like Barnabe Googe and George Crabbe. Hence modern American poetry has never had any difficulty in assimilating money as a subject. It has only had to look toward tradition.

Business, however, is in many ways a modern concept. Certainly the ancients formed partnerships and corporations, but these were small and personal affairs when contrasted to the enormous organizations of today. Wealth can be personified in the wealthy, but how does one deal with a business once the founder has passed away, the company has merged into a conglomerate, and its real control has been divided between a dozen inconspicuous directors and a hundred thousand stockholders? Acquired, reorganized, and diversified, the company no longer has any immediately comprehensible identity. It exists in a world of market forces and economic principles remote from the myths and symbols of traditional poetry. Business, then, is an abstract collective noun as difficult to deal with tangibly as "liberty," "the people," or any other political buzzword.

Money has been a subject which has often interested American poets, possibly because they usually have had so little of it. For many poets, it must possess the irresistible lure of the unattainable. That the penurious young Eliot made so little mention of money in his poetry testifies not only to his patrician breeding; it may also be the best argument for considering him a British rather than an American poet. It is rather a writer like Pound who typifies the real native attitude—money is the root of all evil and all good. And who can deny its intrinsic appeal to a poet, for is not money literally the one true metaphor, the one commodity which can be translated into all else? Everything seems to have its price, and that price is denominated in money. It is hardly a coincidence that Pound's *Cantos*, whose unifying principle is metamorphosis, should eventually have discovered money as its theme. It was only one step from Ovid to economics.

But while money itself was a subject very interesting to poets, few of them really knew much about it. Not simply the subtleties of the money markets but even the basics of economics, "the dismal science," were lost on them. Yet what they did know about money was important: it bestowed power. It was not money but the possession of it that interested them. Gradually in the forties and fifties American poets began exploiting the theme that novelists had discovered half a century before—namely, that while America has no kings or popes or princesses, it does have its millionaires and billionaires. The Rockefellers and Mellons are our Romanovs and Medicis, and the legends that surround men like Howard Hughes are hardly less amazing than those around King Vlad of Transylvania.

In most of the poems in which American writers seem to be dealing with business, they are usually talking about wealth or, more specifically, about the wealthy. Significantly, they deal with money in much the same way they deal with madness or genius. It is a gift or curse from the gods. For example, when Robert Lowell, who came from one of Boston's most distinguished families, discusses the effect of money on his relatives, he sees wealth as a puzzling personal attribute, almost exactly analogous to his own poetic gift. As if in a pun, a fortune becomes a fate. Therefore, Lowell's presentations of the two businessmen in his immediate family—his grandfather, who made millions in hydraulic mining out West, and his father, who worked for Lever Brothers—are the stories of two individuals struggling with curses in the form of wealth. Likewise Randall Jarrell's remarkable monologue for an imaginary multimillionaire, appropriately entitled "Money" (which, like Lowell, he based on a relative—an uncle who was a prosperous but hardly Croesean candy manufacturer), deals almost abstractly with power and personality. It could as easily be about a warlord or a king as about an industrialist.

Stevens was right. Money *is* a kind of poetry: an epic as encyclopedic as the *Cantos*. Consider just a few variations. Money, the long green, cash, stash, rhino, jack, or just plain dough. Choke it up, fork it over, shell it out. To be made of it! To have it to burn! Put it on a barrelhead. Grease it on a palm. It feathers a nest, holds heads above water, burns holes in pockets, and makes both ends meet. Just one long shot can make a big killing. *Musae Americanae, canamus paulo maiora*: let's raise the bidding and up the ante. No, I won't deny it. Who else is our national muse but lithe Miss Liberty who has paraded in alluring deshabille across two hundred years of currency and graced our pocket change with her universally crowned head.[1] As any coin collector knows, latter-day Eisenhowers and Susan B. Anthonys are no true substitutes. If there is a native genius for language and metaphor, he will be found discussing money. In lump sums or loose change, greenbacks or double eagles, megabucks or buffalo heads, our national vision is most easily translated into dollars and cents. Though rates of exchange may fluctuate, the subject is always the same. But money, dear reader, is not business, and now let us return to the business of this essay.

III. WAYS OF SURVIVING

Reading over this account of a literary apprenticeship, I find that it often mentions very small sums of money. There is good reason for the mention, considering that money is the central problem of a young writer's life, or of his staying alive.

(Malcolm Cowley, *"And I Worked at the Writer's Trade"*)

Most critics, I suspect, will hardly be concerned about the absence of business from the world of modern American poetry. They will probably feel instinctively that its omission is proper. And this feeling will not necessarily come from political motivation. The world of commerce will seem to them the territory of novelists rather than poets. It reflects a world of common experience, not the particular and private experiences supposedly at the center of poetry. If pressed, they might argue that its omission also comes from the personal backgrounds of our best poets. Few, they would assume, had much experience in the business world, so how could they write about it with any authority or interest?

We Americans have strong preconceptions about our poets. They must be people out of the ordinary; they must be strong, even eccentric individuals. Most often they are pictured either as scholars or vagabonds, Longfellows or Whitmans, Allen Tates or Allen Ginsbergs. The popular arts are full of such images. Consider the dreamy-eyed, wavy-haired Leslie Howard wandering through America with a knapsack in *The Petrified Forest*. To a surprising degree, even the more serious arts share these stereotypes—witness Bellow's *Humboldt's Gift*, Jarrell's *Pictures From an Institution*, Nabokov's *Pale Fire*, and the various Beat novels. Significantly both academics and bohemians are perceived as living outside the economic and social systems which characterize our nation. They are cut off, usually by choice, from the daily lives of the American middle class. And we have been trained to respect them for this separation.

One anecdote will serve to summarize the conventional wisdom about business and poets. Allen Tate's brother, Benjamin Nathan Tate, was a self-made tycoon who had formed two coal companies in Cincinnati and sat on the Board of Directors of several large companies including Western Union. When Allen left Vanderbilt in 1922, Benjamin decided to start his brother on a business career by securing him a job in one of his coal offices. "In one day I lost the company $700 by shipping some coal to Duluth that should have gone to Cleveland," Tate later explained. Benjamin soon agreed that Allen should seek a literary career and, much to his credit, supported the poet at several crucial periods in his life. The moral is easily drawn. The poet is an impractical, dreamy sort of fellow incapable of holding down a real job. Too bored with business to pay attention to the most basic details of a job, a poet can be nothing but a poet.

But these stereotypes simply do not hold up to scrutiny. As often as not, American poets have sprung up in the most unexpected places, including corporations. Stevens is not the inexplicable exception he is usually made out to be. Rather he is the exemplary figure for a certain type of American poet, a type he did not even originate.

Although one now thinks of Stevens as the archetypal businessman-poet, Stevens himself would have looked back to Edmund Clarence Stedman as a role model. Stedman, a now forgotten poet, was probably the most influential critic and anthologist of poetry in turn-of-the-century America, and his work was still a powerful presence during Stevens' youth. Born in Stevens' adopted Hartford in 1833, Stedman entered Yale at sixteen only to be expelled before graduation (though in that sweet irony that follows poets' careers, twenty-two years later the University awarded him an honorary degree). After several unsuccessful attempts at journalism Stedman came to Wall Street in 1863 where he soon opened up a brokerage firm. His financial and poetic careers prospered together. In his own poetry Stedman was a leading spokesman for the Genteel Tradition, but in his criticism he exhibited a broad appreciation for other poetry which found its fullest expression in his once definitive collection , *An American Anthology* (1900), which celebrated the nation's third century by defining the poetic achievement of its past. In town he presided over New York literary life while out in his country manor in the newly-established artists' colony of Bronxville he entertained little-known young poets like E. A. Robinson with his reminiscences of Whitman. He died at the height of his fame and prosperity in 1908.

Stedman has had many successors beyond Stevens and Eliot. Richard Eberhart was for many years one of the chief executives of the Butcher Polish Company in Boston and still sits on its Board of Directors. The late L. E. Sissman was a director and eventually a vice-president of Kenyon and Eckhart, a Boston advertising agency, where he worked on accounts in the financial and food industries. Even the late Archibald MacLeish, a lawyer by training, spent a decade as editor of *Fortune*, the major American business magazine of the thirties and forties.

A. R. Ammons, who has won the Pulitzer Prize, the Bollingen Prize, the National Book Award, and the National Book Critics Circle Award in poetry, was a salesman for a scientific glass manufacturer in New Jersey when his first book appeared. He had left elementary school teaching a few years earlier and joined the sales department of his father-in-law's company, Friedrich and Dimmock, Inc. "It was total isolation," he later recalled, but when making sales calls in the Paterson area he did manage to visit the invalid William Carlos Williams and take him out for an occasional drive. He spent ten years in business before leaving to teach at Cornell.

In his early thirties James Dickey also left teaching for a successful stint in business. He joined the McCann-Erickson advertising agency in New York in 1956 as a junior copywriter on their newly acquired Coca-Cola account. When the advertising agency moved the account to their Atlanta office, Dickey was promoted and transferred along with it. Three years later, having established himself in his new profession, he switched agencies to increase his salary and responsibilities, becoming copy chief of a small Atlanta agency. Two years later Dickey made another career jump, this time to become Creative Director at Burke Dowling Adams, Atlanta's largest agency. While making his career in advertising, Dickey also published his first book, *Into the Stone and Other Poems*, on the strength of which he won a Guggenheim fellowship which inspired him to quit business for writing.

Robert Phillips also left academics for advertising. After six years of college teaching, Phillips joined the creative department of Benton & Bowles as a copywriter in 1964, then moved through McCann-Erickson and Grey Advertising before becoming a Vice-President for J. Walter Thompson, America's largest domestic agency, where he has had major responsibility for the enormous Ford Motors and Eastman Kodak accounts. In his early forties, David Ignatow spent eight years helping manage the Enterprise Bookbinding Company, a family business. After his father's death he briefly became president of the firm before liquidating it. Ignatow then took two other jobs in the printing industry before receiving a Guggenheim Fellowship which eventually led him into teaching.

There are many more examples. The late Richard Hugo spent thirteen years working for the Boeing Company in Seattle until the publication of his first book brought him the offer of a teaching position. In 1964 Ted Kooser left graduate school at the University of Nebraska and took a temporary job at Lincoln Benefit Life. He has worked there as an insurance underwriter ever since.

William Bronk managed a family lumber and fuel company in upstate New York. R. M. Ryan works as a
stockbroker in Milwaukee. Richard Grossman spent nearly
ten years working for Gelco, a family-controlled leas-
ing company in Minneapolis. James Weil also helped
manage a family business for many years in addition
to running a private literary press. Terry Kistler, the
poet who is a past chairman of Poets & Writers, manages an investment firm. The late Ronald Perry was
Director of Advertising and Public Relations for Out-
board Marine International. Art Beck, the mysterious
and talented San Francisco poet, is a pseudonym for a
local banker. If one also added poets who practiced
law like Melville Cane, Archibald MacLeish and Lawrence Joseph (a distinct profession which in some re-
spects is more closely related to academics than to business), the list would be even longer. And there are
undoubtedly many other businessmen-poets unknown
to me. [2]

There have also been some would-be poets among
American businessmen, most notably Hyman Sobiloff.
A great philanthropist and mawkishly sentimental poet,
Sobiloff sat on the board of half a dozen large companies, and must have had a yearly income considerably
greater than that of the top forty American poets combined. He also bore the curious distinction of being
the only American poet to have ever been nominated
for an Oscar. Sobiloff, however, recognized that his
verse was less than perfect and paid Conrad Aiken,
Anatole Broyard, and later Delmore Schwartz to give
him weekly poetry lessons, though he did have to park
his limousine around the corner to avoid infuriating
Schwartz.

There were then at least half a dozen important American poets, and many minor ones, who were also busi-

nessmen. While this is an interesting fact in itself, it is also one that requires some qualification lest it be misleading. The exceptional careers these poets pursued while writing stand in such sharp contrast to the more conventionally "literary" careers of their contemporaries that it is easy to overlook the similarities. For both the lives and the works of these businessmen have more in common with the mainstream of American poetry than one might suspect. It is first necessary to recall that none of them chose to make careers in business. Initially all of them attempted some conventional literary career. The young Stevens began enthusiastically as a journalist in New York. Eliot studied philosophy and then, like Dickey and Ammons, taught briefly. Eberhart studied at several universities and later became private tutor to the son of the King of Siam. Phillips served as a university administrator and teacher. But soon, because of exhaustion, failure, dissatisfaction or simply poverty, all of these poets left their vocations for business jobs. In a sense, like most people, they "fell into" their new careers. Business was the most convenient alternative that society offered them when their earliest ambitions went sour, and they made what their parents and family probably called a sensible choice.

That poetry was a long-standing vocation in the minds of these men has an importance beyond biographical accuracy. It is a necessary element in understanding their development as writers. When one sees how these well-educated men had professed poetry since youth, it becomes obvious that it is both naive and ill-informed to portray them as primitives emerging from the dark woods of corporate life suddenly able to speak with the tongues of men and angels. Too many critics have expressed a sort of innocent amazement that businessmen could actually write poetry, not to mention good and even great poetry. In different ways the public images of Stevens and Dickey have been especially distorted by this type of mythologizing. And it is easy to see why. The businessman-by-day / poet-by-night contrast makes good copy. Everyone enjoys stories of double lives and secret identities. Children have Superman; intellectuals have Wallace Stevens.

Even first-rate critics found it impossible to avoid sensationalizing the paradox of the mild-mannered insurance executive who wrote uncompromisingly modernist poetry at home. Witness Delmore Schwartz's mischievous glee in beginning his discussion of Stevens' poetry with a description of his office life. But was Stevens' gift to create supreme fictions while working in Hartford truly more surprising than Ezra Pound's ability to write majestically of life's beauty while living in a degrading Pisan concentration camp? I think not. The course of Stevens' career, like those of the other businessmen-poets, was hardly unusual. Was it really surprising that a Harvard man, formerly editor of the *Advocate* and a fledgling writer in New York, would eventually become a major American poet? Rather it seems a classical background for an American writer of that generation. What was most odd about Stevens was not his occupation, but rather that he never visited Paris or Rome, since most corporate vice-presidents do that.

For some American poets, then, business was just one more way of surviving. While it was not the career that any of them originally wanted, it did support them until that other more difficult career became a reality. Let the naive think that the support they needed was only financial. Certainly a job in business paid the bills, but it also provided each poet with much more than money. At least outwardly, it gave direction to his life, providing him with a sense of place and purpose in his society. It gave him attainable goals—raises, promotions, pensions—in contrast to the seemingly unattainable goals of his artistic life. (Witness Eliot's pride at each of his promotions in the Lloyd's Bank international department during his early London years.) The routines of office life might have been anaesthetizing, but this very feature also had its advantages for a poet. The pattern each job imposed on his life helped numb the anxiety he felt between poems, in those long, dry periods when it seemed he would never write again. For a job is more tangible than talent. It can't vanish suddenly the way that inspiration often seems to. And in a small way it gives the poet the success and security which poetry does not readily allow. In short, business provided these men with the same security and satisfaction that many of their contemporaries found in teaching. Young poets chose between both careers looking for the same rewards. Which direction they went in was ultimately a matter of temperament and values.

IV. THE FIRST VOICE

The first voice is the voice of the poet talking to himself—or to nobody.

(T. S. Eliot, "The Three Voices of Poetry")

Stevens, Eliot, Ammons, Dickey, and the other poets I have mentioned form an extremely diverse group. They differ as much in the types of companies they worked for as in the poetry they wrote. They come

from different parts of the country and different levels
of society. They share no obvious spiritual or literary
affinities. Their careers exhibit little similarity except
that they all wrote poetry while working in business.
Yet if one studies the lives of the poets about whom
some biographical information is available, curious re-
semblances begin to emerge.

All of these poets were successful in their business
careers and soon achieved a comfortable, secure standard of living. Yet once they had achieved any level
of fame, they immediately quit their jobs (all except
Stevens, that is, for whom real fame came very late in
life). And finally and most significantly, although they
wrote much of their best work during their years of
employment, none of them had anything to say about
their experiences at work, at least in their poetry. While
their working lives may have had an important influence on the course of their writing, this influence was
never directly manifested. They maintained a disinterested silence about their workaday worlds. Confessional
poetry may be a dominant mode in American poetry,
but while it has unlocked the doors to a poet's study,
living room, and bedroom, it has stayed away from
his office—unless, perchance, the office happened to
be located in a university English department.

Given the strongly personal and often autobiographical character of most American poetry, it seems aston-
ishing that these men did not use the images and situations of their daily occupations as what Marianne Moore
called the "raw material" of their poetry (which, as
she pointed out earlier in the same poem, should not
"discriminate against business documents"). Their aver-
sion to using this part of their lives is an indication, I
believe, of how strongly the prevailing fashions in
American poetry have determined what is written even

by its most gifted poets. It is also proof of Northrop
Frye's conjecture that what a poet writes more often
comes from other poetry than from life experience. And
finally their collective taciturnity suggests that in the
creative process of our businessmen writers there is a
form of voluntary censorship which often determines
what and how the poet will write.

Such a criticism is not primarily intended to demonstrate the paucity of political and social commitment
in modern American poetry, though this very real lack
may be taken as a sign of the problem I am discussing. Instead, these observations point to a larger complaint—namely, that not only has our poetry been unable to create a meaningful public idiom, but that it
even lacks most of the elements out of which such an
idiom might be formed. At present, most American poetry
has very little in common with the world outside of
literature—no reciprocal sense of mission, no mutual
set of ideas and concerns, no shared symbolic structure, no overlapping feeling of tradition. Often it seems
that the two worlds don't even share a common language. At its best our poetry has been private rather
than public, intimate rather than social, ideological rather
than political. It has discussed symbolic places rather
than real ones, even when it has given the symbols
real names. It dwells more easily in timeless places
than historical ones. For many reasons—some of them
compelling—most of our poets have rejected the vernacular of educated men and tried to develop conspicuously personal and often private languages of their own.

Much was gained in this process of refinement—greater
accuracy and intensity in language, intellectual rigor,
and surprising originality. Much was also lost, not the
least of which was the poet's audience. But long before this audience disappeared, a more important thing

had already happened: the poet had lost his sense of addressing a public, lost the belief that he and they had anything significant in common. This failure of assurance changed everything he wrote. There still could be occasional public statements or popular successes, but they seemed incidental to the general course of the art. Readers still existed, but no longer did they form a cohesive or important group. Nor did they matter economically. They were too few and too scattered to reward the poet with either wealth or fame. At times they almost seemed to exist in spite of him, and he in spite of them.

Paradoxically, the poet in business has thrived in this neglect. His job, like the academic's, has sheltered him from the economic consequences of writing without an audience, and possibly even tutored him in surviving alienation. Every day at the office reminds him what an outwardly futile spiritual life he leads. If they knew about his writing, his business associates would surely see no more value in such unlucrative endeavors than his fellow poets would see in his drab job. The poet then is doubly dismissed—by his peers in both professions. Meanwhile he is doubly busy with both vocations. If he survives as an artist, he will certainly be able to face the neglect of an invisible public without much additional difficulty. If he perseveres as a poet, he will be writing primarily for himself, but performing for such an appreciative and discerning audience has its advantages (though fame and wealth are not among them). Writing for one's self makes autobiographical exposition unnecessary. The poet can plunge immediately into the particular idea or experience that interests him. The organization can be complex, the ideas difficult, and the symbolism private. It doesn't matter as long as the poet himself can follow them.

They belong to a private world which is the poet's mind. His poems are what Stevens described in "The Planet on the Table":

> Ariel was glad he had written his poems.
> They were of a remembered time
> Or of something seen that he liked.
>
> Other makings of the sun
> Were waste and welter
> And the ripe shrub writhed.
>
> His self and the sun were one
> And his poems, although makings of his self,
> Were no less makings of the sun.
>
> It was not important that they survive.
> What mattered was that they should bear
> Some lineament or character,
>
> Some influence, if only half-perceived,
> In the poverty of their words,
> Of the planet of which they were part.

V. THE UNCOMMON VOICE

Then surely the splendour of the language is something in excess of the sense, adding enormously to our pleasure but not assisting (rather obstructing) our understanding.

(Donald Davie, "Essential Gaudiness: The Poems of Wallace Stevens")

I am a man of fortune greeting heirs.

(Wallace Stevens)

Office life, investments, interest rates, corporate politics, annual reports—these are not subjects which would
seem especially congenial to poetry, and one can understand how a poet, even one for whom these topics
were matters of daily concern, would ignore them. Certainly Eliot, Stevens, Ammons, and the others managed to ignore them and still write distinctly personal
poetry. But must one conclude then that there was no
fruitful interchange whatever between these poets' literary and professional lives? Could there not have been
a less obvious connection? Knowing that these poets
made careers in business, would it not be reasonable
to assume that some of them at least might have written poetry more closely related to the language and
concerns of the average man than did their academic
bohemian contemporaries? Yet this is clearly not the
case.

It is surprising to notice how consistently extreme
these poets often were in developing distinctly private
and literary languages. While poets as dissimilar as
the academic, Yvor Winters, and the bohemian hermit,
Robinson Jeffers, kept their diction and syntax scrupu-
lously within the bounds of common speech, the businessmen, Stevens and Eliot, pushed vocabulary and
grammar not only to the limits of comprehensibility
but quite often beyond. Stevens in particular sometimes
wrote with the wild, inventive abandon of a Shake-
spearean clown who has suddenly found himself the
protagonist of a tragedy. Nonsense can be serious stuff,
and from this point of view Stevens is the finest nonsense poet in American literature, an Edward Lear for
epistemologists. This unfortunately is an aspect of his
talent too often missed by his more sober academic
commentators.

Another nonacademic professional, Dr. William Carlos Williams, often remarked that while his daily work as an obstetrician exhausted him, it also exercised a good influence on his poetry. Working with common people filled his ears with the contemporary, spoken American English he would use so distinctively in his poems. Surprisingly, for Stevens, Eliot, Ammons, and the others the similar experience of working in business had the opposite effect. Rather than pushing their work in the direction of colloquial language, their professional lives seem to have given them a deep dissatisfaction with the general spoken idiom as a medium for poetry. Perhaps after a full working day of sensible, no-nonsense talk in the office, these poets received a secret, rebellious pleasure in letting themselves go at night by writing extravagantly simply for the joy of it.

Only after work could Stevens, who wore conservative grey suits and drank coffee at the office, write "Tea at the Palaz of Hoon," which begins:

> Not less because in purple I descended
> The western day through what you called
> The loneliest air, not less was I myself.

And being himself at home meant compulsively inventing foreign-sounding words and names, prizing paradoxes, and giving his difficult poems brilliant but mysterious titles.

Returning home from an eight hour day of tabulating the balance sheets of correspondent foreign banks, Eliot wrote some of the most allusive and elusive poetry in English, poems more difficult than any he had written while a student of philosophy. Few great poems in our language are as difficult as those Eliot wrote while working at Lloyd's. The difficulties of *The Waste Land* are well known, but even Eliot's minor poems of this period often read like purposefully forbidding private jokes. One poem begins:

> Polyphiloprogenitive
> The sapient sutlers of the Lord
> Drift across the window-panes.
> In the beginning was the Word.

The poem continues with neologisms and conspicuously unusual diction (often rhyme words designed to call attention to themselves)—"superfetation," "mensual," "piaculative," "epicene." As in Stevens, one must often pause to determine what is going on beneath the playful verbal surface. In a poem like the one above, "Mr. Eliot's Sunday Morning Service," the social commentary has been transformed into an exercise in private sensibility. Significantly, Eliot also developed his gift for nonsense poetry during this period.

Stevens and Eliot left a valuable heritage of how language could be used aggressively in poems, and the later businessmen-poets have been conspicuous among their heirs. Ammons and Dickey, for example, have both shared the interest in exploiting language for its own sake. While Robert Creeley, a bohemian academic, was adapting Williams' "American idiom" to distill a poetry made up of the sparsest conversational diction and syntax, his exact contemporary, A. R. Ammons, while still a salesman, developed the same idiom into an extravagantly different style. Whatever one thinks of Ammons' long, carefully syncopated sentences, his ostentatious puns, or his sometimes knotty diction, it is impossible to deny that his poetry uses language in a forceful and individual way. Likewise James Dickey's poems often seem to carry themselves on by the sheer energy of their verbal invention. Whether he is imitating the sermon of a fervent woman evangelist or recreating the wandering mind of a drunken telephone lineman, Dickey puts his trust (sometimes undeservedly) in the force of the speaking voice and allows it to spill relentlessly from line to line. There is, in short, a degree of verbal aggression in the work of both Dickey and Ammons that one does not often notice in the poetry of their contemporaries.

The poetry of William Bronk is uncommon in a somewhat different way, though it too can be seen in relation to the work of Stevens. Like Stevens, Bronk really has one principal subject underlying his poetry—the perception of reality. His characteristic form is the short, imageless poem:

> We aren't even here but in a real here
> Elsewhere—a long way off. Not a place
> To go to but where we are: there.
> Here is there. This is not a real world.

Concise, abstract, and earnest, Bronk's poems are as extreme as Ammons' or Eliot's most difficult work in their rejection of the imprecision and ease of common speech. They are poems of solitude and isolation, as austere as a mathematical equation. Every word bears the weight of deliberate reflection. Bronk is not an ingratiating poet. He does not want to be. In order to appreciate him one must accept his work totally on its own terms. Otherwise it seems trivial or pompous. Bronk will not meet on the reader's terms. The whiteness of the page is his universe, not ours. Like Ammons or Dickey or Stevens he tries to become a god and create the world of a poem on that whiteness.

These examples are not presented to prove that working in business played the primary role in developing these poets' particularly extravagant or abstract styles. That development was the result of each writer's personal background—their taste, education, personality, and ambitions. What is important was that business had no overtly countervailing effect of simplifying their style or determining an accessible public subject matter. The paradox is simply that these "men of the world" wrote out of a much more private universe than their supposedly sheltered academic counterparts. Perhaps because they worked in isolation, or because their private calling to poetry had so little to do with their daily work, these men had trouble addressing any audience but themselves. Their poems are soliloquies rather than speeches, poetry which the reader does not so much hear as overhear. Contrast strongly idiosyncratic poets like Stevens or Dickey or Ammons with an academic poet and the difference becomes immediately apparent. Take, for example, William Stafford, who is usually considered one of the most personal and quiet American poets writing. Do any of the three poets above speak with such calm self-assurance to average readers as does Stafford? Listen to this short, characteristic passage from "A Ritual to Read to Each Other":

If you don't know the kind of person I am
And I don't know the kind of person you are
A pattern that others made may prevail in the world
And following the wrong god home we may miss our star.

He might even be addressing Stevens.

VI. SOME CONCLUSIONS

"Though Stevens found it tiresome when others pointed to his dual career as businessman-poet, that afternoon he himself called attention to it and the way he handled it. Louis Martz, his campus host that day, recalls "...he opened up his briefcase and he said, 'Now you see everything is neatly sorted out here. Over here in this compartment...is my insurance business with the farmers, and over here in this compartment is my lecture and some poems that I want to read. I keep them completely separated.' At other times, though Stevens might argue just the opposite, stressing the seamlessness of his career..."

(Peter Brazeau, "Wallace Stevens on the Podium: The Poet as Public Man of Letters")

The purpose of this study so far has been to challenge some assumptions normally made about American poets and to raise a few unorthodox questions about the relationship between life and art. The discussion has centered on a curious collection of modern poets who were also businessmen—a group whose very existence no scholar has previously noted. Sticking close to biographical facts and textual examples from these writers, it has pointed out a few unexpected features and demonstrated the difficulty of making easy judgments about the problematic interaction between their two careers. The issues raised in this discussion, however, extend far beyond this small group. Ultimately they concern how any serious artist survives in modern society. Looking at poets who worked in business merely focused the discussion on one of the more extreme and paradoxical examples of the alienated modern artist. In further exploring the broader issues raised by this odd group of individuals, I will try to deal with the more general problem of how American poets, who cannot make a living from their art, still manage to write and develop.

First, it is necessary to recapitulate the key questions raised thus far in this discussion. How did their business careers affect the lives and works of these poets? Why did these men write nothing about their working lives? What personal and artistic changes did they undergo in the years they spent in jobs that were alien if not antagonistic to their vocations as poets? Were these jobs only ways of surviving until fame caught up with them? Is anything even gained by segregating them off as a distinct group of writers and comparing them to other poets whose lives seem more typical? These are serious questions that anyone, who looks closely at the lives of these poets, must ask. And for the most part they are impossible to answer directly. The facts, as they exist, point towards an almost absolute separation between their business careers and imaginative lives. But can this really be all there is to say about the matter? Common sense instinctively demands a more direct relationship between life and art. Parts of the same man's life can't be split apart as easily as Stevens claimed to Louis Martz. While it is certainly true that for many years these poets led strictly divided lives, there must also have been deeper connections between their two careers. Here the critic must become a speculator using not only scholarship and analysis but also inference and intuition. My conclusions here are admittedly both tentative and subjective, but the investigation seems nonetheless worthwhile. Risks are sometimes necessary to achieve difficult goals. One law of investment remains constant between business and poetry—the higher the risk, the higher the potential reward.

There is no need to dwell on the unfortunate effects of business careers on each of these poets. The personal difficulties these men faced are obvious. Their careers took up the greater part of their time and energy. Coupled with the responsibilities of family life (all of these poets were married), their careers forced their reading and writing into odd hours (late evenings, weekends, brief vacations) and probably prevented them from reading and writing as much as they would have liked. Stevens and Eliot both complained about this deprivation, and it is reasonable to assume that one would hear similar complaints from Dickey, Ammons, Bronk and others if one had access to their letters and journals. In Eliot's and Stevens' cases at least, the strain of managing two careers also put severe pressure on their marriages. Likewise their business careers isolated them to a greater or lesser degree from the society of other writers, artists, and intellectuals. Unless like Eliot they had the friendship of a Pound, they lived very much on the margins of the literary world. Working in regular jobs, they did not have the flexibility or leisure to participate fully in either the formal or informal artistic life of their times. There was little freedom to travel, give readings, lecture, edit magazines or anthologies, accept residencies at universities, nor even much time for mixing at the parties, festivals, and conferences where writers and artists so often meet. In a real sense business turned these poets into outsiders in the literary world.

These are considerable disadvantages. Time to think, time to read, time for idle but intelligent conversation—all of these are essential for most young writers' development, and it is foolish to think that without them a poet's performance won't suffer in some way. Likewise it is hard, discouraging work to write in isolation

during one's few spare hours after working a full day
in an office (or a classroom). How inconceivably private the act of writing must have been for Stevens draft-
ing out poems night after night in the dull solitude of
suburban Hartford.

From another perspective, however, these unsuppor-
tive conditions might seem like advantages. For example, while working in business might have cut these
poets off from the literary world, it also sheltered them
from it. Working obviously helped them economically.
It gave them an income independent from writing, free-
ing them from most literary hackwork. They did not
have to review uninteresting books, write matter-of-
fact lectures, teach unwanted classes, or quickly sell
every poem and essay. They could afford to choose
what they wrote and where they published.

An outsider has another advantage. While he may
feel intense pressure to prove himself as a writer to
the people he rightly or wrongly perceives as "insid-
ers" (editors, reviewers, academics, self-supporting
writers), he has the advantage of setting his own pace.
Paradoxically, this doubly busy man enjoys a leisure
which professional poets both inside and outside the
academy do not. The outsider can wait however long
it takes to mature as a writer, whereas the professional
poet must try to speed up the process. Hence Stevens
could wait until he was forty-three before publishing
Harmonium, perhaps the most remarkable first book in
American poetry, and then could afford another thirteen years of silence before bringing out a second collection. Likewise Ammons managed a decade of quiet
growth between the publication of his first, privately-
printed volume and his second, widely-acclaimed book.
And Eliot, in another way, could carefully conserve
his energy, waiting months or years between perfectly

achieved poems. By contrast, for the creative writing teacher the pressures of "publish or perish" may be fatal. The same university job, which frees a young poet from many financial worries, can also add the irresistible pressure to write too much too soon, and the writing may become slick, automatic, and superfluous. Of course, poets inside the academy can survive these pressures, but it is not easy, the demands of tenure, promotion, and prestige and money being as great as they are.

There may even be advantages in missing the society of other writers. One may lose the fun of talking with professional wordsmiths or miss the confidence of knowing the people whose names one sees on bylines and editorial mastheads, but one also doesn't waste ideas in conversation. Talking is easier than writing and much more immediately gratifying. More than one poet has poured his genius into conversation at the expense of his poetry. Also, a person working in business is not constantly besieged by the latest artistic fads. A poet's sense of his own direction might sharpen best if he is not forced to defend or discuss it every day in a classroom or cafe. Witness how steadfastly Stevens followed his independent imaginative course during the frenetically political thirties. Would he have been able to maintain his quirky integrity had he not been working in a Hartford insurance office? Eliot, Ammons, Bronk, and Dickey show the same stubborn independence in following their own sensibilities. Whatever their faults, they are clearly strongly individual writers.

Eliot saw an additional advantage in being constantly busy with another career. It kept one from writing unnecessary poems. Eliot frowned on poets who wrote when they had nothing new to say. Nor was it necessary, he felt, to make one's self write—since the really important poems would force themselves out. When George Seferis, the modern Greek poet, visited Eliot in London, he complained that his duties as a diplomat left him no time for writing. Eliot chided him, saying that this was actually a blessing and his poems would be better for the wait. The unconscious, he told Seferis, is working all the time.

As usual, Eliot had a point. For some poets at least, long silences are an essential stage in their creative growth. The classic examples are Rilke and Valery, for whom many years of poetic silence became the necessary preparation for writing their greatest work. Their cases are extreme, but silences of more modest duration have often proved necessary for many authors, especially at turning points in their careers. A few poets like Hardy or Lawrence apparently manage to write continuously throughout their lives, but for most poets, even great ones, writing is an exhausting, intermittent process. A competent poet can usually turn out some lines of verse for any occasion, but a serious poet at some crucial point in his artistic development may hesitate to write at all. His old style of writing may no longer seem authentic or appropriate, and a new form of expression that answers his particular needs may still seem impossible to find.

How poets overcome these imaginative challenges in life is an interesting study. Stevens, whose confidence was shattered after the uneventful debut of *Harmonium,* stopped writing for years and devoted himself to office work and private reading. Eliot, on the other hand, abandoned poetry at the height of his career after the triumphant reception of *Four Quartets,* turning his creative attention entirely to writing for the theater. Many poets, however, undergo less dramatic transitions which nonetheless demonstrate the courage to endure months or even years of self-doubt while they wait between poems. Like Rilke they will not write when there is nothing to say. They know that they cannot fake the real thing. Instead they let the work mature slowly in the back of their minds or shape itself through innumerable drafts and revisions. It is essential for these poets not to force themselves to write too much or too quickly.

Business has proven a helpful shelter for this careful and introspective kind of writer. Their jobs kept them sufficiently occupied to take away some of the guilt and self-questioning of not being able to write. For other poets teaching or translation has filled a similar need, but these undertakings may be too closely related to writing to offer comfort for everyone. To businessmen-poets like Stevens and Eliot, the steady rhythm of office life provided a sense of security and relief. While such regulation would have been unbearable to extroverted poets like Pound or Auden, for some of their more private contemporaries it obviously worked, and the proof is in their poetry.

Outside careers also sheltered these men from other dangers. In some way hard to pin down, their jobs protected them from the occupational hazards of writing poetry. For whatever reasons, the profession of poetry is a dangerous one in America, perhaps because it is so damnably difficult to succeed in any meaningful way. Some poets have literally killed themselves for fame, destroying themselves slowly in public before distastefully appreciative audiences. Suicide, alcoholism, drug addiction, poverty, and madness are all too often fellow-travellers of poetry in this country, as the biographies of our poets tragically demonstrate. This essay is not the place to speculate on why this should be so, but a glance at the lives of writers like Vachel Lindsay, Hart Crane, H.D., Delmore Schwartz, John Berryman, Weldon Kees, Robert Lowell, Winfield Townley Scott, Sylvia Plath, and Anne Sexton show it to be the case. Nor is this self-destructiveness new. Baudelaire noticed this distinctively American curse in the life of Poe, and it creeps less overtly even into the lives of writers like Robert Frost, Conrad Aiken, Randall Jarrell, Elizabeth Bishop, and Theodore Roethke.

Somehow working in business gave the poets I have discussed a saner perspective on their careers as writers. It gave them other accomplishments that helped soften the recurrent sense of frustration and failure any poet at times experiences. It also tutored them in the difficult virtue of patience. But most importantly, working in nonliterary careers taught them a lesson too few American writers learn—that poetry is only one part of life, that there are some things more important than writing poetry. This is an obvious statement to anyone but a writer, yet it is one that few American poets have ever learned because it addresses life and not art. It has nothing to do with writing poetry, and knowing it will never help a writer gain fame or perfect his craft. But learning it may help him or her survive.

F. Scott Fitzgerald's dictum that "there are no second acts in American lives" is too often true about our poets. But it need not be so. The young Eliot survived a disastrous marriage, the agonizing physical and mental decline of his wife, and his own mental breakdown. The middle-aged Stevens weathered the public failure of *Harmonium* and the more bitter private failure of his family life. Yet both kept their sense of artistic purpose intact, and both went on to write their most ambitious and influential work because they possessed a hard-earned realism about their lives. They did not define themselves as men by poetry alone but recognized other ambitions and responsibilities—even when the resulting actions were painfully at odds with their literary dreams. They knowingly sacrificed time and energy away from their writing. Paradoxically those compromises saved them as artists. By refusing to simplify themselves into the conventional image of a poet they affirmed their own spiritual individuality, and the daily friction of their jobs toughened the resolve. Ultimately the decisions they made forced them to choose between abandoning poetry and practicing it without illusions. Anyone who studies the lives and works of the men who combined careers in business and poetry finds this hard-won sense of maturity and realism at the center. Their lives may not always provide other poets with overtly inspiring examples, but their careers offer pragmatic and important lessons in spiritual survival. In a society which destroys or distracts most artists, they found a paradoxical means to prosper—both as men and writers. In American literature that is not a small accomplishment.

---

1 One of her heads deserves special mention—that on the so-called Mercury dime, minted between 1916 and 1945, which was modeled after a young woman named Elsie Viola Kachel, also known as Mrs. Wallace Stevens.

2 Indeed there were. Since first publishing this essay I have received letters from numerous poets who work in business. Some of the more widely published writers include Miriam Goodman, Larry Rafferty, Michael Malinowitz, James Autry, John Barr, and Suzanne Doyle.

POETRY AND RELIGION

By Mark Jarman

> Man needs a metaphysics;
> he cannot have one.
> —Frank Bidart

> ...logic doesn't stand a chance, a prayer.
> —Andrew Hudgins

Just as poetry persists in the face of widespread indifference, so has a sense of the religious in poetry continued to exist despite the indifference of most poets to religion. It might be better to modify the word *indifference* or to refract it into ignorance, nostalgia, and animosity. Nevertheless, the religious impulse in poetry endures; many poems being written today show that urge to be tied to or united with or at one with a supernatural power that exists before, after, and throughout creation. I plan to draw most of my examples from contemporary American poetry, with examples from the English past during the greatest period of devotional verse, and from modern American poetry wherein that breakdown of an institutional and monolithic religious view began to be clear. Even the more or less devout among religious poets today suspect the institution of religion, and not as Dante and Milton did, because of its corruption, but because of the requirements of orthodoxy against which the individual struggles.

I do not believe that there is one genre of religious poetry being written in America today, as there was

in England in the 17th century, despite the appearance
of the recent anthology *Contemporary Religious Poetry,*
edited by Paul Ramsey; in fact, aside from a smatter-
ing of nuns and priests, his anthology includes many
who profess no religion and might have written their
religious verse inadvertently. Still, religion is important to contemporary poetry. For poets who have grown
up with strong religious training, it provides a background, usually a violent one. The desire for atonement, secularized by the romantic movement, takes a
characteristic form in American poetry about nature.
The imagination, in Wallace Stevens' terms, provides a
substitute for God for some poets and the need for alternative, non-Christian myths fills the gap for others.
When the above alternatives fail, poets may still try to
make a peace with present circumstances and regard
grace or mercy with almost theological reverence. T.S.
Eliot's "Ash Wednesday" and "Four Quartets," two of
the greatest achievements at uniting religion and poetry in this century, loom over the vestigial modes of
the religious poem in our time. Even contemporary
readings of Eliot's poems, emphasizing their secular
themes, suggest that they embody all the approaches
to religion and poetry taken by Eliot's grandchildren
and great grandchildren. Finally, there are the exceptions—poems written out of genuine religious conviction that do not beg the question of belief but, in fact,
call non-belief itself into question.

I

Batter my heart, three-personed God; for You
As yet but knock, breathe, shine, and seek to mend;
That I may rise and stand, o'erthrow me, 'and bend
Your force to break, blow, burn, and make me new.
I, like an usurped town, to 'another due,

Labor to 'admit You, but O, to no end;
Reason, Your viceroy 'in me, me should defend,
But is captíved, and proves weak or untrue.
Yet dearly 'I love You, 'and would be loved fain,
But am betrothed unto Your enemy.
Divorce me 'untie or break that knot again;
Take me to You, imprison me, for I,
Except You 'enthrall me, never shall be free,
Nor ever chaste, except You ravish me.

(John Donne)

The language of overthrow, assault, abduction, and
rape still gives Donne's poem its vigor; for him and
his first readers, violence is redemptive, Christ's sacrifice for us is harrowing. Like Saint Theresa, Donne invites
a sexual assault; some argue that he meant the poem
to shock the readers of his own day. Yet today the
language of violence, with some exceptions, still has
an impact. The taking and holding and retaking of towns
recalls the feudal importance of the city state, but the
news from the Middle East is full of similar battles.
The Platonic argument for Reason as a viceroy might
seem especially dated, both for the French notion of
the king's representative, but also for the belief that
reason represents a higher power. What is current still
is the mingling of abduction, divorce, chastity, rape;
we still see these actions played out romantically in
the popular media, even though we have an increasingly complex political response to them. To wit, violence against a spouse or lover is never justifiable. We
suspect sexuality that includes violence, even among
consenting adults. We can read Donne's poem within
its 17th century context as playing with a radical paradox, making the most carnal of metaphors out of God's
grace, and see it as the poem of a believer who may
even relish the discomfort his final metaphor will give

the puritanical. What is striking today, as it was then, is the combination of violence, and especially sexual violence, and religion.

For Donne this combination sprang from the intensity of his religious feeling. For the contemporary American poet steeped in some religious background, this combination of religion and violence springs from the intensity of his feeling *about* religion. More often than not it is an intense feeling about religion's failure to explain or redeem the world. Still, the most highly charged language available to the poet is the language of faith. Sometimes it is the problem of still having a religious bent that hangs the poet up.

In Frank Bidart's "Confessional," the poet confronts the division between a unified religious view of experience and the belief that such a view is impossible. Religion is the problem in the poem; when the speaker's mother has had her conversion experience, she kills her son's pet cat to demonstrate denial of the world. Clearly the speaker's mother is mad. It is less clear if the speaker is conversing with a priest or with an analyst whose job is to show him that "forgiveness," that virtue neither mother nor son could show to each other, "doesn't exist." The speaker contrasts his relationship with his mother and St. Augustine's with his mother, St. Monica. He calls "The scene at the window at Ostia / in Book Nine of the *Confessions*" one "to make non-believers / / sick with envy..." The speaker envies the supernatural closeness of Monica and Augustine. After the scene in which they meditate on the lives of the saints, Monica feels her relationship with her son, converted now to Christianity as she had wished him to be, is "complete" as we might say in contemporary psychological terms; thus satisfied, she dies nine days later. But it appears that the poet Bidart, who paraphrases the *Confessions* so beautifully, is sick with envy for another thing—the immediate experience of God without the veil of nature. He must conclude, speaking now as the listener, priest or analyst, *"Man needs a metaphysics; / he cannot have one."* How violence is manifested may be at the heart of this problem. Killing a pet cat is a far cry from "NO REMISSION OF SINS / WITHOUT THE SHEDDING OF BLOOD"; the psychological violence between mother and son also yields no salvation. When he learned that his mother miscarried his stepbrother or sister the day she saw a man fall from a tree and lie screaming on the ground at a golf course, the speaker recalls that he was "GLAD." Perhaps, salvation through violence and the completion of relationships happens only to others, like St. Augustine and *his* mother, people in other times and other places, characters so distant that the idea that forgiveness does not exist or that man cannot have a metaphysics has no effect on them; the pathos is contemporary and ours alone.

A number of poets share Bidart's nostalgia for faith, especially those who have recognized its transforming power in others and have some experience of it in their own lives. But they approach the subject obliquely, as if they would not be taken seriously otherwise. Bidart contrasts stark denial and its equally stark irresolution with the richness of resolution and belief, yet concludes that the latter is impossible. Andrew Hudgins in "Prayer" shows the embedding of religious experience, most of it Southern fundamentalism, in his life, and its strongest vestige in him today—prayer, "of all the things I've given up to logic / ...the one I can't / let go..." In a two-part poem, he devotes the first part to ringing changes on ecstatic religious utterance as he recalls hearing a woman in church holler, *"Hep me, Jesus! Hep me, Jesus!"* then hearing another in a backwoods Baptist revival cry *"Hurt me, Jesus! Hurt me, Je-*

sus Lord!" and finally in a cheap motel hearing a woman scream *"Fuck me, Jesus! | Fuck me, Jesus!"* To the last he responds wryly, "It must have been a prayer." But in part two of the poem he confesses that having learned his girlfriend had been raped at seventeen, he cannot convince himself that it doesn't bother him and that, implicitly, he will not leave her, even though she says she will understand if he does. He confronts the impotence of prayer, as he employs it, and the fact that "when I put my hands on friends and say, / *Be healed*, nobody yet has been healed." Though the analytical, logical voice of Bidart's confessor might intone, "Prayer is useless," Hudgins compares his urge to pray to "the virtues of a vicious circle, why / a mother suckles her contagious child, / or why the victim has to be rebuked." Hudgins does not appeal to Donne's viceroy, Reason, but to its opposite. Against this, "logic doesn't stand a chance, a prayer." Hudgins describes a persistent faith that is still useless against violence.

In terms of the world, it has always been so. The world's urge toward violence ends, in Christian mythology, in the murder of God Himself. It is an article of faith, based on the accounts of a few witnesses, that the man who admitted to being God was resurrected from the dead. No amount of belief in Him averted the catastrophe. The orthodoxy of the Christian church, both Catholic and Protestant, maintains that the event was necessary, even while condemning those who brought it about. "NO REMISSION OF SINS / WITHOUT THE SHEDDING OF BLOOD." No chastity without ravishment. Yet how can we see metaphorical redemption in literal fact?

Violence within a religious context still shocks us, even when we know that violence is an essential part of religion. Thus, David Dooley's "Revelation" is as disturbing as any of Flannery O'Connor's stories for much the same reason; it drops the catalyst of violence into a world of religious faith and produces a monstrous shape. Dooley's poem narrates the story of a clergyman who takes a kid, probably a young male prostitute, in off the streets and tries to give him a new life, only to learn that the boy has murdered a little girl in the neighborhood and stowed her body in the basement room where he has been put up. The poem is full of the vocabulary of religion, but when the preacher sees the child's body and remarks, "Precious Jesus, the blood," Dooley demands that we think twice: once about the statement and the literal fact of the victim's blood; once about the precious blood of Jesus which, if we think of it at all, we remember only in figurative terms, even though it, too, was a literal fact. Here, the redemptive blood and the convicting blood have nothing to do with one another. The minister lets the boy escape, giving him his car to get away, then to himself tries "to name all of the authorities who must be notified." The violence at the heart of Christianity, which allows Donne to create his great paradox, no longer maintains its metaphorical meaning in the contemporary poem that includes religion. Its literalness is a sign that religious poetry, like Donne's, is impossible.

II

LOVE (III)

Love bade me welcome: yet my soul drew back,
          Guilty of dust and sin.
But quick-eyed Love, observing me grow slack
          From my first entrance in,

Drew nearer to me, sweetly questioning
       If I lacked anything.

"A guest," I answered, "worthy to be here":
       Love said, "You shall be he."
"I, the unkind, ungrateful? Ah, my dear,
       I cannot look on thee."
Love took my hand, and smiling did reply,
       "Who made the eyes but I?"

"Truth, Lord; but I have marred them; let my shame
       Go where it doth deserve."
"And know you not," says Love, "who bore the blame?"
       "My dear, then I will serve."
"You must sit down," says Love, "and taste my meat."
       So I did sit and eat.

(George Herbert)

Aggressive violence is not the only metaphor, of course, for the way God calls his own. Herbert's famous "Love (III)" presents an entirely different human milieu, in which God offers his grace courteously, requiring only humble acceptance (rather than humble refusal). By taking the mystery of the Eucharist and turning it into a simple domestic meal, Herbert expresses a desire for a gentler atonement than Donne's. In American poetry, in most poetry since the Romantic era, this desire is clearest in poems about the natural world.

The poet William Matthews has observed humorously that American literature is "thick with forest Christians" and that the theme of many nature poems is "I went out into the woods today and it made me feel, you know, sort of religious." The satire is effective because of its self-evidence. Matthews' lampoon depicts American poetry of the natural world, but it certainly doesn't eradicate it. Perhaps, it will render the too fluent poet of nature a little more self-conscious. What interests me, however, is how in approaching the mystery with religious respect American poets anthropomorphize nature, even to the point of domesticating it, as Herbert does Love, in order to make it inviting, and most importantly, inviting to us.

James Dickey does this in "In the Tree House at Night." Having built his ladder up into the tree, he and his brothers, "one dead, / The other asleep from much living," rest above "lakes / Of leaves" and "fields disencumbered of earth / That move with the moves of the spirit." In this case, Dickey makes the spirit of nature one with that of the dead brother; it "touches the tree at the root" and sends "A shudder of pure joy" up the trunk. As important as the biographical detail is (Dickey has another poem about his brother who died before he was born), the drama of the poem is to invest nature with a believable spirit, e.g. a dead brother's, so that communication with nature can seem human, specific, domestic, and not merely oceanic; Dickey does have poems, of lesser quality, with larger and vaguer aspirations. The idea that his dead brother's spirit, once he has located himself deep and high inside the natural world, may be inhabiting his own body allows him these powerful lines which still convey the conventional romantic goal of nature poetry:

> My green, graceful bones fill the air
> With sleeping birds. Alone, alone
> And with them I move gently.
> I move at the heart of the world.

The dead brother has been reincarnated in the tree and Dickey, through an act of Keatsian empathy, knows how that feels, and thus in a complicated interplay makes a metaphor of atonement. It is the religious impulse that leads to such a poem, one of gentle invitation and

submission, but the impulse is separate from any recognizable religion.

"Sleeping in the Forest" by Mary Oliver is a quieter,
less dramatic, but even clearer expression of the desire for atonement, but the desire is for unification with
nature rather than with God:

I thought the earth
remembered me, she
took me back so tenderly, arranging
her dark skirts, her pockets
full of lichens and seeds. I slept
as never before, a stone
on the riverbed, nothing
between me and the white fire of the stars
but my thoughts, and they floated
light as moths among the branches
of the perfect trees. All night
I heard the small kingdoms breathing
around me, the insects, and the birds
who do their work in the darkness. All night
I rose and fell, as if in water, grappling
with a luminous doom. By morning
I had vanished at least a dozen times
into something better.

This is a poem of faith just like Donne's or Herbert's,
but based on a fundamental belief that we share, at
least as American readers, that nature or the earth is
better than the world where we actually do our living.
Earth, personified as having not only memory but "dark
skirts" and "pockets," appears as a classical female deity,
"Mother Earth." She accepts the speaker, like Herbert's
Love, "tenderly." But the actual atonement occurs while
the speaker sleeps, like Jacob's vision of the angelic
ladder. Now Oliver loses her humanity and becomes
"a stone" which presumably has "thoughts" that inter-
pose between it and "the white fire of the stars." I

hesitate to look too closely at Oliver's poem, since it is
deeply flawed as a poem, but its flaws are part of its
faith, too. The stone is on a riverbed, but perhaps it is
a dry riverbed; the stone's thoughts are compared to
moths. And the trees the moths play about are perfect.
Dream logic justifies all. Thus, thought and hearing
unite the poet with nature: thought, hearing, and sleep.
It is a sleep like water, perhaps like the river's water
that might move a stone up and down all night (one
can't look too closely), in a dream where the speaker
grapples with "a luminous doom." The most interesting phrase in the poem, it suggests that literal unification with nature would result in doom for the poet;
but dreamed of this way, it takes on an inviting lumi-
nosity. The poet dreams of a dozen transformations
into something better than what she is on waking and,
implicitly, on having to leave this setting. She has gone
out into the woods and felt more than "sort of religious." Nevertheless, "Sleeping in the Forest" is a defi-
nite example of American forest Christianity.

Robinson Jeffers' late poem "Vulture" offers something a bit sterner than either Dickey's or Oliver's poems,
but with the same fundamental belief. Jeffers' refusal
to anthropomorphize gives the poem its austerity. Yet,
in the pantheistic view of nature I have been describing, the idea of reconstitution as reincarnation is strong;
certainly it is implicit in the Christian sacrament of
communion. Jeffers' poem resonates across religious
boundaries, even though he presents his view as an
alternative to them all:

> I had walked since dawn and lay down to rest on a bare
>   hillside
> Above the ocean. I saw through half-shut eyelids a vulture
>   wheeling high up in Heaven,
> And presently it passed again, but lower and nearer, its
>   orbit narrowing, I understood then

That I was under inspection. I lay death-still, and heard
the flight-feathers
Whistle above me and make their circle and come nearer.
I could see the naked red head between the great wings
Bear downward staring. I said, "My dear bird, we are
wasting time here.
These old bones will still work; they are not for you."
But how beautiful he looked, gliding down
On those great sails; how beautiful he looked, veering
away in the sea-light over the precipice. I tell you
solemnly
That I was sorry to have disappointed him. To be eaten
by that beak and become part of him, to share those
wings and those eyes--
What a sublime end of one's body, what an enskyment;
what a life after death.

Did I say he did not anthropomorphize the bird?
But what is an address to an inhuman presence, concrete or abstract, but a recasting of that inhuman other
into human terms? Still, the eating here does not involve suffering, but organic recycling. No wonder Jeffers has been claimed, or reclaimed, by the environ-
mentalists. He says mostly the right things about the
natural world, the orthodox things. Jeffers could be
called a prophet for their movement; he could be called
a priest of nature poetry; depending upon how you
see the sad development of the wild land around Tor
House, he might even be thought of as a martyr, and
partly because of the decline of his reputation. But his
reputation did not decline because of his romanticism
or his religious faith in the natural world as an expression of God, in fact, as God itself. It declined because of his loathing for man, his absolute contempt
for man's place in the grand scheme of things. Even
forest Christians might find this hard to swallow—but
Jeffers was one of them.

III

Those—dying then,
Knew where they went—
They went to God's Right Hand—
That Hand is amputated now
And God cannot be found—

The abdication of Belief
Makes the Behavior small—
Better an ignis fatuus
Than no illume at all—

(Emily Dickinson)

We say God and the imagination are one...
How high that highest candle lights the dark.

(Wallace Stevens)

For poets who make a religion of nature, albeit one rooted in the romantic faith in one's intuitive, singular response to experience without the intercession of orthodoxy or institutionalized ritual, I have tried to show that at least one of the aspirations is the same—atonement or a oneness that implies forgiveness. Just as Love's meal will make one better, so will sleeping out in the forest at night. Note that missing from these examples is the desire to be ravished or ravaged by a greater power. There is good reason for this, but I'll go into that later. The subject of this section is how a poet makes an alternative to religion or to a given monolithic belief; that is, here I wish to discuss the role of the imagination and the poet as its priest.

Emily Dickinson's poem of 1882, written four years before her death, makes "The abdication of Belief" a practical ethical problem; to have no belief shrinks the compass of one's "Behavior." The key word is "Belief"; Dickinson offers, with true American horse sense, the preferability of a deceptive hope, a fool's fire, to none at all, for it is that which gives illumination. Again, she does not appeal to reason, although she makes a reasonable appeal. She recognizes the necessity of an illumination to live by. Remaking the imagination has been as much an American project as reclaiming the continent.

In contemporary terms, the substitution of the imagination for a traditional belief in God has included the replacement of Christian and Judaic myths with myths reclaimed from the past or from other cultures. Leslie Silko's "Prayer to the Pacific" invokes an ancient native American myth of origin.

Thirty thousand years ago
    Indians came riding across the ocean
    carried by giant sea turtles.
Waves were high that day
    great sea turtles waded   slowly out
                from the gray sundown sea.
Grandfather Turtle rolled in the sand   four times
        and disappeared
           swimming into the sun.

And so   from that time
      immemorial,
            as the old people say,
rain clouds drift from the west
      gift of the ocean.

In "Prayer to the Pacific" Silko refers to the Pacific as being "Big as the myth of origin," then enters into the animistic faith that endows the natural world with spiritual identity. At the same time she identifies herself with her own native American ancestors. Quite apart from the quality of the poem, its religious foundation must enjoy our assent; we must not quarrel with it. Thus, we may read Leslie Silko's revival of an Indian myth with none of the doubt we might experience reading a contemporary poem of equal faith about the birth of Christ, because she has remade the religious imagination without asking us to accept it as part of an orthodoxy or institution.

Quality of the composition, the excellence of the art, is, however, indivisible from authentic religious feeling in poetry. In this way, Robert Pinsky's "The Figured Wheel" is a masterful Ecclesiastical *memento mori*, while at the same time appropriating a symbol and sentiment from the old Peter, Paul and Mary hit, "The Great Mandala":

> Take your place on the Great Mandala
> As it moves through your brief moment of time.
> Win or lose now, you must choose now.
> And if you lose you're only losing your life.

So went the song, which was also a parable protesting the war in Vietnam. Pinsky's poem achieves a greater semantic thickness, and thus extends the significance of the mandala far beyond the limits of the popular song:

The figured wheel rolls through shopping malls and prisons,
Over farms, small and immense, and the rotten little
    downtowns.
Covered with symbols, it mills everything alive and grinds
The remains of the dead in the cemeteries, in unmarked
    graves and oceans.

...the wheel hums and rings as it turns through the births
    .of stars

And through the dead-world of bomb, fireblast and fallout
Where only a few doomed races of insects fumble in the
    smoking grasses.
It is Jesus oblivious to hurt turning to givewords to the
    unrighteous,
And it is also Gogol's feeding pig that without knowing it
    eats a baby chick

And goes on feeding.

As a metaphor for the irresistible force of the cos-
mos, Pinsky's figured wheel, whereon even his own
death and annihilation are "figured and pre-figured,"
is undeniable, for he combines the old myths of Jesus
and the mandala itself with the new myths of science
and global unity: the wheel is covered with "Hopi gar-
goyles and Ibo dryads" as well as "wind-chimes and
electronic instruments." To write a religious poem, a
poem in which some binding belief is at work, a poem
in which as Philip Wheelwright states in the *Princeton
Encyclopedia of Poetry and Poetics* there is "an imaginative fusion of the elements of experience and a responsive faith in a reality transcending and potentially sanctifying the experience," the author must possess some
grain of faith that the concrete details of his metaphor
represent a transcendent reality. Pinsky's poem has to
be considered a religious poem, though certainly not a
devotional one like one of Donne's or Herbert's addresses to a personal, loving, though mysterious God;
Pinsky creates a terrifying juggernaut, offering no salvation from ultimate destruction; yet the wheel's all-
inclusiveness invites our belief. It offers a kind of mercy,
but only to:

...dead masters who have survived by reducing them selves
    magically

To tiny organisms, to wisps of matter, crumbs of soil,

Bits of dry skin, microscopic flakes, which iswhy they are
    called "great,"
In their humility that goes on celebrating the turning
Of the wheel as it rolls unrelentingly...

The adverb "magically" has a whiff of Emily
Dickinson's "ignis fatuus" but the relative clause, "which
is why they are called great," contains Pinsky's own
brand of irony—a necessary cynicism in the face of his
monolithic metaphor. If we assent, finally, to the religious view of "The Figured Wheel," then we accept
an imaginative substitute for many religious myths,
both Western and Eastern. An affirmation of art lurks
throughout Pinsky's poem. If "God and the imagination are one," as Stevens says in "Final Soliloquy of
the Interior Paramour," then it is through art that we
worship them.

Christianity and its traditional icons rarely enter contemporary poetry as a source of devotional attention
or religious celebration except as art or as a stimulus
to the imagination to make art—its religion; for if the
imagination is God, then for poets, poetry is its church.
In Jorie Graham's "Pietà" the purpose is to communicate the visual effect of a picture in the belief that, if
successfully communicated, it will put one in touch
with some transcendent reality, whose nature is relative. After a description of light on the broken body of
Jesus, of how Mary holds him, how the soldiers cast
lots for his garment, "blazing where the light snags on
the delicate / embroidery, and black where the neck-
hole gapes," the resurrection is prefigured in the statement that the body, missing the garment, is "the form
/ gone." Formal qualities compel Graham throughout
the poem, because, whether abstract or figurative, form
in a piece of art compels feeling and creates meaning.
At the end of the poem, we are asked if we hear "the
spirit of / matter." And "the proof of god" becomes a

"cry sinking to where it's / just sound, part of one sound, one endless sound—maybe a cry maybe a / countdown, love—" The word "countdown" is charged with its contemporary meaning, for Graham associates the death of Christ with the annihilation of earth (Graham plays on this analogy throughout her recent work). She asks us to believe in this death as representative of all deaths and not as a divine act in which our sins are forgiven and death is defeated. For Graham, art is the highest good, the transcendent reality that will itself be lost if we destroy ourselves. This recognition has separated the violence in Christianity into another, terrible category, and set apocalypse apart as an end to avoid and not accept as the completion of a divine plan.

Christopher Buckley's "Why I Am in Favor of a Nuclear Freeze" enunciates this division, this belief that nuclear annihilation has nothing to do with a divine scheme, or with the idea of Omega, the end of time, built into Christian myth and other religious systems. Buckley reminisces about being with a friend as teenagers, hunting doves on his friend's father's ranch, and talking about various things, including their days in parochial school.

We even talked of the nuns who terrified us with God and
        damnation. We both recalled
that first prize in art, the one pinned to the corkboard
in front of class, was a sweet blond girl's drawing
of the fires and coals, the tortured souls of Purgatory.

Not to acknowledge the crucifixion as suffered for our sakes leads to condemnation to far worse suffering. This way of scaring people, especially children, repels the two friends. But armed with their 12 gauge shotguns, they shoot doves, and at one point the poet accidentally discharges his gun, narrowly missing his friend's head and his own foot. Then, when they come upon "two tall ears" in the dry grass, he admits "we together blew the ever-loving Jesus out of a jack rabbit / until we couldn't tell fur from dust from blood..." One of their nuns would call this gratuitous violence a manifestation of original sin. Yet Buckley's conclusion is much the same and meant to suggest the larger potential for a final violence against ourselves and nature. Recalling that day of hunting with his friend, now a family man with children, who, like the speaker, doesn't hunt any more, the poet asks about the rabbit, "why the hell had we killed it so coldheartedly?" The poem's final statement illuminates its title: "it was simply because we had the guns, because we could."

Granted, the poem is a personal statement explaining why the poet is, as he says in the title, in favor of a nuclear freeze. But a Roman Catholic grounding in the agonies of damnation and the essential corruption of man also ties together the elements of the poem. It is a poem with a religious background, and plays with the poet's alienation through phrases like "ever-loving Jesus" and "why the hell"; still, it may also be seen as a religious poem. For though it makes the distinction clear between Omega and annihilation it implies that with the right, or the wrong, weapons, man will cause destruction, because of his innate depravity, his original sin.

The poem as prayer against nuclear annihilation has become a genre unto itself. Still, it is curious to note how often such poems play against the Christian notion of the end of days. Chase Twichell's "When the Rapture Comes, I Will Depart Earth (Sign seen in a car window in Kansas)" takes a secular view of this idea; that is, Twichell offers no particular religious background for her statement, but she uses religious vocabulary when she writes "What should we pray / to the smoke and bone of the grass? / That its death light our way into otherness?" And she ends with a secular prayer, an appeal more to those of like mind, those who would regard the sign in the car window as silly at best and at worst somewhat frightening:

> When the rapture comes
> let the car continue through the woods
> unharmed by miracles.
> And if a fierce, atomic heaven falls,
> let it stop us in an ordinary act.

Finally, poems like Buckley's and Twichell's appeal to us to forego notions of transcendent reality, especially religious ones, for they depend inevitably on the end of *this* reality, the one in which we are at home with our ordinary acts, "unharmed by miracles."

IV

> There is not any haunt of prophecy
> Nor any old chimera of the grave...
>   ...that has endured
> As April's green endures...

—Wallace Stevens

> The poem is about the majesty of our
> planetary world, than which no greater
> majesty is available to the human senses;
> no world beyond nor world to come
> that perception can find or imagination invent.

—John Crowe Ransom on "Sunday Morning"

Poetry that takes the imagination as God and presents atonement as the creation of art or the experience of it also holds the earth as the highest reality. Thus, John Crowe Ransom reads Stevens' "Sunday Morning." Thus we find the total destruction of nuclear war abhorrent both for its fact and for its fictional part in the myth of the end, of Omega, and in any religious belief that would subvert existence as we have come, finally, to appreciate it, including especially the Christian belief in judgment. And yet spiritual yearning still exists, and being at one with a painting or a landscape or a natural phenomenon, some inhuman force, itself mortal or inorganic (Jeffers' granite, for example), does not satisfy that yearning. Often its expression hearkens back nostalgically to a former assurance. Charles Wright is the master of this sentiment and its language:

> Ancient of Days, old friend, no believes
>   you'll come back.
> No one believes in his own life anymore.

("Stone Canyon Nocturne")

In his most recent volume, *Zone Journals*, he reiterates his regret and adds a comment about the limitations of language and therefore of the imagination.

> —Words, like all things, are caught in their
> finitude.
> They start here, they finish here
> No matter how high they rise—
> my judgment is that I know this
> And never love anything hard enough
> That would stamp me
> and sink me suddenly into bliss.

("Night Journal")

When Wright does recognize and admit to feeling the sort of transcendence or unity a religious poet depicts, it is with natural cycles, in traditional American fashion, though not exactly as in the nature poetry of Dickey or Oliver. "Bays Mountain Covenant" offers an austere, Zenlike resolution, still taking the natural world as the paradigm.

> Sir you will pardon him you will wave if he now turns
> To the leaf to the fire in the swamp log to the rain
> The acorn of crystal at the creek's edge which prove
> Nothing expect nothing and offer nothing
> Desire no entrance and harbor no hope of change
> Foxglove that seeks no answer nightshade that seeks
>   no answer
> Not to arrive at and be part of but to take
> As the water accepts the whirlpool the earth the storm.

Only Jeffers might have taken the imagination and its earthly dominion to this logical end. Wright's spirituality, like his, is austere, even forbidding.

For lesser mortals, those moments when we call on the assistance of a power greater than ourselves or feel that still point in the turning world when we are capable of blessing because we feel blessed, the language of our religion, whatever religion it might be, comes into play, because it is the language that is most highly charged with feeling. Lest that sound like circular reasoning, let me restate myself to say that religious language, whether it is Christian or Buddhist, exists because it expresses religious feeling most powerfully. It was invented, manmade, to describe states attributed to a divine presence.

Sydney Lea's "Sereno" begins as a poem of the American in the wild, feeling that solitary union the American poet seeks with nature. Then the poem changes to another issue entirely. Hunting duck in December, in the northeast, the poet is suddenly struck by the unusual warmth of the wind, "wafting / forgiveness here." Just as he lets his quarry go, so he lets go a catalogue of forgiveness, including himself in the list:

> I forgive all beings in their desperation:
> murdered, murderer; mothers, fathers wanting something
> the children they bring forth can't give;
>
> Myself for my own childhood cruelties—
> the way I taunted Nick Sereno
> (*serene*, a thing that neighbor never was,
>
> Dark hungry victim, bird-boned butt of my deceptions...
> the time I decoyed him out onto the raft
> and cut him loose, and jumped.
>
> I cut the frail hemp tether, and off he drifted, quacking
>   fear).
> And I forgive the fact that cruelty can circle:
> grown he paid me back one night in a steaming gin mill.

Lea opposes Bidart's assurance that forgiveness doesn't exist; he knows "There is more to all this than I allow." There is, indeed. The idea of forgiveness is rooted deeply in the belief in a merciful God; to forgive, even if aided by circumstances conducive to feeling good, like a warm wind in December, is still a spiritual discipline. It's not easy.

It's not easy invoking the elements of a faith we may have grown to mistrust or grown away from simply because of the pressures of life, especially in a culture that either ignores the religious or offers it up in the crudest, most simplistic, and bigoted forms. Many of Garrett Hongo's poems deal with the deracinated Japanese of Hawaii and the mainland U. S. who have kept traditions alive, sometimes in the face of deliberate persecution. In "O-Bon: *Dance for the Dead*" he recognizes that the most potent way to redeem the memories of his dead father and grandfather, to keep familial feeling alive, is through invocation of Buddhist ritual. Yet he confesses:

> I have no story to tell about lacquer shrines
> or filial ashes, about a small brass bell,
> and incense smoldering in jade bowls, about the silvered,
> black face of Miroku gleaming with detachment,
> anthurium crowns in the stoneware vase
> the hearts and wheels of fire behind her.

He has tried to observe rituals:

> ...pitched coins and took my turn
> at the *taiko* drum, folded paper fortunes
> and strung them on the graveyard's *hala* tree...

Though he has hewed to the requirements of faith, still "the cold sea chafes the land and swirls over gravestones / and the wind sighs its passionless song through ironwood trees." Rarely does the earth send the warm wind at the right time to inspire us with blessedness. Our only approach to the divine, to a force powerful enough to forgive us, appears to be a route of ritual and language whose potency is as mysterious as the goal itself. And as unpredictable:

I want the cold stone in my hand to pound the earth,
I want the splash of cool or steaming water to wash my feet,
I want the dead beside me when I dance, to help me
flesh the notes of my song, to tell me it's all right.

Hongo ends his poem with a supplication to spirits out of his reach. Their paradoxical response, if it comes at all, comes without warning and often without invitation. T. S. Eliot represents it as the intersection of the timeless moment and the temporal world. He is the great poet of this experience and I turn now to him.

V

This is the time of tension between
dying and birth

("Ash Wednesday")

Who then devised the torment? Love.

("Little Gidding")

In his essay, "Grace Dissolved in Place: A Reading of 'Ash Wednesday,'" Vereen Bell argues that "what happens or fails to happen in 'The Waste Land' produces the experience of 'Ash Wednesday,' and what happens or fails to happen in 'Ash Wednesday' issues eventually in the disconsolate theological affirmations of the plays and the 'Four Quartets.'" Or, in other words, "(a)s 'Ash Wednesday' was latent in 'The Waste Land,' so the 'Four Quartets' is latent in 'Ash Wednesday,' an alternative when the quest in 'Ash Wednesday,' perhaps because the result is foreseen, fails." The quest Bell speaks of is for "redeemed time," for "grace dissolved in place," and "not a transcendence of time altogether," as a religious reading of the poem might seek. Bell's stated intention is to do a secular, psychological reading; by so doing, he helps us better to understand what persists in our poetry and links it to religious poetry. The plea "Ash Wednesday" ends with— "Suffer me not to be separated / And let me cry come unto Thee"—is, Bell claims, for a union of flesh and spirit in the natural world, *this* world; or, as T. S. Eliot himself writes, "even among these rocks." Certainly that describes the yearning for a greater wholeness or spiritual integrity that marks the poetry I have discussed so far.

But what of the "disconsolate theological affirmations" Bell alludes to in "Four Quartets"? Bell quotes these lines about "the gifts reserved for age" in part II of "Little Gidding."

> ...the cold friction of expiring sense
> Without enchantment, offering no promise
> But bitter tastelessness of shadow fruit
> As body and soul begin to fall asunder.

These lines are spoken by the "dead master." The poet meets him "In the uncertain hour before morning." The master extends his advice, which is practical as well as theological, from the realm of experience, which Eliot himself has already entered. But not all of the "theological affirmations" of the poem are "disconsolate," unless one refuses to accept redemption on their terms.

"Burnt Norton," the most secular of the four poems because of its avoidance of theological language, presents the "grace dissolved in place" that Bell perceives as the heart of "Ash Wednesday." It is there in the rose garden, where "rises the hidden laughter / of children in the foliage..." In "Burnt Norton" Eliot describes "the still point of the turning world" in a number of paradoxes. Finally, Eliot resorts to Dante's metaphor of the prime mover (drawn from Aquinas).

> Love is itself unmoving,
> Only the cause and end of movement,
> Timeless, and undesiring

Except in the aspect of time
Caught in the form of limitation
Between un-being and being.

"Love," the mover of all things, unmoved by "the tension between dying and birth" in "Ash Wednesday" and all the riot of experience that swirls and hurries over the brown land of "The Waste Land," reveals itself to Eliot in "Burnt Norton" because of his oblique approach, through paradox. Still, his appropriation of the Thomist meaning of Love and his syntax, which is reminiscent of the beginning of the Gospel of John, testify to the power of religious language, even when approached indirectly and perhaps precisely because of that indirect approach.

"East Coker" continues this approach, maintaining that "To arrive where you are, to get from where you are not, / You must go by a way wherein there is no ecstasy," and proceeds with the famous allegory of redemption as an act of surgery:

The wounded surgeon plies the steel
That questions the distempered part;
Beneath the bleeding hands we feel
The sharp compassion of the healer's art
Resolving the enigmas of the fever chart.

Here we learn that "the whole earth is our hospital / Endowed by the ruined millionaire," Adam. Here also, turning bizarrely on the medical metaphor, Eliot introduces his memorable depiction of Purgatory:

If to be warmed, then I must freeze
And quake in frigid purgatorial fires
Of which the flame is roses, and the smoke is briars.

The surgical poet here has exposed the violent heart

of Christianity, where suffering is the way to salvation. The paradox works against common sense, as all paradoxes do; but even when we resolve it intellectually and recognize its innate truth, we still must make sense of another paradox—the strange contract or covenant between this God, the wounded surgeon, and his patients:

> The dripping blood our only drink,
> The bloody flesh our only food:
> In spite of which we like to think
> That we are sound, substantial flesh and blood—
> Again, in spite of that, we call this Friday good.

Here is a disconsolate affirmation, indeed.

"The Dry Salvages" adds to it, but not as powerfully (it is the weakest of the four poems), extending a metaphor of seafaring and addressing us, the readers, as "O voyagers, O seamen" who "suffer the trial and judgment of the sea." Eliot brings Krishna in here, too, and alludes to his admonition to Arjuna in the *Upanishads* that there is no death because the killer cannot truly kill and thus the battle must be fought. As with "East Coker," part IV is the lyrical passage containing the Christian element of the poem; it addresses the Queen of Heaven in Dante's terms as "daughter of your son" or "Figlia del tuo figlio" and beseeches her to:

> ...pray for those who were in ships, and
> Ended their voyage on the sand, in the sea's lips
> Or in the dark throat which will not reject them
> Or wherever cannot reach them the sound of the sea bell's
> Perpetual angelus.

Yet in "The Dry Salvages" Eliot comes closest to describing the attainable goal for the spiritual aspirant:

> For most of us, there is only the unattended
> Moment, the moment in and out of time,

The distraction fit, lost in a shaft of sunlight,
The wild thyme unseen, or the winter lightning
Or the waterfall, or music heard so deeply
That it is not heard at all, but you are the music
While the music lasts. These are only hints and guesses,
Hints followed by guesses; and the rest
Is prayer, observance, discipline, thought and action.

I think most of the poets I have discussed in this essay would recognize and agree with the above description, especially since the "unattended moment" occurs on earth at its best and in conditions when we are at our best. Many might balk at the monastic overtones of passing the rest of the time in "prayer, observance, discipline, thought and action," but only the word "prayer" keeps these terms from being those of artistic practice.

Eliot's greatest problem in "Four Quartets" is how to make a palatable metaphor out of redemptive suffering or the cleansing pain of Purgatory's "refining fire." He must also justify Love's role in the creation of suffering, since Love is the still point, the godhead, the first cause, from which all effects come. Part IV of "Little Gidding" is the lyrical, hymnal movement of this "Quartet":

The dove descending breaks the air
With flame of incandescent terror
Of which the tongues declare
The one discharge from sin and error.
The only hope, or else despair
 Lies in the choice of pyre or pyre—
To be redeemed from fire by fire.

Who then devised the torment? Love.
Love is the unfamiliar Name
Behind the hands that wove
The intolerable shirt of flame
Which human power cannot remove.

> We only live, only suspire
> Consumed by either fire or fire.

That dove has made an appearance earlier as "the dark dove with the flickering tongue" in the meeting with the dead master in section II of "Little Gidding." It has been seen as one of the German bombers besieging England during World War II. This lethal dove, associated also with the Holy Spirit, connotes violence; it brings the "flame of incandescent terror" and purgation, "the one discharge from sin and error." As Eliot transforms German bombers into doves, dark or holy, so he takes Purgatory's flames and makes them the petals of a rose, "infolded / Into the crowned knot of fire..." His poem finds its way back to its beginning, and it bears with it a great weight of wisdom delivered with perfect, even effortless expression, after so much "periphrastic study":

> ...the end of all our exploring
> Will be to arrive where we started
> And know the place for the first time...
> At the source of the longest river
> The voice of the hidden waterfall
> And the children in the apple-tree
> Not known, because not looked for
> But heard, half-heard, in the stillness
> Between two waves of the sea.
> Quick now, here, now, always—
> A condition of complete simplicity
> (Costing not less than everything).

Though Eliot can say that "all shall be well" upon arrival, upon attaining this simple "grace dissolved in place," the absolute cost of this "complete simplicity" is problematic at best.

At the end of this century, is it possible to think of

suffering as Christianity has thought of it and as Eliot
describes it here, as redemptive? The sufferings of the
century include wars and genocide and individual acts
of violence against which even the most devout have
been helpless. Furthermore, is it possible to believe that
the conflagration of the final and greatest suffering will
be redemptive at all? The meaning of Omega has been
divided from its religious promise for as long as we
perceive it as synonymous with holocaust. A cost that
would be "not less than everything" would leave nothing to redeem. Is it no longer possible to see history in
religious terms, as a function of the personality of God,
a God capable of judgment and mercy and expecting
our obedience? Moments of grace are still moments of
grace; we have no other way to describe them except
in theological terms. But wariness as to whom we owe
them and what might be demanded of us—everything?—
has estranged poets to the point that even those who
approach the devotional, the religious, in their poetry,
do so obliquely, almost in code, afraid to name a God
detached from history. Eliot's "Four Quartets" prefig-
ures much that we see of the religious in contemporary poetry. Yet because it portrays suffering—the sine
qua non of Christian belief—as religiously redemptive,
it divides its readers into believers and non-believers.

VI.

I know you are there. The sweat is,
I am here.

--John Berryman

John Berryman's "Eleven Addresses to the Lord" in
his book *Love & Fame* are remarkable for their simplic-

ity, a characteristic that Berryman achieved in many of his poems before he ended his life in 1972, and their genuine power and religious sentiment. In the eleventh of the addresses, the poet asks God that he be an acceptable and ready witness "at the end of time." The poem serves as a believer's eloquent response to many of the reservations stated and implied in this essay so far:

> Germanicus leapt upon the wild lion in Smyrna,
> wishing to pass quickly from a lawless life.
> The crowd shook the stadium.
> The proconsul marvelled.
>
> "Eighty & six years have I been his servant,
> and he has done me no harm.
> How can I blaspheme my king who saved me?"
> Polycarp, John's pupil, facing the fire.
>
> Make too me acceptable at the end of time
> In my degree, which then Thou wilt award.
> Cancer, senility, mania,
> I pray I may be ready with my witness.

Though a contemporary poet may no longer possess the intellectual framework to invest divine meaning in metaphor, as the metaphysical poets did, still he may look to examples of faith. By dramatizing acts of witness he can point to them as examples of Paul's definition of faith in Hebrews 11:1: "Now faith is the substance of things hoped for, the evidence of things not seen." But how is this different from begging the question, when the argument can no longer be logical, reasonable, or even widely disseminated as it was during some previous Age of Faith? In fact, the appeal is emotional, not rational, but the method—witnessing—is still part of our social make-up. From the testimony in the courtroom to the customer's statement of satisfaction with the product, the scale of testifying or witnessing runs from the sublime to the ridiculous. Unlike the metaphysical argument for the existence of a supreme being, this drama in which an individual swears on his own experience persists effectively in our culture. Its most powerful manifestation is steadfastness in the face of suffering and death.

A contemporary religious poet like Berryman must be careful not to assume his suffering will be redemptive. In his eleventh "Address to the Lord" he points to the deaths of other Christians and requests that he, too, will be acceptable, as they presumably were, after death. He proposes three unhappy fates for himself— "Cancer, senility, mania"—and we know that the fate he chose for himself was unhappier still. He prays that he will be a ready witness or, in other words, that his conviction will remain unshaken, that despite suffering he will somehow remain intact. He puns on his own academic career, saying "Make too me acceptable at the end of time / in my degree, which then Thou wilt award." Thus he regards his own capacity for suffering and belief as something God will acknowledge and award retroactively. In this ambiguous and rich conceit (as close as we come to Donne and Herbert), we can see the ancient structure of faith as Paul describes it. Since its substance is invisible, we can glimpse evidence of it only in actions. If it is actually present in ourselves, God will recognize it, though others may marvel. The early Christian martyrs Germanicus and Polycarp embody their faith in acts appropriate to their maturity. The wild young man embracing his fate, Germanicus wishes "to pass quickly from a lawless life." Polycarp, the stoic, older scholar, asks a rhetorical question with an obvious answer. Berryman prays only that he "may be ready." Berryman invites our admiration not for secular acts of courage in the face of death but for acts of courage based on faith in God, who will be made manifest "at the end of time." Here the idea of that end is also clarified; since it must come, there will be no escape. How it will come is not the issue (although as I have pointed out it has become an issue in our day). What is important is that because time will have an end, the readiness is all.

Paul Mariani probes the ambiguous nature of modern faith in "Then Sings My Soul," the last poem in his book *Prime Mover*. Like Berryman, he discovers its evidence in the example of another human being, although not a saint, and also in his own surprising emotional response to that example:

> Who can tell a man's real pain
> —or a woman's either—when they learn
> the news at last that they must die? Sure
> we all know none of us is going anywhere
>
> except in some pineslab box or its fine
> expensive equal. But don't we put it off
> another day, and then another and another,
> as I suppose we must to cope? And so
>
> with Lenny, Leonardo Rodriguez, a man
> in the old world mold, a Spaniard
> of great dignity and fine humility,
> telling us on this last retreat for men
>
> that he had finally given up praying
> because he didn't want to hear
> what God might want to tell him now:
> that he wanted Lenny soon in spite
>
> of the hard facts that he had his kids,
> his still beautiful wife, and an aged
> mother to support. I can tell you now
> it hit us hard him telling us because

for me as for the others he'd been
the model, had been a leader, raised
in the old faith of San Juan de la Cruz
and Santa Teresa de Avila, this toreador

waving the red flag at death itself,
horns lowered and hurling down on him.
This story has no ending because there is
still life and life means hope. But

on the third day, in the last Mass, we were
all sitting in one big circle like something
out of Dante—fifty laymen, a priest, a nun—
with Guido DiPietro playing his guitar

and singing an old hymn in that tenor voice
of his, all of us joining in at the refrain,
Then sings my soul, my Savior God to thee,
How great thou art, how great thou art,

and there I was on Lenny's left, listening
to him sing, his voice cracked with resignation,
how great thou art, until angry glad tears
began rolling down my face, surprising me....

Lord, listen to the sound of my voice.
Grant Lenny health and long life. Or,
if not that, whatever strength and peace
he needs. His family likewise, and

his friends. Grant me too the courage
to face death when it shall notice me,
when I shall still not understand why
there is so much sorrow in the world.

Teach me to stare down those lowered horns
on the deadend street that shall have no alleys
and no open doors. And grant me the courage
then to still sing to thee, *how great thou art.*

Mariani gives us a fuller, contemporary, human situation with a larger sense of community than does Berryman. In this case, the example is not a martyr but an ordinary man, Lenny Rodriguez, whom his friends had mistaken for an extraordinary model of faith, like San Juan de la Cruz or Santa Teresa de Avila, and cast in the romantic role of "toreador / waving the red flag at death itself, / horns lowered and hurling down on him." Both Mariani's and Berryman's poems have a homiletic structure, although Mariani's is more narrative and Berryman's more elliptical, and Mariani makes a proposition first and Berryman first gives examples. Both end with a prayer, as a preacher's sermon would end, which is both personal and on behalf of their audience, their congregation or community, i.e. their readers. Since Lenny Rodriguez turns out not to be a Germanicus or a Polycarp, but another like the fifty laymen he is on retreat with, the problem of how to face death is more clearly existential in Mariani's poem. Lenny has stopped praying because he does not want to hear God tell him death is coming soon despite all of his obligations. He has chosen not to be ready, in defiance, returning spite for spite. Germanicus made his leap of faith and Polycarp faced his death stoically, with the fortitude of 86 years. But Mariani's question is one of immediate concern: "Who can tell a man's real pain / —or a woman's either—when they learn / the news at last that they must die?" What we put off daily, in order "to cope," is facing the death which has not yet come. Lenny Rodriguez's confession of estrangement throws the speaker, and presumably the others, into a state of introspection. "If Lenny's feeling this way, how must I feel?" might be their sentiment.

This is much closer to the emotion of the common person than to the saint. When the poet hears Lenny beside him singing, "How Great Thou Art," "his voice cracked with resignation," he recognizes also just how the normal sinner submits—broken and "cracked," "resigned," before a power he acknowledges as insuperably "great." Of course, the terms of the hymn are in hopeful praise of this power, whose greatness is synonymous with benevolence, and who is called not only "God" but "Savior." The soul, the immortal part, sings to Him, because the mortal part has submitted at last. This response has nothing to do with reason; but as Andrew Hudgins explains it: "logic doesn't stand a chance, a prayer." Rodriguez's estrangement from this all too demanding God is reasonable; its logic distresses his admirers. Mariani describes the emotional breakdown or, rather, the emotional triumph that unites the soul with God. And the poet's own response—"angry glad tears"—surprises him.

Mariani's prayer is different from Berryman's. It makes no mention of final judgment, of "the end of time." It keeps the issue personal, drawing its metaphorical structure from the experience and model of Leonardo Rodriguez, "a Spaniard / of great dignity and fine humility," the romantic "toreador" facing death. The poet asks for courage to face death the bull and hopes that he will still be able to praise God when death shall "notice" him. What is most affecting, however, is the first line of this prayer: "Lord, listen to the sound of my voice." In that line is the Christian belief that a personal God exists to hear one's witness, one's prayer, a God who understands one's suffering, even one's despair, because He suffered and came near despair Himself. When a Christian faces his personal end, he hopes that his death will mean more than physical termination; he hopes that God will take it personally, as he will himself. The cracked resignation of Lenny Rodriguez's voice leads Mariani to say to God, "Listen to me now, too."

Christianity sees suffering as redemptive, because the central event in Christian belief is the triumph over suffering and death—Christ's resurrection. I have alluded to this as the violence at the heart of Christianity and I have also referred to the contemporary use of Christian iconography and art, in poems like Jorie Graham's "Pietà," that make a statement about this violence but for artistic rather than religious purposes. But religious poems themselves may take events, icons, or art as subjects of meditation; though the formal properties of the art compel the poet, the end or aim is recognition or reaffirmation of faith. Such a poem is Clare Rossini's "Fra Angelico's 'Crucifixion,' Cell 42, Convent of San Marco."

> Under the sagging gentility of Christ,
> Mary staggers towards the emptiness
> That looms beyond the picture plane, her hands
> Covering her face. Martha turns to follow,
> Her sympathetic hand stalled in space
> Inches from Mary. On the rock that runs
> Across the fresco's foreground like the bared
> Spine of the world, Dominic is kneeling,
> His hands locked in prayer, his eyes fixed on
> The shaded features of his expired god
> As if he were reading a meaning there.
> Only John manages to protest, lifting
> One hand beseechingly towards the soldier
> Who heaves his lance at Christ's sealed, pearl-gray side.
>
> Above them, nothing: no father-God
> Parting clouds, revealing banks of angels
> Singing; beyond them, no hills droning off
> Suggesting places where angelus bells
> Rock slowly in dusk-swathed towers. No,
> This is the world with the fat burned off,
> Honed to rock, a scattering of grievers,

The muscles rippling through the soldier's arm.
And now we hear it as the Fra did, the sound
Of flesh slowly parting before metal—

An almost imperceptible sound,
Like a curtain in the distance being torn.

One act of religious meditation is to regard the moment of utter hopelessness that the crucifixion was; thus, Fra Angelico painted it in cell 42, in the Convent of San Marco, in Florence. Whoever occupied that cell certainly had a disconsolate image to contemplate, especially when compared to the rainbow-striped wings of the annunciation angel on the wall down the passageway. The line that unites the painting's context in the convent, its situation, the death of Christ, and its meaning is "This is the world with the fat burned off." This amazing line—figurative and colloquial at once—bursts forth, uniting self-denial, sacrifice, and American pragmatism, even mixing in a witty play on metabolism, all to emphasize the fact of the body. The attenuated Christ, with his ascetic's flesh, obviously meant to be an example to the Dominicans who studied this picture (they were not known for asceticism), hangs dead above the "bared / Spine of the world," which has been "Honed to rock." This is the foundation for what Bell calls Eliot's "disconsolate theological affirmations." Christ is dead, Mary turns away, Martha reaches to console her, John protests uselessly as the soldier, the one potent character in the picture, "heaves his lance at Christ's sealed, pearl-gray side," his own arm muscles "rippling" with power. Meanwhile, in a touch notable in Renaissance Italian paintings, St. Dominic himself kneels before the event, *in* the event as it were, with Christian piety, fully knowledgeable of all that this means in a way Mary, Martha, and even John presumably are not. Here Rossini interprets, keeping the occasion dark, describing Dominic's "eyes fixed on / The shaded features of his expired god / As if he were reading a meaning there." Her interpretation is due to the oblique approach I have also discussed that poets are likely to take in the religious poem. No consolation can even be suggested until the full desperation of the moment has been recognized.

Again, Rossini points out that no pastoral Italian landscape has been painted in the background of this picture, suggesting the church's manifestation and the resurrection's triumph. However, she makes her own imaginative leap beyond meditation on the picture to a scriptural allusion and thus, lightly, deftly, and exactly, crosses the divide between self and God that the picture dares one to cross. Imagining how the lance blade sounded as it pierced Christ's flesh, she compares it to "An almost imperceptible sound, / like a curtain in the distance being torn." The synoptic gospels report that at the moment Christ gave up the ghost, the veil in the temple was torn. Matthew adds that the earth shook and the dead were raised, and Luke that the sun was darkened. All are signs of heaven's dismay, the tragic recognition that Man has indeed murdered God. Rossini engages our understanding of this very subtly, for she says we hear this action—the piercing of the lance—as "the Fra did." She assumes that we hear what she hears, in fact: the relation between this human death and its divine consequence, one that Fra Angelico would have recognized. Thus while including all the readers of this poem, her "we" actually draws a smaller circle around Christian believers like herself and Fra Angelico; that is to say, readers who are actually outside the circle of belief may be included without realizing it as they, too, make the connection between the images in the final four lines.

Rossini's critique of the Fra Angelico painting makes her poem, on the surface anyway, more an appeal to reason than the poems by Berryman or Mariani. But her actual subject is the painter's subject, the first example of Christian witness, the sacrifice that set all other Christian sacrifices in motion, made them possible, and gave them meaning. Rossini's final assertion is quiet, not so dramatic as Berryman's and Mariani's closing prayers to their Lord, and yet it is vital to the poem's religious foundation. Without it, the poem would still be a poem but not necessarily a religious poem, one that expresses the belief of the poet in, to use Philip Wheelwright's terms again, "a reality transcending and potentially sanctifying...experience." Specifically, without the final lines, the poem would not be a Christian poem and thus part of a tradition that includes much of Western civilization's greatest literature.

It is inconceivable that a religious poem can be written by accident. Yet the religious impulse in poetry today moves many poets who would not call themselves religious. Obviously the need to see one's experience as linked to a transcendent reality and thus sanctified by that connection continues to affect some poets strongly, as I have tried to show. But the religious poem of a believer has a quality of conviction that still resonates with extraordinary power, especially when one considers the risk the poet has taken to witness, in effect, in a poetic mode that has passed out of fashion.

THE FEMINIST LITERARY
MOVEMENT: 1960-1986

By Carole Oles and Hilda Raz

She must learn again to speak / starting with I / starting
with We.

(Marge Piercy, "Unlearning to not speak" 1973)

These lines from Marge Piercy's poem suggest what
our discussion of the feminist literary movement will
take as its organizing principle. Our reading and thinking have led us to see collaboration as essential to the
movement. We will demonstrate how it unifies, strength-
ens, guides feminist poets over what may be hostile,
painful, fearful terrain as they explore that hitherto
unacknowledged half of American poetry of this century—the story of *their* lives.

We use the word collaboration fully cognizant that
it may also suggest negative political associations. Some
feminist poets and critics believe the record of their
strategies for survival has until quite recently recom-
mended collaboration in ways treasonable to the self.
Our sense of the word "feminist" in this discussion
refers to women's turning their loyalties, sympathies,
and affections to themselves and to each other in their
mutual interest. Women poets we will designate "feminist" have decided to end cooperation with others against
themselves. They are committed to changing the ways
in which they function in the society. And in this we
must be clear: feminism is no literary movement. It is
a life movement which has literary implications for any

work with life as its subject. X may be a symbolist or surrealist poet, but that label doesn't necessarily suggest how X will vote on abortion rights.

Our approach to the subject relies on the poems themselves as documents, rather than on external events or commentary. Feminist views of "history" support "anecdote as authority,"[1] since history has so largely ignored and distorted women's lives and work.

Surveying the company of feminist poets in twentieth- century America requires an adjustment of the parameters of our discussion to a manageable dimension. Therefore, we will cite only cursorily the works of poets published before 1960. We justify this demarcation, concurring with many feminist critics, by the profusion of groundbreaking poetry volumes published during and since that decade. A similar list has been proposed by Alicia Ostriker.[2] Our list includes works of varying intensity within the feminist spectrum: Anne Sexton's *To Bedlam and Part Way Back*, Sylvia Plath's *The Colossus and Other Poems* (in the British edition), H.D.'s *Helen in Egypt*, Maxine Kumin's *Halfway*, Carolyn Kizer's *The Ungrateful Garden*, all published in 1960 and 1961. Sexton's *All My Pretty Ones* and the American edition of *The Colossus* in 1962; in 1963 Adrienne Rich's *Snapshots of a Daughter-In-Law* and Gwendolyn Brooks's *Selected Poems*; Denise Levertov's *O Taste and See* in 1964; in 1965 Plath's *Ariel*, Kumin's *The Privilege*, and Kizer's *Knock Upon Silence*; Muriel Rukeyser's *The Speed of Darkness*, Brooks's *In the Mecca: Poems*, Nikki Giovanni's *Black Feeling, Black Talk*, Audre Lorde's *The First Cities*, and Alice Walker's *Once*—all in 1968. The following decade delivered May Swenson's *Iconographs: Poems* in 1970; Sexton's *Transformations* in 1971; Robin Morgan's *Monster*, Pat Parker's *Child of Myself*, and Kumin's *Up Country* in 1972; Lorde's *From A Land Where Other People*

Live, 1973, *New York Head Shop and Museum*, 1975, and *Coal* in 1976; Rukeyser's *Breaking Open*, Walker's *Revolutionary Petunias*, and Rich's *Diving into the Wreck* in 1973; Leslie Marmon Silko's *Laguna Woman*, and Paula Gunn Allen's *The Blind Lion* in 1974; Susan Griffin's *Woman and Nature: The Roaring Within Us* and *The Work of a Common Woman: The Collected Poetry of Judy Grahn 1964-1977* in 1978.

In addition, this same period brought forth a number of little magazines and small collective presses publishing either exclusively or primarily the poems of women. We number among these The Feminist Press (1973), Alice James Books (1973), Persephone Press (1976), The Seal Press (1976), Kitchen Table: Women of Color Press (1981) and the magazines *Aphra* (1969), *Calyx* (1970), *Moving Out* (1970), *Amazon Quarterly* (1972), *13th Moon* (1973), and *Conditions* (1976). *The International Directory of Little Magazines and Small Presses*, 19th edition, 1983-84, lists under the heading *Women* two hundred twenty-six entries. Of fifteen magazines and presses selected at random from the list, all began publishing in the 70s.

The quantity of poetry written by feminist poets from the 60s on, the newly established outlets for publication, and the palpable community of writers and readers, merit books on the subject. Our task here, however, is to point to some of the major outlines of that work and that movement, and to provide bibliographical signposts for readers who wish to travel farther.

We will cite poems in terms of feminist attitudes toward the female body, the collective self, nature, the working self, and women as part of an international community. The significance of collaboration for feminists as it extends to literary criticism and joint literary projects, including magazines and presses, will form part of our consideration.

Many women are singing together of this.

(Anne Sexton, "In Celebration of My Uterus" 1969)

The feminist poet's acceptance of the implications of her gender in our society is perhaps nowhere so vividly expressed as in the poems of Anne Sexton, with considerable hazard to her critical reputation, as Maxine Kumin describes in her introduction to *The Complete Poems*. James Dickey said Sexton dwelled on "the pathetic and disgusting aspects of bodily experience"; and Robert Lowell found much in the poems "embarrassing." What interests us about Sexton is her sense of the collaboration between her female body in all its aspects and creativity. "I am filling the room / with the words from my pen. / Words leak out of it like a miscarriage."[3] The work she is at such pains to produce is expelled prematurely, unformed. Yet her diction sets the tone for a generation of feminist poets. Sexton's fearlessness in writing about taboo subjects— abortion, menstruation, gynecological exams, masturbation—and in using taboo language to demystify the female body, allows her to tell the truth about women's lives.

The same attempt, with the same objective, appears in Susan Griffin's "The Song of the Woman with Her Parts Coming Out," in which Griffin repeats the words lesbian, pee, cunt, vagina, dyke, sex, toward taking away their power to condemn the speaker and silence her.[4]

The desire to tell the truth about women's bodies/ experiences informs much of Adrienne Rich's work. For feminist poets over two decades, Rich has often in spite of herself been seen as the lodestar. Critic Catharine Stimpson writes, "As Rich grounds women's thoughts and feelings in their bodies, she naturalizes them . . . unequivocally, lyrically, she asks women to think through the material flesh and their own bodies."[5]

Woman's experience of birthing enters many poems by feminists, and perhaps the image at the close of Rich's "The Mirror in Which Two Are Seen as One" is primary to an understanding of the responsibility the feminist poet assumes: "Your mother dead and you unborn / your two hands grasping your head / drawing it down against the blade of life / your nerves the nerves of a midwife / learning her trade."[6] The truth of a woman's body is invoked in the service of her own delivery /deliverance.

The redemptive power of the female body goes beyond the poet's giving birth to herself. In the poem "We Need a God Who Bleeds Now" Ntozake Shange writes of a female deity as the restorer of the planet; she "spreads her lunar vulva & showers us in shades of scarlet / thick & warm like the breath of her / . . .the planet is heaving mourning our ignorance / . . .i am / not wounded i am bleeding to life / / we need a god who bleeds now / whose wounds are not the end of anything."[7]

Even in its absence, childbirth forms a matrix of the poet's consciousness of her own body. Jane Cooper's "Waiting" acknowledges that she will never bear children and portrays the body first as violin, then as music hall "waiting to be torn down."[8] She concludes that compassion will be the singing to fill that hall, that body.

Another part of the feminist poet's acceptance of her body involves rejection of the conventional, largely male-produced notions of the female physical ideal. Kathleen Fraser's "Poem In Which My Legs Are Accepted" establishes a new ideal based on the real physical accomplishments of the speaker's legs—in this instance their strength, acrobatic skill, and loyalty.[9] Again the

language of birth expresses their ultimate acceptability, when the legs are "locks in a new canal between
continents. / The ship of life will push out of you."
Carole Oles's "The Price of Breast in Las Vegas" also
rejects the male's stereotypical physical ideal for women,
by graphic description of the mutilation it indirectly
wreaks upon them.[10] Marge Piercy's "The Friend" presents another version of the theme, when male urges
female "burn your body. / it is not clean and smells
like sex. / it rubs my mind sore." The difference in
this poem is that the female is still collaborating in the
bad old sense: "I said yes."[11]

Feminist recognition and rage address too the more
violent consequences of male attitudes toward the female body. For example, Piercy's "Rape Poem" equates
rape with a series of violent crimes and injuries, and
portrays women's fear of rape lurking behind seemingly innocuous scenes and events. In the last lines of
her poem, rape becomes murder of "those who dare /
live in the leafy flesh open to love."[12] Adrienne Rich's
poem "Rape" like Piercy's describes the rapist as an
ordinary man, rather than aberrant beast. She goes further, seeing the male authority cop as complicitous,
turning the victim into the offender: "to him, you are
guilty of the crime / of having been forced."[13] The feminist
poets' effort to integrate body and mind has required
that they examine again and again the myriad ways in
which the society—and that means the wielders of power,
men—has at once idealized, denigrated, and violated
their bodies. June Jordan in "To Sing a Song of Palestine" extends the notion of rape to include the viola-
tion of countries: the conflict of populations in Israel
and Palestine is, she says, like gang-rape of the land—
"How many different men will fit / themselves how
fast / into that place?"[14]

A poet who pushes some of the society's myths about the female body to their grotesque extremes, Cynthia MacDonald uses wit to accomplish deadly serious ends. Poems such as "Wanted" tear ironically and fabulously the confusions behind traditional identifications, mocking men's fears about the outbreak of women's lusts by comparing them to a disease she calls "Ural Mountain / Spotted fever." In curing it, the men become hairless, the women grow beards—"Our civilization is falling apart."[15] Good news.

we were the rev- / olution crawling forward on each other's / bellies.

(Marilyn Hacker, "Taking Notice" 1980)

The conviction of feminist poets that women are "allies and portions of one another"[16] finds expression in poems of their relationships with other women—as mothers, daughters, sisters, lovers, ancestors, and prototypes.

Poems dealing with mothers and daughters show that relationship to be as problematical as the relationship of father and son. Another layer of complication exists for the female in that the first lover, the mother from whom she is torn at birth, is like herself. In the work of most feminist poets the complexities of that relationship are sounded. The desired end for women, rather than slaying or besting the father, is to return to feed and be fed by the relationship with the mother.

Maxine Kumin's "Life's Work" exemplifies both what unites and differentiates one mother and her daughter. Both need definition through defiance of "the firm old fathers," but whereas the mother sacrificed a career as pianist, the daughter went on swimming competitively despite her father's disapproval. In the poem the daughter has grown old enough to consider what her mother lost, and to empathize with her. She has both separated from the mother, and returned sufficiently to her so that she hears the "dry aftersound" of her sacrifice.[17]

Separation of the female self from the mother is treated in "Dusting" by Julia Alvarez. The child writes her name on domestic surfaces, only to have her mother follow behind her—erasing, polishing the wood and mirrors until her daughter's prints disappear. Alvarez concludes her poem with a refusal "to be like her, anonymous."[18] This poem appears in the first section of Alvarez's book, *Homecoming*, among a group describing the poet's training in housekeeping by her mother. The poems treat the mother and the domestic tasks at once with love and distaste; that child desires to write her own name large and let it stand for all to read, as now it does in the poems she signs. In the last poem of this section, "Orchids," Alvarez pays homage to her aunt, who raised twenty-two varieties of orchids until she married in her thirties. Though the aunt thinks of her remarkable accomplishment in retrospect as a "good diversion," Alvarez celebrates "the single-minded labors / of the single woman artist."[19]

Poems of women's connections to each other are also prominent in Carolyn Kizer's work. Lessons of the mother portrayed in "The Intruder"[20] and "The Great Blue Heron,"[21] for example, sustain the poet in her life; poems to a friend Jan appear scattered through *Mermaids in the Basement*, significantly subtitled *Poems for Women*. "For Jan as the End Draws Near" shows the two women as having had "nearly forty years / to crack our dismal jokes and love each other" and indulge their fantasies of being old crones together in a cabin in the woods of California, or in more recent poems, on a Greek island.[22] Kizer's poem "The Blessing" addresses her daughter in a mode that suggests how women's roles as mothers and daughters often blur; moreover, that overlapping forges stronger bonds. The poem opens with Kizer speaking to "Daughter-my-mother," then shifts in the third section to "Mother-my-daughter" and Kizer explores how "I lean on the bosom / of that double mother, / the ghost by night, the girl by day." The poem ends with Kizer's promise that she will "whisper blithely" in her daughter's dreams at some future time, as her mother's ghost does in her own.[23]

Women's connections to each other may generate imagery based on traditional women's activities. Alice Walker's "For My Sister Molly Who in the Fifties" invokes domestic chores as signs of the sister's loving attachment to her siblings in a catalogue that includes artistry in mashed potatoes, cooking, cleaning, patiently answering children's questions, correcting grammar and deportment, reading and storytelling, making dresses, braiding hair. Molly was for the poet, "SOMEONE OVERHEAD / A light A thousand watts / Bright and also blinding." When Walker says at the end of the poem "And she left us," the poet is conscious of how that departure freed her, even in the context of the grief it caused her, who would do the same in her own time.[24] Adrienne Rich in "Transcendental Etude" extrapolates the technique of the quilter, not for nostalgia's sake, but as a method of joining the parts of women's lives, to indicate "the many-lived, unending / forms in which she finds herself." The poem traces the progress of woman torn from woman at birth, to the female lovers rejoined with themselves and their mothers, "a whole new poetry beginning here."[25]

The proliferation of lesbian poetry during the past three decades in America must be seen as one important strain in the feminist literary movement. This new poetry Rich has done so much to make finds a voice in the work of Audre Lorde and others. Lorde's "On a Night of the Full Moon" expresses erotic delight in a lover's female body.[26]

Marilyn Hacker's poems continually struggle after the means by which two women can live together in a world that wishes them to be invisible. Judy Grahn's "A Woman Is Talking to Death" presents clearly the dangers to a lesbian who is visible. Discharged from the military, beaten in a hamburger joint, humiliated by the police to whom she reports the incident, the speaker knows too well her fears are not groundless.[27]

But the power and danger of the lesbian also emerge in the poem. The speaker must confront her own fears; then she can confront Death, who comes in a multiplicity of guises in male-dominated society. Every force in that society dictates woman's disconnection from herself and other women. Yet it is the prime motive of the poet to make that connection—"Yes I have committed acts of indecency with women and most of them were acts of omission. I regret them bitterly."[28]

The acts of women against women are sometimes acts of commission. Michelle Cliff in "The History of Costume" reflects upon ways the male-based culture has dictated women's adornment of themselves. She and her mother walk through the museum exhibit, reacting to the finery on display. "And then the wigs: the hair of another women... To wear the feathers of a large flightless bird. To cover a head with hair that has been sold." The exploitation and distortion that begins with men and women continues between women. This poem closes, fittingly, with the image of a mother and daughter in mourning.[29]

A discussion of the theme of women's multifarious connections with women would be incomplete without mention of the pluralism that both informs and divides feminism, hence the feminist literary movement, despite the efforts of some feminists to speak with unanimity. A continuing discourse of separation exists between white women and women of color. In an open letter to Mary Daly in 1980, Audre Lorde takes issue with Daly's omission of non-European women from her study of female ecology, *Gyn / Ecology*. Lorde maintains, ". . .to imply that all women suffer the same oppression simply because we are women, is to lose sight of the many varied tools of patriarchy. It is to ignore how those tools are used by women without awareness against each other."[30] Lorde continues, pointing out the tradition of mutual support and strength found in the female bonding of African women. The potency of Lorde's position comes across in a poem called "Who Said It Was Simple" in which presumably white middle-class women preparing for a political rally are complaining about the difficulty of getting "girls"—and the tone and context suggest the girls are black—to work at home for them while they march against oppression.[31]

Feminist scholars are working to provide both the texts of poems by women of color, and examinations of their traditional and radical contexts. Gloria T. Hull, Barbara Smith, Paula Gunn Allen, Hortense Spillers and others, provide them in publications such as *Conditions: 5, The Black Women's Issue*. Poetry and criticism by women of color have been largely unavailable to white audiences beyond the feminist community. Any reader outside that community must look to feminist sources for information, and this includes scholars, since the traditional data bases contain severely limited listings of these works. Hull's statement in *Shakespeare's Siters* might in this context apply to all women of color: "Black women poets are not 'Shakespeare's sisters.' In fact, they seem to be siblings of no one but themselves."[32]

Racial, sexual, and religious divisions in feminist alliances are elaborated in Barbara Smith's introduction to *Home Girls*, her anthology of black feminist writing. Smith examines negative myths about feminism and divisions among women of color, positing her belief that all oppressions are one, a notion not shared by all feminists of color. She questions whom it serves to allow internal divisions to fracture the feminist movement, asking "Who benefits most? Undoubtedly, those outside forces that will go to any length to see us fail."[33]

It may be easier to forge bonds with foremothers than with contemporary sisters. Homage to women in the poems of feminist writers may take the form of re-imagination of historical foremothers. Ruth Whitman's *Tamsen Donner* recreates the Donner party's ill-fated journey west from the point of view of the wife of its leader. Through disappointments, physical deprivations and the pain of loss, the shrinking of the party and its dreams, Tamsen's unflinching loyalty remains intact. In the context of her refusal to eat human flesh we feel her "Hunger. The lightness of it . . . It would be easy to join the air and float into nothingness."[34] The last poem in the collection again speaks to posterity, as Tamsen, whose body was never found, says: "If my boundary stops here / I have daughters to draw new maps on the world . . . / they will speak my words thinking they have invented them."[35]

Carole Oles speaks in the voice of nineteenth century astronomer Maria Mitchell to describe her double commitment to research and to teaching women. Oles's book *Night Watches* also gives voice to Maria's ghost, who comments on the status and behavior of contemporary women. In "Maria Mitchell in the Great Beyond with Marilyn Monroe," the childless astronomer bears witness to the childhood molestation of the actress, rescues her name: "Come walk with me . . . now you live everywhere at once / whose ambition was to be men's earthly star. / Here are stars you can trust: / . . . / Say these, Norma Jeane. / We are women learning together."[36] Margaret Gibson's *Memories of the Future* consists of daybooks imagined by Gibson to be written by Tina Modotti, actress, political activist, photographer, in the last years of her life. Gabrielle Daniels writes about Millicent Fredericks, Anais Nins's housemaid, "I have learned / from such self-denial, / martyrs and saints are made / or forgotten."[37]

In addition to full-length books of poetry dedicated to reviving women buried by history, many individual poems by women have honored a variety of foremothers. Two poems by Rita Dove, "Belinda's Petition" and "The House Slave," are spoken by women brought to America in the eighteenth century as slaves. Before daylight the house slave hears "the laggards" outside being beaten by the slavemaster, "sometimes my sister's voice, unmistaken, among them."[38] Jane Cooper's "Threads: Rosa Luxemburg from Prison" remembers this protester of the Kaiser's war policy, who spent most of World War I as a political prisoner in Germany. She was released shortly before the Armistice, then picked up by government authorities again, beaten, shot, and thrown into a canal. The poem takes the form of Rosa's letters to Sophie Liebknecht, the wife of her co-revolutionary. Near the end of the poem, Rosa writes, "Thus passing out of my cell in all directions / are fine threads connecting me / with thousands of birds and beasts / You too, Sonitchka, are one of this urgent / company / to which my whole self throbs, responsive."[39] The poem allows Cooper to talk about war and so-called civilization as well as to honor Rosa Luxemburg.

Some poems memorializing foremothers speak collectively rather than personally. Donna Kate Rushin's "The Black Back Ups," first identifies and honors the black women singers "behind" white male vocalists. Then she expands her homage to other black women who supported their bosses: the maids, laundresses, actresses, and commercial gimmick, Aunt Jemima. Between stanzas cataloguing the lives of these women, Rushin sings the refrain "And the colored girls say / Do dodo do do dodododo."[40] A tour de force, the poem closes with the disintegration of the refrain, and a final "do"—both the last back-up note, and a pun.

Sandra Gilbert alternates sections about personal experience and women relatives with sections dealing with historical models for women in *Emily's Bread*. Poems called "Daguerreotypes," for example—suggesting both nineteenth century photographs and stereotypes—portray traditional roles of women: the governess, the fallen woman, the wet nurse, the lace-maker. Another section of the book, "Still Lives," fixes women in conventional female work such as cooking, dressing up, and fantasizing escape from the house. Shifting to first person from the third person of "Daguerreotypes," Gilbert implies a temporal and not merely spatial meaning for "still."

The sense of self as part of a community is central to the work of feminist poets. Yet many also revise the old myths, toward a redefinition of the realities of women's lives. Muriel Rukeyser, for example, conflates old and new myths in "The Private Life of the Sphinx" (1948) and its revision, "Myth" (1973). In the later version, Oedipus is a querulous old man, who stumbles onto the Sphinx by recognizing her smell. When he

asks her why he was punished, why he failed to recognize his own mother, the Sphinx recalls his answer
to the riddle, Man, and his omission of Woman. "'When
you say Man,' said Oedipus, 'you include women /
too. Everyone knows that.' She said, 'That's what /
you think.'"[41] The Sphinx, monstrous in nature, de-
prives power from more than her laughter.

An important work of revisionist mythmaking written earlier in this century is H.D.'s *Trilogy*, an extended
creation that empowers women in a context outside
the contemporary patriarchy's constraints. Through the
agency of a magus, Kaspar, the poet merges two proto-
typical women—Mary Magdalene and the Virgin Mary—
with herself. By choosing to place her narrative outside the country torn by male-waged war and devas-
tation, she creates a synthesis of female subjectivity in
a spiritual rather than a temporal context.

Rachel Blau DuPlessis writes, "Criticizing the nature
of myth is one of the reevaluations that women writers . . . undertake, for their own lives allow them to
see the culturally repressive functions of archetypes,
and their own experiences of personal and social change,
recorded in poems about consciousness and politics,
belie the illusion of a timeless, unhistorical pattern that
controls reality."[42] She goes on to distinguish between
archetypes and prototypes, the former fixed and binding, the other open to transformation.

In this context we note the title of Anne Sexton's
book of revisionist tales, *Transformations*. Retelling the
classic stories of the Brothers Grimm, she uncovers the
heart of their meaning. The forms of children's tales—
their paraphernalia—give way as she makes parables
of control and destruction. Examples of this kind of
revisionist poem abound. A sequence in Marilyn Hacker's
Assumptions, "The Snow Queen," transforms the An-
dersen tale into a female quest for identity. Along Gerda's

journey, she finds mothers and alter egos to help define herself; The Robber Woman and Robber Girl, society's
outcasts, present valuable models for survival.

In Celia Gilbert's re-telling of the Eurydice myth,
Eurydice follows Orpheus earthward "reluctantly, . /
As one who would be forced / To know old pains and
sorrow." Orpheus has sung of mankind's sorrow, but
not of Eurydice's; nothing in their life together calls
her back. Orpheus turns because of his uneasiness about
her "shrouded silence," his sense that they have "outgrown each other." When she must remain in the un-
derworld, Eurydice says, "And I was free"—as is the
poet, of the freight of archetype and history.[43]

We are nature seeing nature.

(Susan Griffin, *Woman and Nature* 1978)

In feminist poems, women identify the male culture's
distinction between a taming civilization and a teeming nature. Sandra Gilbert's "What He Hates / What
He Loves" depicts the female speaker in terms identified with teeming nature, what he hates. The imagery
of the poem underlines the consequences, to a woman
whose body is described in terms of moisture and swamp,
of proximity to a male whose body is described in terms
of embers and flame. "Your sweet swamp dries up. /
You forget your own name." The poem offers a short
gloss on history: the male is "climbing out of the snow
of his past" into the Phaeton myth, and the female is
"hiding in the damp shed at the edge of the swamp,"
calling through the silence. Later in the poem, the woman
shows him their child's scar (he never saw the blood
or the wound), and the family dog's dead body; "he
says, 'Let's change the subject' "—- after having named
other men his "comrades." The bodies he turns *to* in

the poem are, like his, "sealed up, rough, dry."[44]

The image structure of this poem signals the act, for many feminist poets, of changing the subject from the male presentation of history, to the heresy of female embodiments. In 1970 May Swenson published the shaped poem "Bleeding," one of the series called *Iconographs*. She presents a dialogue between two voices, neither identified by gender: the knife that separates flesh, and the cut being defined and enlarged. "Stop bleeding you make me messy with this blood," says the knife. "If only you didn't bleed said the knife I wouldn't have to do this. / I know said the cut I bleed too easily I hate that I can't / help it I wish I were a knife like you and didn't have to bleed."[45] Women's bodies are part of the natural world, bleeding and soiling what they touch. Women's voices say "I feel I have to bleed to feel" and men's voices answer, "I don't I don't have to feel." The ellipses of the text duplicate on the page the cut made by the knife, a wound both sexual and societal.

Like Swenson, Maxine Kumin participates in her natural world unsentimentally. In Kumin's "The Excrement Poem" we see again the use of taboo language, an earthy subject treated in an open, direct manner with some wry humor ("of considerable heft, something awesome"[46]). The poem opens with an identification of the speaker with all creatures, and then celebrates the wastes of the body and the natural functions it performs in order to survive. "Thinking of Death and Dogfood" considers the mutual mortality of Kumin's horse Amanda, who will "go to Alpo or to Gaines," and herself, who will be transmuted to potash to "sweeten the crops."[47] Kumin observes in nature the same "dark obedient order" that operates in her own life.[48] This identification consoles, as she sees that the physical world will go on

without Amanda, without her; they both take their in-
evitable places in the life continuum. This nature is
not to conquer or turn from, but to join.

The sense of collaboration between feminist poet and
nature characterizes Carolyn Kizer's "A Muse of Water," which addresses the masters of civilization who
have used water for their own ends. Women are seen
as nursing mothers, then attendants of "tiny gods, /
imperious table-pounders, who / are final arbiters of
thirst"[49] —Kizer's wit at play in the obvious reference
to male arbiters of taste. As if the plundering were not
enough, the male then invokes water as inspiration for
his poems, even while his misuse of water diverts it,
evaporates it. Then he blames the water for disappear-
ing when in fact it has been "Plundered by man's in-
satiate want." This poem sparkles with the wit and
formal parody displayed in Kizer's mother lode poem
"Pro Femina." It closes with a directive to the masters
of civilization, inviting them to a significantly deserted
beach "where ghosts of curlews [not the living birds]
wade" urging "Here, if you care, and lie full-length, /
is water deep enough to drown."[50] Whereas in Kumin—
humanity's pollutions notwithstanding—the noble shit
and its maker prevail, in Kizer the powers that commit the abuse against water may be called finally to
answer to it with their lives.

As early as 1935, Muriel Rukeyser worked similar
themes in "Sand Quarry with Moving Figures." A father takes his daughter to visit the family business;
this quarry, ruining the land, will make them rich. The
girl in the poem is terrified and runs from her father
and his promise of a bracelet to be bought with prof-
its. The quarry's pit is clearly an image of rape: of the
land, and obliquely of the girl who recoils from the
"stubble and waste of black / and his ugly villages."[51]

June Jordan expands women's sense of connection to nature when she chooses natural images to define her identification with political victims: she says, in response to their suffering and as a declaration of solidarity, "I am fallen / I am the cliff"[52] that in an earlier poem was held by trees "against the edges / of a life-long avalanche."[53]

A groundbreaking book treating these themes in an expanded and formally innovative way is Susan Griffin's *Woman and Nature: The Roaring Inside Her.* Griffin's central thesis is that while Western man has set himself apart from nature, women have continued to be seen and to see themselves as part of nature.

Griffin develops her central notion through four sections of the book, basically a dialogue between women and the cultural authorities. The first book, "Matter," delineates "a history of scientific, religious, and philosophical notions about nature or matter, juxtaposed chronologically with a history of ideas about women."[54] Book Two, "Separation," speaks of the consequences of dividing men from women, body from mind. The last two books, "Transformation" and "Her Vision," examine the material of Book One in a new voice and with a changed vision. Griffin incorporates the techniques of essay, drama, and poetry into an amalgam of compressed power that builds throughout the four sections of the book. A creative work, *Woman and Nature* also redefines by implication the strategies of scholarship.

The subject of form in women's poems, however, might be called by some feminists an intellectual luxury. Women's working is for them a more compelling issue. Sandra Gilbert and Susan Gubar quote historian William Chafe: ". . .twice as many women were at work [in 1960] as in 1940, and 40% of of all women over sixteen held a job."[55] The numbers of women entering the workplace a little over two decades ago must, of necessity, have had an effect of feminist poetry.

On a postcard a row of black women stand— / track-women of the B & O— / with shovels ready to dig a rail-road bed. / It is wartime and manpower is short.

(Michelle Cliff, "Women's Work" 1980)

Cliff's poem traces the subject of women's work through time and space from nineteenth century Jamaica and Scotland to fifteenth century Bologna, to Chicago in the early 1900s. The work Cliff finally undertakes, given her knowledge of women's history, moves beyond description "to ignite the fuse of our knowledge." By the close of the poem, she's redefined the title of the poem— her work is *for* women.

The Work of a Common Woman represents Judy Grahn's portrayal of women whose work is not creative, but mundane—among them a white collar boss, and a waitress. Ella, "a copperheaded waitress . . . / flicks her ass / our of habit, to fend off the pass / that passes for affection. / She keeps her mind the way men / keep a knife—keen to strip the game."[56] In these poems, Grahn compares working women to crow, nails, rattlesnake, thunderstorm, the reddest wine, monkey, new moon: the elemental and dangerous.

In "Climbing" and "Substation" Joanne Ward speaks as a female lineman who takes jeers and sexual jibes from male co-workers. (A biographical note in *13th Moon* says she works for Seattle City Light as an "Electrical Helper.") The "mustachioed linemen / with the power in their hands / that can kill or save us all" tell her and the other women workers that they're "slow and stupid / cunts and bitches / who don't belong."[57] But the women endure, to find their bodies growing strong and calloused, their tongues sharpened. The rewards are great, perhaps even for the men, for at the end of the poem "We begin to learn, woman to woman, now, / and woman to man, / that taut ropes have always burned through / our dreams, / and our muscles will hold."[58]

Donna Kate Rushin's "The Tired Poem: Last Letter from a Typical Unemployed Black Professional Woman" confronts issues of black men's treatment of black women, the black woman's role and stereotypes within her community, and the bind education seems to put her in. The speaker concludes she erred "the day you decided to go to school."[59] Waiting at a bus stop, she refuses to provide a $10 sexual service for a man. She tries to explain to him her reasons, suggesting he should look for someone he cares about, but he becomes belligerent. She raises her voice, the bus comes, and when "the second-shift people file on" they "look at you like you're crazy." The man yells and turns away, the bus leaves her alone on the street, "And then, / It is / Very / Quiet." The end of the poem slows to a stop, with line-breaks sputtering into silence. Education has left her alone on the street—literally, in her alienation from black men, and in her unemployment. The speaker's perception of narrowing options reflects the difficulties of being in transition in a society more comfortable with static, if corrupt, positions.

The downward turning touch / the cry of time / fire falling without sound / plunge my hand in the wound

(Alicia Suskin Ostriker, "Exile," *during the evacuation of Phnom Penh 1975*)

but you can learn / from the edges that blur O you
who love clear edges / more than anything watch the edges
that blur

(Adrienne Rich, from "Contradictions: Tracking
Poems"1983-1985)

In 1968 Rich wrote that the oppressor's language was
the only one she had to speak in, noting a problem
central to feminist poets whose perceptions depend on
a clear understanding of the attitudes words imply.

In her poem "Jacklight," Louise Erdrich uses language
confusion to examine attitude confusion. The Chippewa
work for *flirting* also means *hunting,* and *rape* has the
same word as *bear killing with hands.* The poem de-
pends too on a confusion of voices. The plural speaker
is both women and the collective voice of hunted animals. Drawn from the safety of home into the glare of
a circle of truck headlights, both women and animals
are in danger. The poem turns on a reversal: luring
the hunters—by lust, by greed—into the woods where
the victims are at home, they reappropriate their power
and save their lives.

Muriel Rukeyser, born thirteen years after the beginning of this century, noticed the ways in which the
female self is often confused and damaged by the patriarchy, divided, "split -open." Personal sundering she
saw as a reflection of cultural divisions. Rukeyser wrote
in the 30s of various oppressions, and continued her
political resistance to war and injustice in poems protesting the Vietnam War, such as "Don Baty, The Draft
Resister," and "Welcome from War." "Breaking Open,"
published in 1973, recalls Rukeyser's being jailed for
her political activism. It states her conviction on the
one hand that "Anything you can imagine . . . Rational

man has done" and on the other that transformation is possible, "The country of our waking / breaking open."[60] Against enormous historical odds, Rukeyser continued to present a vision of hope, setting consciousness, the healing human touch, delight and laughter, as the way to peace and justice. Unlike some feminists who affirm international ties, Rukeyser sees the breach between male and female as reparable.

The image of the self extended beyond the borders of body and nation presents new possibilities for international connection and mutual responsibility. In her last poem, "The Gates," Rukeyser speaks of her trip to "the prison gates—also the gates of perception, the gates of the body"—as advocate for a Chinese poet imprisoned by his government. In a vision that connects her to his mother and his wife, her own son to his son, she remembers her friend Anne Sexton, newly dead, and wonders "How can we meet the judgment on the poet, / . . . How shall we speak to the infant beginning to run? / All those beginning to run?"[61]

June Jordan envisions a similar connection between women and international oppressions when she speaks of war sites in Lebanon, Grenada, Guatemala, Chile, Nicaragua, South Africa. She too sees women's bodies as part of the image structure of shelter: land and home, "A woman's body as the universal / shelter . . . as the space created / by the mothers of our time."[62] She conflates the rapes of three women, a white, a black, a Portuguese, to declare "I am raising my knife / to carve out the heart / of shame / / The very next move is not mine." In this way Jordan establishes a personal and political pattern of response to violence. At the conclusion of her book of poems *Living Room*, she declares, "I was born a Black woman / and now / I am become a Palestinian."[63] Her use of elevated diction signals the power to assume an identity in which the personal becomes the political, and the language of Hitler can be usurped in order to beg for "her" people *Lebensraum*, living room.

The ways in which feminist poets use the oppressor's language often hold it up for scrutiny, thereby unfreezing it from the meanings the oppressor attaches. Rich and Jordan parody official jargon; the government that says, "Those who have ceased"[64] —cultures and peoples destroyed by the spread of civilization—is the target in Rich's "Turning the Wheel." She calls this jargon, "amnesia-language." Jordan hits the stereotypes of black language by using "we ain't got no fried chicken" as a refrain in one poem.[65] In another, "A Song for Soweto," she translates part of the vocabulary of violence in an attempt to transform the nature of experience. *Blood* becomes *water, grave* becomes *grass, dust* becomes *homeland*.[66]

Linda Hogan writes from a traditional American Indian perspective in a tone that venerates the earth and sees the human body as its extension. In her poem "The Sand Roses," she invokes a vision to merge nations and peoples: "Beyond skin and stone and nations / all of earth's creations dance together / . . . / drawing the dances all over the globe / like a magnet / with her sand roses of America, / Indian roses, / the Russian dancing roses of flesh, / Africa, / the opening roses of the eye's pupil / the singing mouth / genital roses..."[67]

It is no coincidence that the feminist literary movement as we date it explodes in print about the time the United States is waging an undeclared war in Indochina, bombing villages in North Vietnam and Cambodia. An important sense of women's international connections and responsibilities arises from outrage at that American aggression.

In Carolyn Kizer's "The First of June Again" the speaker

is witness; the poem's title indicates the likelihood that the events described will go on and on, as they have occurred in the past and continue into the present. Kizer identifies the wagers of war as the same plunderers of nature who abuse the water and make the great redwoods fall, with the approbation of the governor of California. All violence is seen as one. An image of regeneration, the magic fungus rings springing up on the redwood stumps, comes back to haunt in the poem when Kizer recalls the mushroom cloud of the A-bomb.

Alicia Suskin Ostriker's powerful *The Mother / Child Papers* juxtapose the individual experience of birth and motherhood with the violent events of the same period: in this instance, the Kent State killings and the bombing of Cambodia. Nowhere does the blood imperative of women for survival become so compelling as in the relationship between one woman and her child, in these poems a son, who from birth the obstetrician calls a good soldier. The co-opting of life by the government of war-makers—the same committees Rukeyser wrote of in poems of the 30s and 40s—is what feminists resist. By merging the voices of the infant and mother, and the moment of his birth with the deaths at Kent State and in Cambodia, Ostriker presents a vision of simultaneity and extended responsibility.

War is one oppression against which feminists rally in their poems. Hunger and poverty are others. In Alice Walker's "A Few Sirens," the poet is at home writing poems, but acutely aware of suffering experienced around the world. Moving out from the sirens of the ghetto, where people lose jobs and housing, Walker considers the countries where children die of starvation before age five. She contrasts these devastating scenes with American children who starve themselves, anorexics. The end of the poem addresses the insensitivity of the unhungry to the plight of the starving through an image of the particular, "a dead child / starved naked / among the oranges / in the market-place" and asks if there wasn't a time when that sight would have "spoiled / the appetite."[68]

Other feminist poets have written of world hunger and injustice, notably Adrienne Rich in the poem "Hunger" dedicated to Audre Lorde and Lorde her-self in "The Evening News." Rich's poem goes beyond the depiction of hunger in graphic imagery, to a stated position that no revolution has ever chosen to elimi-nate hunger from human experience because "that choice requires / that women shall be free."[69] When women have power, they will decide to feed the world. In Lorde's poem, she asserts her connection with South African political activist Winnie Mandela. At the opening of the poem, Lorde is kneading bread and thinking about "our wars / being fought by our children."[70] The frame of the poem uses the language of official instructions, rules of the road: first rule, "attend quiet victims first"— defining the poem as a women's survival manual.

New formal patterns often are required for poems that envision social change. New forms, sustained only in individual book or single poem, rely on the sound of the spoken word. Dialects, rap, ellipses, the absence of conventional punctuation, syntax, and metaphor signal the collapse of formal diction and traditional meters in the works of some feminist poets. Others depend on a radical text embedded in a traditional form. Anne Waldman's "Fast Speaking Woman" establishes a chant rhythm that encourages readers and listeners to add to its text. The poem, then, becomes a model for its extension and has a growing number of collaborative authors.

What Rich calls blurring of edges manifests itself in

a variety of formal strategies, recombinations. Kizer's use of form is variable; she tends to employ regular, traditional meters and longer lines in poems that call into question or mock aspects of the patriarchy. The highly structured and regular line of "Pro Femina," for example—an alternately six and seven-stress line—both packed and relatively long, gives the sense of a poet who has plenty to say and vigorously hammers it out. Kizer's melding of various forms in her recent volume *Yin* includes a prose homage to her mother as her muse.

Jane Cooper's *Scaffolding* also includes a prose memoir "Nothing Has Been Used in the Manufacture of this Poem that Could Have Been Used in the Manufacture of Bread" (1974). In it she discusses publication and silences, the relationship between love and work, and the distortion of work through formal revision.

However, use of received or patriarchal forms can make a conscious political statement. Marilyn Hacker, a stunning practitioner of sonnet, villanelle, rondel, and other more or less arcane traditional forms, employs these "venerable vessels for subversive use."[71] Tension between the direct, woman-centered content of the poems and the patriarchal, canonical forms constitutes a reappropriation. Hacker's poems are the strongest proponents of reclamation of these forms which attract other feminist poets such as Julia Alvarez and Marie Ponsot.

The work of Michelle Cliff exemplifies another use of formal strategies. In single poems, Cliff frequently alternates prose passages of personal recollection, journal entries, dreams, catalogues, newspaper excerpts or, as in "Claiming an Identity They Taught Me to Despise," an advertisement for raffle of a horse and a servant girl. Collaborations in poetry such as Olga Broumas and Jane Miller's *Black Holes, Black Stockings* represent the merging of the poets' perspectives and voices. The Broumas-Miller collaboration shows obvious divergence from male collaborations such as poetry correspondences in which each of two voices remains separate.

The feminist imperative to develop new forms carries over to feminist criticism. Rachel Blau DuPlessis's essay "For the Etruscans" (1981) uses the Etruscans as a figure for women. By refusing to establish and maintain the conventional distance between critic and reader, she breaks down hierarchical assumptions implicit in male critical diction. The essay begins with the author's questioning her academic training, and continues with personal musings in a style that omits formal connections. It includes sentence fragments, words in capital letters to indicate intensity of feeling, and the use of exclamation points. The essay unfolds as a dialogue, with herself and in response to quotations from other sources, both published and unpublished. Susan Gubar's discussion in "The Blank Page" ranges freely among a variety of poets, fiction writers, and feminist theorists. She uses examination of a story by Isak Dinesen as the occasion for a feminist discourse on the consequences of female art, passivity, and receptiveness.

Nomagic here. / Only the heat of my desire to fuse/ what I already know / exists. Is possible

(Cherríe Moraga, "The Welder" 1981)

For us, Moraga's words incorporate the paradox that the blurring and fusion of boundaries, the attendant heat of that process, necessarily precede the building of a welded structure or community.

The collaborations which characterize the feminist

literary movement are represented by anthologies such as *This Bridge Called My Back* (1981) edited by Cherríe Moraga and Gloria Anzaldúa. At the time of its second printing in 1983, it had sold 20,000 copies, an estimable number by any poetry anthology standards. Despite the statistic, this book is only a beginning in the effort to give voice to the writings of women of color. *Home Girls: A Black Feminist Anthology* (1983), mentioned earlier, is another. Both these volumes include poetry and prose, as if to reject the exclusivity of genres.

Anthologies of poetry by women that appeared during the period we have considered gathered the work of a range of poets; they have been variously attentive to the inclusion of women of color and lesbians of any race. Louise Bernikow's *The World Split Open* (1974), published with an introduction by Muriel Rukeyser, stopped at 1950. Two anthologies that spanned into the 70s are *No More Masks!* and *Rising Tides*, both published in 1973. *Extended Outlooks*, originally published in 1981 as an issue of the *Iowa Review,*brought together the work of poets writing in the 70s and 80s, as well as more familiar names from the preceding decades. The editors also published hitherto unpublished work by H.D., and reprinted poems. We are not distinguishing here between feminist work and work by women. Merely putting between covers the work exclusively of women poets seemed an act of some editorial bravado. The non gender-identified anthologies of the same period maintained what Joanna Russ cites in *How to Suppress Women's Writing*, University of Texas Press, 1983, as a predictable if lamentable ratio—1 in 4. We found that Russ was optimistic.

Collaborative feminist publication ventures during the 70s and 80s appear in the form of literary magazines and cooperative presses dedicated to publishing and distributing the poetry of women. Some of these, *Kitchen Table: Women of Color Press*, for instance, state a racial commitment. Special issues of *Calyx* and *Sinister Wisdom* are devoted to the work of women of color as well. The collective Alice James Books has published fifty-four titles, eight by men. Mary Bigg's article on women's literary magazines in the United States, published in *13th Moon*, reexamines the careers of women editors from 1912 to 1972—Harriet Monroe, Margaret Anderson, Martha Foley, through Gina Covina and Laurel Galana—in order to evaluate their roles in supporting the women authors of their time.

Sandra Gilbert and Susan Gubar are two of the most visible critical collaborators representative of the scholarly enterprise so essential to reclamation and revisionist reading of literature by women. Their two books of criticism, *The Madwoman in the Attic* and *Shakespeare's Sisters* have altered the ways in which canonical writing by women is read and understood. Their mammoth contribution to feminist literary studies, *The Norton Anthology of Literature by Women: The Tradition in English*, has been hailed and derided, but nowhere met with disinterest. The authors were cited among *Ms.* "Women of the Year" in January, 1986; in the accompanying article, they discussed the methods and nature of their extraordinary collaboration.

Sandra Gilbert and Alicia Suskin Ostriker are models for another kind of collaboration we want to acknowledge among feminist writers. Academics as well as poets and critics, they weld the powers of the mind and imagination, to the invigoration of both. Adrienne Rich, June Jordan, Barbara Smith, Maxine Kumin, Audre Lorde, Judy Grahn, Marilyn Hacker, Minnie Bruce Pratt, Alice Walker, Ntozake Shange, and Carolyn Kizer, among others, work as editors, publishers, reviewers, teachers and critics, authors of fiction, poetry, essays and plays.

Collaborations between poets of the period we have discussed include the well-known one between Maxine Kumin and Anne Sexton, who co-authored children's books and sustained each other in a working poetry friendship for seventeen years. This double collaboration is documented through references to each other in their poems, as well as in Sexton's published correspondence and Kumin's introduction to Sexton's *Collected Poems*.

The Broumas / Miller collaboration begun with *Black Holes / Black Stockings* may produce other joint works. Friendships among feminist poets may produce associations in their writing for future scholars to trace. What we know for certain is that these women are reading each other and committing themselves to mutual support: Rich writes the Introduction to Grahn's *The Work of a Common Woman*, Hacker commissions for *Woman Poet: The East* an interview between Rich and Lorde, Ostriker reviews contemporary women's poetry in the *New York Times*, Lorde writes the introduction to Philippine poet Mila Aguilar's *A Comrade is as Precious as a Rice Seedling*, and so on. Indeed if feminists ceased to call attention to each other's work in these ways, many of the names we mention here would be missing.

Feminist scholars have an opportunity for inquiry into numerous matters concerning American poetry from the 1960s on. Some subjects that occur to us as inviting examination are: the further development of an inclusive feminist poetics; a thorough consideration of feminist poets' rejection of formal syntax, punctuation, and structures as a political statement with artistic implications; the use of taboo language to defetishize the female body; and patterns of imagery that may cross over from poet to poet—for example, the significance of *lioness* and *roach* in the writings of Rich and Griffin, Rukeyser and Lorde. Alicia Suskin Ostriker's *Stealing the Language* provides a solid inquiry into the characteristic themes and forms of American women's poetry. Another study might look at the ways an ostensibly single voice represents a communal one, to be mapped via biographical research. June Jordan claims lineage from Walt Whitman in writing a people's poetry; Sexton writes a song of herself; Lorde writes rules of the road; Judy Grahn cites the Whitman catalogue as a stylistic feature of lesbian feminist poems.

The extent to which feminist literature has remained outside the literary establishment's notice is suggested by the fact that 1970 was the first year the MLA's Commission on the Status of Women offered sessions providing a feminist approach to literature. Twelve years later, what Audre Lorde called the first book on black women's studies was published, Gloria T. Hull, Patricia Bell Scott, and Barbara Smith's *All the Women Are White, All the Blacks Are Men, But Some of Us Are Brave*. After three more years Elaine Showalter's collection, the first book of feminist critical essays, *The New Feminist Criticism*, appeared. In the interim the poems of May Swenson went out of print. Clearly the work of feminist poets and critics also involves vigilance and rescuing women's poems—by gathering them into anthologies, by publishing critical assessments.

We think that whatever label poetry by women carries into the final decade of this century—*feminist, postfeminist, womanist*—when read seriously and attentively, this poetry must affect both the techniques available to poets and literary scholars, and the canon of twentieth and twenty-first century American poetry.

[1] Rachel Blau DuPlessis, "For the Etruscans," in *The New Feminist Criticism*, ed. Elaine Showalter (New York: Pantheon Books, 1985), 277.

[2] Alicia Suskin Ostriker, *Stealing the Language: The Emergence of Women's Poetry in America* (Boston: Beacon Press, 1986), 7.

[3] Anne Sexton, "The Silence," *The Complete Poems* (Boston: Houghton Mifflin Co., 1981), 318.

[4] Susan Griffin, *Made from This Earth* (New York: Harper & Row, 1982), 206-8.

[5] Catharine Stimpson, "Adrienne Rich and Lesbian/Feminist Poetry," *Parnassus* (Fall/Winter 1985): 249-68.

[6] Adrienne Rich, *Diving into the Wreck* (New York: W.W. Norton and Company, 1973), 22.

[7] Ntozake Shange, *A Daughter's Geography* (New York: St. Martin's Press, 1983), 51.

[8] Jane Roberta Cooper, *Scaffolding* (London: Anvil Press Poetry Ltd., 1984), 90.

[9] Florence Howe and Ellen Bass, eds., *No More Masks!* (Garden City, NY: Anchor Press/Doubleday Anchor Books, 1973), 253.

[10] Carole S. Oles, *The Loneliness Factor* (Lubbock: Texas Tech University Press, 1979), 8.

[11] Marge Piercy, *Circles on the Water, Selected Poems* (New York: Alfred A. Knopf, 1982), 39.

[12] Ibid., 164.

[13] Rich, *Diving*, 44.

[14] June Jordan, *Living Room* (New York: Thunder's Mouth Press, 1985), 45.

[15] Cynthia Macdonald, *(W)holes* (New York: Alfred A. Knopf, 1980), 27.

[16] Ostriker, *Stealing*, 93.

[17] Maxine Kumin, *Our Ground Time Here Will Be Brief, New and Selected Poems* (New York: Viking Press, 1982), 102.

[18] Julia Alvarez, *Homecoming* (New York: Grove Press, 1984), 19.

[19] Ibid., 41.

[20] Carolyn Kizer, *Mermaids in the Basement* (Port Townssend, WA: Copper Canyon, 1984), 11.

[21] Ibid., 14.

[22] Ibid., 34.

[23] Ibid., 16.

[24] Alice Walker, *Revolutionary Petunias and Other Poems* (New York: Harcourt Brace Jovanovich, 1973), 16.

[25] Adrienne Rich, *The Dream of a Common Language* (New York: W.W. Norton and Company, 1978), 77.

[26] Audre Lorde, *Chosen Poems, Old and New* (New York: W.W. Norton and Company, 1982), 21.

[27] Judy Grahn, *The Work of a Common Woman: The Collected Poetry of Judy Grahn 1964-1977* (New York: St. Martin's Press, 1978), 125.

[28] Ibid.

[29] Michelle Cliff, *Claiming an Identity They Taught Me to Despise* (Watertown, MA: Persephone Press, 1980), 32.

[30] Cherríe Moraga and Gloria Anzaldúa, *This Bridge Called My Back, Writings by Radical Women of Color*, 2nd ed. (New York: Kitchen Table: Women of Color Press, 1983), 94-97.

[31] Lorde, *Chosen Poems*, 49.

[32] Sandra Gilbert and Susan Gubar, eds., *Shakespeare's Sisters, Feminist Essays on Women Poets* (Bloomington: Indiana University Press, 1979), 165.

[33] Barbara Smith, ed., *Home Girls, A Black Feminist Anthology* (New York: Kitchen Table: Women of Color Press, 1983), xix-lvi.

[34] Ruth Whitman, *Tamsen Donner* (Cambridge, MA: Alice James Books, 1977), 72.

[35] Ibid., 75.

[36] Carole S. Oles, *Night Watches: Inventions on the Life of Maria Mitchell* (Cambridge, MA: Alice James Books, 1985), 67.

[37] Moraga and Anzaldúa, *This Bridge*, 76.

[38] Rita Dove, *The Yellow House on the Corner* (Pittsburgh: Carnegie-Mellon University Press, 1980), 33.

[39] Cooper, *Scaffolding*, 121.

[40] Smith, ed., *Home Girls*, 63.

[41] Muriel Rukeyser, *The Collected Poems* (New York: McGraw-Hill Book Company, 1978), 498.

[42] Rachel Blau DuPlessis, *Writing Beyond the Ending, Narrative Strategies of Twentieth-Century Women Writers* (Bloomington: Indiana University Press, 1985), 134.

[43] Celia Gilbert, *Bonfire* (Cambridge, MA: Alice James Books, 1983), 21.

[44] Sandra Gilbert, "What He Hates/What He Loves," *13th Moon* 6, nos. 1,2 (1982): 84.

[45] May Swenson, *New and Selected Things Taking Place* (Boston: Little, Brown and Company, 1978), 104.

[46] Kumin, *Our Ground Time*, 72.

[47] Ibid., 139.

[48] Ibid., 151.

[49] Kizer, *Mermaids*, 104.

[50] Ibid.

[51] Rukeyser, *Collected Poems*, 14.

[52] Jordan, *Living Room*, 44.

[53] Ibid., 24.

[54] Griffin, *This Earth*, 82.

[55] Sandra Gilbert and Susan Gubar, eds., *The Norton Anthology of Literature by Women* (New York: W.W. Norton and Company, 1985), 1673.

[56] Grahn, *Common Woman*, 65.

[57] Joanne Ward, "Climbing," *13th Moon* 6, nos. 1,2 (1982): 47.

[58] Ibid.

[59] Smith, ed., *Home Girls*, 256.

[60] Rukeyser, *Collected Poems*, 527.

[61] Ibid., 573.

[62] Jordan, *Living Room*, 45.

[63] Ibid., 134.

[64] Adrienne Rich, *A Wild Patience Has Taken Me This Far* (New York: W.W. Norton and Company, 1981), 52.

[65] Jordan, *Living Room*, 75.

[66] Ibid., 57.

[67] Linda Hogan, *Seeing Through the Sun* (Amherst: The University of Massachusetts Press, 1985), 61.

[68] Alice Walker, *Horses Make a Landscape Look More Beautiful* (San Diego: Harcourt Brace Jovanovich, 1984), 30.

[69] Rich, *Common Language,* 12.

[70] Lorde, *Chosen Poems*, 101.

[71] Carole S. Oles, "Mother Wit," review of *Assumptions*, by Marilyn Hacker, *The Nation*, 27 April 1985, 58.

PSYCHOANALYSIS AND CREATIVITY THE ROLE OF THE PRECONSCIOUS

By Frederick Feirstein

In Freud's early topography of the mind, the preconscious is the intermediate system that bridges the unconscious and conscious. It is a perceptual system that looks inward to the derivatives of the instincts, the archaic heritage of our species' symbols, and the particular symbols of the repressed unconscious. It also looks outward to the stimuli of consciousness and the commonly shared symbols of society.

As Susan Deri, making use of Winnicott, points out, developmentally the preconscious is the heir of the transitional space, that growing gap between the child and his mother which both connects him to her and gives him room to play privately and creatively. He expresses his connectedness and separateness by what he does with his transitional objects (blankets, teddy bears, etc.) This expressiveness will later become the model for mature creativity—a form of play that both reaches inward to his private world and outward to a reader, an audience. We can see this origin of creativity not only in the act of creativity but also in the themes of connectedness and separateness or connectedness versus separateness that often find their way into literary work.

If the early playing is damaged, for instance, by an intrusive mother who invades her child's privacy and makes his symbols her own, or by a depressed one who neglects the child, doesn't give his play an audience, then the child's preconscious, and later his adult creativity, will be damaged. As Lawrence Kubie points out, the preconscious of such a child becomes rigid and inflexible—overly attached to the inner world or too detached from it and overly connected to the facts of reality, to consciousness. Or, to put it in terms of transitional objects, its symbols either remain internal and too private or they're too connected to the outside, to mother, reality, clichés.

So we might say then that the creative person (the scientist, psychoanalyst, entrepreneur, etc. as well as the artist) is blessed with a fluid preconscious. The preconscious is not only genetically well endowed with a rich storehouse of symbols but is one that is nurtured by a good enough mother. As the child played easily in the transitional space, so the creative adult's preconscious has relatively easy access to both its inner world and to reality.

We might also say that creativity, the preconscious at full play, is a normal state deriving also from the phylogenetic origins of REM sleep. During the creative process, the artist goes into a trance-like state resembling sleep where all psychic systems are bridged and function in unison. The artist pulls stuff in from consciousness (as the dreamer does the day's residue) and blends it with material from both the original unconscious—our species' symbols—and from the repressed unconscious with its symbols distorted by conflict and shut out of consciousness.

Not only do the symbols seem to be inherited, the degree of fluidity of the preconscious itself seems to have a genetic basis. We can see this early in the creative child who appears born with spontaneity, playfulness, imagination, sensitivity to others and to his own vulnerability. This kind of personality seems to have thinner boundaries between his psychic systems and between the inner and outer worlds. Sometimes, as Ernest Hartmann shows us, the creative child is vulnerable to nightmares because he has easier access to the demons as well as the angels of our archaic heritage. He's also extremely sensitive to the nuances and even the unconscious of others, as Alice Miller talks about in *Drama Of The Gifted Child*. Such a sensitive child can be damaged severely by the manipulations of narcissistic parents, no matter how they cover their maneuvers up.

Good parents will nurture the creativity of such a child in a couple of ways. Not only will they protect the child's play from their own pathology, but they will protect the child from the child's archaic heritage. Parents can do this by creating distance between reality and the symbols and complexes of the original unconscious i.e. by not acting like the monsters of the child's dreams. They give the child a way to assign the monsters to fantasy as, for example, Bruno Bettleheim shows us in stressing the importance of fairy tales which make the archaic heritage fictional and therefore more distant and manageable.

Later on the fluidity of the preconscious and creativity are developed by education in whatever field the creative person chooses. So, for instance, the poet learns to freely use displacement and condensation in making metaphors. In doing so, his primary processes mature way beyond the primitive state they began with.

The education of the poet, when it's truly nurturing, leads to fluidity, and the poet will be able to range up and down developmental stages and connect up his inner world with reality and make a poem that communicates passionately.

A similar education is available to the psychoanalyst. In learning the language of dreams, transference, countertransference and resistance, the good analyst sits in the transitional space of the session like a creative artist. He is in touch with his patient's displacements and condensations, for example as they're revealed in the language of his symptoms, and is in touch with his own pathology, as the patient evokes it, and is in touch with his and the patient's symbolic language for describing his character. Frequently he will think in images that will help him make metaphoric interpretations, communications effectively connecting to the patient's world.

Finally, what helps the creative person's fluidity is psychoanalysis--particularly when pathology affects his symbolization processes. As I mentioned earlier, we can look at pathology in the preconscious at two extremes. When the preconscious is too rigidly attached to the unconscious then, as Deri shows us, those symbols which reach preconsciousness and are threatening are shoved back down, distorted by conflict and reappear (the return of the repressed) as cryptosymbols, demanding expression, repetitively so.

This is what happens when an artist is blocked. He goes stale and finds that he's repeating himself. Or he may be stuck in the conflicts of a particular developmental level and, for instance, as Chassguet-Smirgel points out, he may be capable of producing only anal art, aesthetically pretty expressions of rage.

At worst, when the artist is so rigidly attached to his unconscious, he shuts out reality and becomes solipsistic. He conveys only a private language that sometimes resembles and sometimes actually is psychotic.

When the preconscious is too rigidly attached to consciousness, we get a very different kind of problem. There the "artist" isn't well attuned to his inner life but instead borrows the stale repetitive symbols of reality that in fact are sometimes symptoms of historical repression. Such symbols (as Jews well know the Holocaust is in danger of becoming) avoid feeling and work as signs, intensifiers as Thass-Thienemann calls them.

Why then would an aspiring artist need to do this, borrow the clichés of consciousness and get so attached to them his work seems to have no inner spirit?

Let me try to offer some explanation by looking again at how fluidity in the preconscious comes about. First of all, it comes from heredity, the endowment of a rich storehouse of symbols and an ease with symbolization processes. Some people who want to be artists but aren't richly endowed can manage to acquire the formulas of consciousness and repeat them from their mildly creative subjectivity. Such people used to be called and maybe still are called hacks. They're people who can successfully pitch and carry out t.v. series that repeat stereotypes, write cheap, even best-selling novels and, if their personalities are sensational enough, sell themselves to the art world. They pander to others but often admit to feeling like shams because they experience a shallow sense of self. They may have been used to pleasing others in childhood, pleasing `narcissistic parents, and become quite adept at it. They may initially rebel, determine to become a great novelist or painter with their own style. But after significant rejection and attendant anxieties and depression, they find it much easier and gratifying to imitate, to produce what's expected of them.

We see this in every field—in the analytic field in the "California style therapies", the quick fix cures. There, instead of going inward and outward to explore human nature, such hacks put in a bit of this and that pop psychology, formulas that lull people for a while.

There are also analysts who hook into academic formulas of this school or that without profoundly learning the spirit of the school or their own insides and so become cerebral therapists, often brilliant-sounding ones theoretically who produce a sham of analysis, as an "artist" can produce a clever-sounding but empty work.

Getting back to the other kind of rigidity, there are also analysts so rigidly attached to their unconscious that they lose all contact with such realities as the AIDS epidemic and in the past The Holocaust. As a friend has pointed out to me, there was very little written about The Holocaust by analysts as it was actually happening.

In summing up: Creativity seems to depend on maintaining fluidity, in not becoming rigidly attached to the unconscious or to consciousness. It comes from an ability to shuttle back and forth between inherited symbols, symbols we make and re-make with developed primary processes (as Pinchas Noy points out) and the facts of human comedy and tragedy.

REFERENCES

Bruno Bettleheim, *The Uses Of Enchantment* (Vintage, 1977).

Janine Chassguet-Smirgel, *Creativity And Perversion* (Norton, 1985).

Susan Deri, *Symbolization And Creativity* (I.U.P., 1984).

Sigmund Freud, "The Unconscious" (1915) in *Standard Edition.*

Ernest Hartmann, *The Nightmare* (Basic Books, 1984).

Lawrence Kubie, *Neurotic Distortion of the Creative Process*
(University of Kansas Press, 1958) .

Alice Miller, *Prisoners Of Childhood: The Drama Of The Gifted Child*
(Basic Books, 1981) .

Pinchas Noy, "A Revision of the Psychoanalytic Theory of Primary Process," *Int..J. Psa.*, 50, (1969).

Theodore Thass-Thienemann, *The Interpretation Of Language* (Jason Aaronson, 1973).

D.W. Winnicott, *Playing And Reality* (Tavistock, 1971).

A BLACK RAINBOW:
MODERN AFRO-AMERICAN
POETRY

By Marilyn Nelson Waniek and Rita Dove

The number of Afro-American poets represented in major anthologies is relatively small; three or four may appear here and there, but to discover others one must seek out the anthologies of Black literature or find individual volumes of poetry. Literary politics have a great deal to do with social politics. Confined to a literary ghetto for many of the same reasons Blacks have been confined to physical ghettos, Black poets have created their own tradition, rooted in a song fundamentally different from its white counterpart. Modern Black poetry is nourished by the work of earlier Black poets, and draws much of its sustenance from the folk sources which have nurtured the race since slavery. These sources include Black music, Black speech, the Black church, and the guerrilla techniques of survival—irony, concealment, double-entendre, and fable.

The most pervasive influence on modern Black poetry has been the idea of the audience. Black poets bear witness to the oft-quoted observation by W.E.B. DuBois that the Black American "ever feels his twoness." That "twoness" can be seen in the work of poets as a division in their address to their Black and white audiences. Most approach this division by choosing to address one or the other group; a few choose to combine their audiences, overlooking the differences between them in a hopeful attempt to speak to the whole of the American people.

The idea of the audience has affected Black poetry in several ways; one is in the choice of language. As the work of the troubled turn-of-the-century poet Paul Laurence Dunbar demonstrated, the Black poet must consciously choose to write either in the standard English preferred by the white audience, or in what Dunbar called the "broken tongue" of dialect or colloquialism. Early in this century, Black poets tended to alternate between the two modes. The work of later poets, most especially those of the Amiri Baraka generation, continues this tendency.

Choice of language is related to a second aspect of the Black poet's view of the audience. The readership of poetry in the United States is very small; to address oneself to only a portion of that already small audience is to limit oneself severely. Those Black poets who address the Black audience often resolve this problem by writing poems intended to be performed, rather than silently read. The older tradition of the *griot* , or storyteller, has been kept very much alive by poets who perform their works on street-corners, at political gatherings, anywhere they can find an audience willing to listen. Indeed, the oral nature of much Black poetry is one of its strongest identifying characteristics, and one of the reasons critics and teachers often find it difficult to discuss more than the sociological backgrounds of individual poems. Performance poetry directed primarily to a Black audience often lacks literary polish. Free of metaphor, of simile, of literary allusion, this poetry relies to a large extent on an extra-literary convention traditional in the Black community: that of call-and-response. The poet, in the role of the caller, expects—even demands—the audience to respond verbally (or at least vocally) to words, intonations, and associations familiar to the community. As the traditional Black preacher expects the congregation to respond, the performance poet requires a sort of "Amen-reaction" from the Black audience. This response is a vital part of the poem, although it is not expressed in the text itself.

Modern Black poetry has, from its beginnings in the Harlem Renaissance, incorporated elements of Black music. The blues and jazz poems of Langston Hughes, the ballads of Sterling Brown, Margaret Walker, and Gwendolyn Brooks, the gospel-song righteousness of Carolyn Rodgers's poems: all of these bear witness to the influence of Black music. Clarence Major, in his introduction to *The New Black Poetry* , points out another, less obvious influence: the emphasis of "the *beat* as opposed to anything melodic." Black poets often strive for syncopation in metrical verse, and even loose free-verse by Black poets often achieves jazzlike rhythmic effects. Both Langston Hughes and the Black Arts poets of the Sixties and early Seventies learned to "worry the line" like blues singers; instead of the literary references of generic poetry, Black poetry tends to allude to spirituals, the blues, and jazz, often going so far as to mention specific jazz musicians or pop singers by name, as if to insure the place of poetry in that richest tradition of Black culture.

Of the other elements of Black culture which make their way into Black poetry, the breath-units of the inspired sermon and the tenacity of faith—if not in Christianity's God, at least in the possibility of an improved future, often expressed in revolutionary terms—can be discerned. In a long and persuasive introduction to *Understanding The New Black Poetry* , Stephen Henderson enumerates several elements of what he describes as "elegant Black linguistic gesture": these include the use of virtuoso naming and enumerating, of virtuoso free-rhyming, of hyperbolic or understated imagery, of metaphysical imagery, and of compression.[1] In her *Negro Digest* essay, "Black Poetry—Where It's At," Carolyn Rodgers adds to the list the use of "signifying" (hyperbolic insult, often describing one's adversary's Mama), of "shouting" (verbal harangue), and of "du-wah dittybop bebop" (which defies explanation).[2] The spoken virtuosity of many Black poets is one way they call up audience response: It's difficult for a Black audience to hear a signifying competition or a talented shouter lay down his rap without adding, "Sock it to 'em," "Right on," or simply, "Amen!"

While many critics argue the existence of one or several Black themes, a most appropriate and encompassing understanding of theme recognizes the sense of mission shared by Black poets. Dismissing the idea that poetry does nothing, many Black poets have persistently believed that poems are tools of power. A sense of cultural responsibility prompts them to affirm the place of poetry in the struggle against social injustice. This is not to say that there is a party-line of Black poetry; rather, this poetry insists that it will be heard or read by individuals who are a part of a real, larger social and political community. Whether they address Black or White audiences, Black poets, as Amiri Baraka points out, "can't go anywhere without an awareness of the hurt / the white man has put on the people. Any people."[3] Taking the side of the people, Black poetry offers them a description of life's possibilities. Even when it addresses political problems, social injustice, or personal pain, its tonal character tends to be enlivening. It draws inspiration from the survival of Black people in a hostile world and from the survival of their faith in a dream.

THE HARLEM RENAISSANCE

The decade following the First World War, known to literary generalists as the "Jazz Age," was an enormously energetic period for Black literature. The "Great Migration" of Southern Negroes to the cities of the North, their increased activism in response to "Jim Crow" laws and lynchings, and the birth of several organizations and publications which encouraged Negro artists contributed to the burgeoning activity of writers who sought to express the yearnings, anger, and pride of the race which critic Alain Locke termed "The New Negro." Harlem became a booming Negro metropolis, and because many of the artists whose voices dominated the period lived there, the period came to be known as "The Harlem Renaissance." The Renaissance saw the publication of many novels and volumes of poetry, among the most important to the history of Black poetry Locke's anthology, *The New Negro* (1925) and *The Book of American Negro Poetry* (1922), edited by poet James Weldon Johnson. The many able writers represented in these pages gave voice to the radical political influence of W.E.B. DuBois and the Pan-Africanism of Marcus Garvey in works which struggled to define the Negro and his place in America and the world. Their mood was one of awakening militancy and pride. The most talented poets of the period were Claude McKay, Countee Cullen, James Weldon Johnson, and Langston Hughes.

Born and educated in Jamaica, where his first two volumes of dialect poems about the Jamaican peasantry were published, McKay emigrated to the United States as a young man, and soon became the poet—in carefully structured sonnets—of pride and rage. While much of his American work deals with the emigrant's nostalgia for his forsaken homeland, McKay's strongest poems—those upon which his reputation is rightfully based—are such sonnets as "The White House," "Baptism," and "If We Must Die." The last- mentioned poem, occasioned by the frequent lynchings which cast their bloody shadow over the post-war years, urges the Negro to answer violence with violence: "we must meet the common foe! / Though far outnumbered let us show us brave."[4] The speaker of most of McKay's sonnets is cast as a romantic hero, an outsider whose soul is tested by the violence of his society. Thus in "The White City," McKay's speaker says he must "Muse my lifelong hate, and without flinch / ...bear it nobly as I live my part,"[5] and in "Baptism" he enters into the "furnace" of American racism, yet assures us that "I will not quiver in the frailest bone." McKay confronts the duality of being Black in a white society without losing a shred of his pride; indeed, he draws strength from rejection and rage, as in "My House":

> I know the dark delight of being strange,
> The penalty of difference in the crowd,
> The loneliness of wisdom among fools,
> Yet never have I felt but very proud.[6]

In his life as in his work, McKay was an outsider; though his writing had a profound influence on the Negritude poets, Senghor and Cesaire, McKay had little personal influence on his American contemporaries. His gift to posterity is a small collection of powerfully militant sonnets and the irony of his weighting their delicate form with such a bitter cargo.

Countee Cullen, like McKay, used the fixed metrical forms of the English tradition. Raised in Harlem as the adopted son of a conservative Methodist minister, and educated at New York University and Harvard, Cullen was widely considered an extremely fine craftsman. The main body of his poetic work reveals a sensitive romantic haunted by the "burden" of being a Negro, which seemed to Cullen to contradict belief in an omnipotent, merciful God. Some of his strongest poems constitute an argument with the Creator, who in the words of his "Yet Do I Marvel," has been cruel, (or ironic, or unwise) enough "To make a poet black, and bid him sing!" Cullen found in his racial identity a troubling ambivalence. In "Heritage" his skin is for him the source of pride, of joy, and of distress; he finds no release from the sense that Africa—the symbol of sensuality and abandon, and the antithesis of "Jesus Christ, / preacher of humility"—paces like a caged lion through his veins. Although Cullen wishes in this poem that "He I served were black" and elsewhere does write of a Black Christ, the poet's sense of himself as an individual who plays "the double part" is clearly expressed in "The Shroud of Color," a dream-vision in which he learns "How being dark, and living through the pain / Of it, is courage more than angels have."[7] Cullen's pensive work expresses more quietly than McKay's the dilemma of being Black in the early part of the century; as with McKay, however, Cullen's contribution to the tradition of Black poetry is largely thematic. It was James Weldon Johnson and Langston Hughes who laid the groundwork for the poets who came after the Harlem Renaissance.

James Weldon Johnson was born in Jacksonville, Florida, to an educated and cultured family, and was graduated from Atlanta University. Johnson was "the Renaissance man" of the Harlem Renaissance. Among the many accomplishments gracing his distinguished career were service in the American diplomatic corps,

the secretary generalship of the N.A.A.C.P., musicals
written in collaboration with his composer brother (with
whom he also wrote the song known as "The Negro
National Anthem"), the publication of one of the more
important novels of the Harlem Renaissance, two land-
mark collections of spirituals and Negro poetry, and
two volumes of his own poetry. Of these, *God's Trombones* , published in 1927, has enjoyed enduring popularity.

In the seven poems of this collection Johnson attempts
to capture the power and virtuosity of the Negro folk
sermon. As he points out in his preface to the volume,
"these poems would better be intoned than read"; to a
listening audience the poems are intensely moving.
Johnson felt that "what the colored poet in the United
States needs to do is something like what Synge did
for the Irish; he needs to find a form that will express
the racial spirit by symbols from within."[8] In his preface Johnson includes instructions to the reader, pointing out that he has arranged lines and punctuation to
indicate the tempos of the preacher, and that "there is
a decided syncopation of speech" in the poems, as in
the folk sermon. Johnson acknowledges the fact that
the audience responses needed to give the poem-ser-
mons "an antiphonal quality" do not appear on the
printed page; the reader unfamiliar with the Negro folk
sermon would do best to read these poems aloud, imagining as he does so the voice of Paul Robeson or perhaps the contemporary actor James Earl Jones, as well
as the murmurs of shared feeling from the audience-
congregation. *God's Trombones* is a collection of performance poems which assumes both a speaking voice
and a vocalizing audience. Like many of Langston
Hughes's poems, these are dramatic monologues which
create both a speaker and a situation.

The folk nature of the poems is evident from the outset, as in "Listen Lord—A Prayer," where the speaker offers a homely view of God, asking him to "open up a window of heaven, / and lean out far over the battlements of glory."[9] God is anthropomorphized, and more: like the Lord of the folk preacher, Johnson's God is personalized, familiar. In "The Creation," God rolls light around in his hands to make the sun and creates man "Like a mammy bending over her baby." The folk preacher puts himself and his listeners in the Biblical situation, as in the spiritual, "Were You There When They Crucified My Lord," in which the folk lyricist insists upon her own presence at Calvary as she describes the scene in poignant detail. Though himself an unbeliever, Johnson's lament for Christ in "The Crucifixion" tenderly brings the scene home in language similar to that of the Negro spirituals:

> Jesus, my lamb-like Jesus,
> Shivering as the nails go through his hands;
> Jesus, my lamb-like Jesus,
> Shivering as the nails go through his feet.
> Jesus, my darling Jesus,
> Groaning as the Roman spear plunged in his side;
> Jesus, my darling Jesus,
> Groaning as the blood came spurting from his wound.
> Oh, look how they done my Jesus.[10]

As the poet worries the refrain the descriptive lines grow more and more syncopated, drawing a murmur of assent from the audience. Here, as in this passage from "The Judgment Day," Johnson's poetry does more than deal with Black subject matter; it is the authentic voice of the folk:

> Then the tall, bright angel, Gabriel,
> Will put one foot on the battlements of heaven

> And the other on the steps of hell,
> And blow that silver trumpet
> Till he shakes old hell's foundations.[11]

The poems of *God's Trombones* are theatrical, although the intonations and gestures of their speaker and the responses of the audience are not indicated in their text. Their form—written and implied—comes closer to expressing their racial element than had heretofore been considered possible or dignified; the poems ensure the survival of a rich and lively oral tradition.

The considerable diversity of Black poetry is clearly evidenced in the humorous use to which Langston Hughes puts the same oral tradition in "Sunday Morning Prophecy," a poem from *One-Way Ticket* (1949):

> ...and now
> When the rumble of death
> Rushes down the drain
> Pipe of eternity,
> And hell breaks out
> Into a thousand smiles,
> And the devil licks his chops
> Preparing to feast on life,
> And all the little devils
> Get out their bibs
> To devour the corrupt bones
> Of this world—[12]

Affectionately known for most of his life as "The Poet Laureate of Harlem," Langston Hughes was born in Missouri and raised in the Midwest, moving to Harlem only as a young man. There he discovered his spiritual home, in Harlem's heart of Blackness finding both his vocation—"to explain and illuminate the Negro condition in America"—and the proletarian voice of most of his best work. If Johnson was the Renaissance man of the Harlem Renaissance, Hughes was its greatest man of letters; he saw through publication more than a dozen collections of poems, ten plays, two novels, several collections of short fiction, one historical study, two autobiographical works, several anthologies, and many books for children. His essay, "The Negro Artist and the Racial Mountain," provided a personal credo and statement of direction for the poets of his generation, who, he says, "intend to express our individual dark-skinned selves without fear or shame...We know we are beautiful. And ugly too."[13] His forthright commitment to the Negro people led him to explore with great authenticity the frustrated dreams of the Black masses and to experiment with diction, rhythm, and musical forms.

Hughes was ever quick to confess the influences of Whitman and Sandburg on his work, and his best poetry also reflects the influence of Sherwood Anderson's *Winesburg, Ohio* . Like these poets, Hughes collected individual voices; his work is a notebook of life-studies. In his best poems Hughes the man remains masked; his voices are the voices of the Negro race as a whole, or of individual Negro speakers. "The Negro Speaks of Rivers," a widely anthologized poem from his first book, *The Weary Blues* (1926), is a case in point. Here Hughes is visible only as spokesman for the race as he proclaims "I bathed in the Euphrates when dawns were young. / I built my hut near the Congo and it lulled me to sleep."[14] Poems frequently present anonymous Black personae, each of whom shares a painful heritage and an ironic pride. As one humorous character announces:

I do cooking,
Day's work, too!
Alberta K. Johnson
Madam to you.[15]

Hughes took poetry out of what Cullen called "the dark tower"—which was, and even during the Harlem Renaissance, ivy-covered and distant—and took it directly to the people. His blues and jazz experiments described and addressed an audience for which music was a central experience; he became a spokesman for their troubles, as in "Po' Boy Blues":

> When I was home de
> Sunshine seemed like gold.
> When I was home de
> Sunshine seemed like gold.
> Since I come up North de
> Whole damn world's turned cold.[16]

American democracy appears frequently in Hughes's work as the unfulfilled but potentially realizable dream of the Negro, who says in "Let America Be America Again:"

> O, yes,
> I say it plain,
> America never was America to me,
> And yet I swear this oath—America will be![17]

There are many fine poems in the Hughes canon, but the strongest single work is *Montage of a Dream Deferred* (1951), a collection of sketches, captured voices, and individual lives unified by the jazz-like improvisations on the central theme of "a dream deferred." Like many of his individual poems, this work is intended for performance: think of it as a Harlem *Under Milk Wood* . Hughes moves rapidly from one voice or scene to the next; from the person in "Blues in Dawn" who says "I don't dare start thinking in the morning," to, in "Dime," a snatch of conversation: "Chile, these steps is hard to climb. / Grandma, lend me a dime."

The moods of the poems are as varied as their voices, for Hughes includes the daylight hours as well as the night. There are the bitter jump-rope rhymes of disillusioned children, the naive exclamations of young lovers, the gossip of friends. A college freshman writes in his "Theme for English B:" "I guess being colored doesn't make me not like / the same things other folks like who are other races." A jaded woman offers in "Advice" the observation that "birthing is hard / and dying is mean," and advises youth to "get yourself / a little loving / in between." "Hope" is a miniature vignette in which a dying man asks for fish, and "His wife looked it up in her dream book / and played it." The changing voices, moods, and rhythms of this collection are, as Hughes wrote in a preface, "like be-bop...marked by conflicting change, sudden nuances...." We are reminded throughout that we should be hearing the poem as music; as boogie-woogie, as blues, as bass, as saxophone. Against the eighty-odd dreams collected here, the refrain insists that these frustrated dreams are potentially dangerous:

> What happens to a dream deferred?
>
> Does it dry up
> like a raisin in the sun?
> Or fester like a sore—
> And then run?
> Does it stink like rotten meat?
> Or crust and sugar over—
> like a syrupy sweet?
> Maybe it just sags
> like a heavy load.
>
> *Or does it explode?* [18]

More than any other Black poet, Langston Hughes spoke for the Negro people. Most of those after him have emulated his ascent of the Racial Mountain, his painfully joyous declaration of pride and commonality. His work offers white readers a glimpse into the social and the personal lives of Black America; Black readers recognize a proud affirmation of self. For some forty years, Hughes was the beloved spokesman of the race he lovingly described as "Laughers":

> Dream singers,
> Story tellers,
> Dancers,
> Loud laughters in the hands of Fate—
> My people.
> Dish-washers,
> Elevator-boys.
> Ladies' maids,
> Crap-shooters,
> Cooks,
> Waiters,
> Jazzers,
> Nurses of babies,
> Loaders of ships,
> Rounders,
> Number writers,
> Comedians in vaudeville
> And band-men in circuses—
> Dream-singers all,—
> My people.[19]

POST-RENAISSANCE POETS

The exuberance of the Harlem Renaissance glowed for a few years, but gradually faded during the Depression into a disillusioned silence. During the thirty-odd years between the Renaissance and the Black Arts Movement, Langston Hughes continued to write, and several new poets, principally Sterling Brown and Robert

Hayden, emerged. These poets, most of them academics, were not a part of Harlem's glittering grandeur; they did not write of the splendors of Africa, nor of the orthodoxy of race which had characterized the Harlem Renaissance. Working in relative isolation and strongly influenced by their Anglo-American contemporaries, they introduced new themes and techniques to Black poetry and took it to a new and wider audience. Their optimistic attempt to integrate Black poetry into the mainstream of American literature ironically prepared the way for the disaffected Black poets of the Sixties.

Born 1901 in Washington, D.C., and educated at Williams College and Harvard University, Sterling Brown taught for many years at Howard University and produced two collections of poetry (his *Collected Poems* , published in 1980, won the National Book Award), four books of criticism, and a major anthology of Afro-American literature. Despite his impressive academic credentials, Brown is primarily a folk-poet, mining Southern Negro culture for its treasures of folk characters, stories, and songs. His realistic portraits of share-croppers, farmers, and workers are myths of disappointment and fortitude. Alternating between vernacular poems in which his characters describe their own lives, and standard English poems which demonstrate more fully his mastery of technique and his depth of thought, Brown's work has a wider range than that of Hughes, though, like Hughes, he borrows musical forms from the folk. His use of blues and ballad forms as well as the work song results in several striking poems such as the title poem of his first volume, *Southern Road* (1932):

> White man tells me—hunh—
> Damn yo' soul;
> White man tells me—hunh—
> Damn yo' soul;

Go no need, bebby,
To be tole.[20]

Like the speaker of this poem, a worker on a chain
gang, Brown's characters tend to be strong men and
women whose resistance to oppressive forces—often
whites, but almost as often the colorless faces of history or nature—makes them outcasts or outlaws. His
"Georgie Grimes" flees from the memory of "hot words,
lies, / The knife, and a pool of blood." In "The Last
Ride of Wild Bill" a numbers-runner leads the entire
police force on a mad chase. While many of his characters try to run away from trouble, Brown also portrays those who cannot escape because, as "Riverbank
Blues" has it, "A man git dis yellow water in his blood."
Their plight, expressed in "Children of the Mississippi,"
is to face annually the ruthless river, to watch it "Take
their lives' earnings, roll off their paltry / Fixtures of
home, things as dear as old hearthgods." Brown writes
of the rural underclass, slaves no longer of human masters,
but of the soil itself. In "Arkansas Chant" he extends
the blame even further: for the Black sharecroppers
the devil is a night-rider and

God may be the owner,
But he's rich and forgetful,
And far away.[21]

Brown frequently borrows folk motifs, among them
the ideas of a smaller heaven for whites ("When De
Saints Go Ma'ching Home"),the American South as hell
("Slim Greer in Hell"), and of ju-ju ("Scotty Has His
Say," "Parish Doctor"). Folk humor suits his bitter vision. More characteristic of his pessimistic world-view,
however, is the following passage from "Episode," in
which a man is destroyed by his own rage:

Oh for a throat to glut his fierce hatred.
Let him rush out, now, drunken and sick,
Find where he can a crashing appeasement,
Let madness have him, let murder be served.[22]

Margaret Walker, a native of Birmingham, Alabama, was educated at Northwestern University and the University of Iowa, and has taught for many years at Jackson State College in Mississippi. Her writing career has suffered from the long silences which characterize the careers of many women writers. Her first book, a collection of poems, was the Yale Younger Poet selection of 1942; her second, a novel, was published in 1965, and her third, another collection of poems, did not appear until 1970. Her poems are much influenced by Langston Hughes and Sterling Brown, and by the oratorical and musical traditions of the Black community. Her ghost story, "Molly Means," is a stirring folk ballad; the long verse-paragraphs of her best known poem, "For My People," borrow much from the tradition of moving oratory:

For my people blundering and groping and floundering in the
dark of churches and schools and clubs and societies,
associations and councils and committees and conventions,
distressed and disturbed and deceived and devoured
 by money-hungry glory-craving leeches, preyed on by
facile force of state and fad and novelty by false prophet
and holy believer...[23]

The most successful poet of the Post-Renaissance period was Gwendolyn Brooks. Raised and educated in Chicago, where she has lived all her life, Brooks has, since the publication of her first book, *A Street in Bronzeville* (1945), combined a quiet life as housewife and mother with a literary career most poets can only dream of. Her exquisite, word-intoxicated poems demonstrate her mastery of craft; her realistic portraits of working-class Black people demonstrate her insight and her sympathy. While her career took a sudden turn in the Sixties and fell under the detrimental influence of younger, more militant poets, the wholeness of style, theme, and vision of her earlier work makes hers an important contribution to American letters.

Brooks' primary concern is to show the value of the individual. Her investigations of the interior lives of her subjects probe beyond their skin-deep identities. Psychological depth and tight control of language and metrical form are characteristic of Brooks' work. In "The Mother," for example, a haunted woman explains to the "dim killed children" whom she has aborted that "even in my deliberateness I was not deliberate," and that "I knew you, though faintly, and I loved, I loved you / All."[24] Although her poems about women are among her best, Brooks writes about men with equal sympathy. "The Sundays of Satin-Legs Smith" is a study of the effects of environment and history on an individual. Satin-Legs Smith is a hard-living dandy, a womanizer, yet the poet extends her sympathy to him, explaining his preferences for flashy clothes, down-home food, and easy women with an understanding which makes him engaging to an audience which might otherwise find him merely ignorant and vulgar. Contemplating his taste in music, she observes that

> ...a man must bring
> To music what his mother spanked him for
> When he was two: bits of forgotten hate,
> Devotion: whether or not his mattress hurts:
> The little dream his father humored: the thing
> His sister did for money...[25]

A sonnet sequence about American soldiers in the Second World War exhibits similar sympathy. In "still do I keep my look, my identity..." a soldier muses that in death, the body itself is uniquely individual, each "Shows the old personal art, the look. Shows what / It showed at baseball. What it showed in school."[26]

Annie Allen , the book for which Brooks won the Pulitzer Prize in 1950, might be called a *Bildungsroman* in verse. Its protagonist, the daughter of a working-class Black family, comes to womanhood during the war. The longest poem in the volume, "The Anniad," ironically contrasts the life of the girl with the exploits of the legendary heroes alluded to in the title, and hints that the work is the epic of an ordinary life. Here again, Brooks is concerned with the development of individual character. As a girl, Annie is a romantic in the tradition of *Anne of Green Gables* ; an adolescent in the first part of "The Anniad," she still watches

> ...for the paladin
> Which no woman ever had,
> Paradisiacal and sad
> With a dimple in his chin.[27]

But the world has no place for Black girls who dream they are Cinderella. Annie settles for an ordinary love affair, though in the room of her lover she imagines herself like a nun in a chapel, and "genuflects to love." War interrupts their love, and he returns a different man, frustrated by his new realization of his social impotence. He takes a mistress, leaves Annie to find solace in nature, and books. When he returns again, Annie is already broken; at twenty-four "almost thoroughly / Derelict and dim and done."

The highly alliterative trochaic stanzas of "The Anniad" are a formal tour de force, though the poem is often unrewardingly difficult. More successful is the sequence called "The Womanhood," deft portraits of a mature and thoughtful woman who faces life's most profound questions with intelligence and concern. She wishes life might be simpler, for both she and her child "want joy of undeep and unabiding thing, / Like kicking over a chair or throwing blocks out of a window." But life is not simple for Black children, and she cannot make it so for herself, or for her child. She has no comforting truths to give to children who cry

> ...that they are quasi, contraband
> Because unfinished, graven by a hand
> Less than angelic, admirable or sure.[28]

She experiences the silent prejudice of being stared at in a fancy restaurant; she is hurt by the contrast of her Chicago with Beverly Hills; she longs for a certainty impossible in the godless post-war world. In the last poem of the sequence and of the book, Annie addresses white America. "Reserve my service at the human feast," she says, "And let the joy continue." Rejecting all forms of discreet oppression, including the request that she be patient, she argues that it is time for all of us to

> ...combine. There are no magics or elves
> Or timely godmothers to guide us. We are lost, must
> Wizard a track through our own screaming weed.[29]

None of Brook's later work is equal in control or depth to the poems in her first three collections, though her willingness to experiment with poems more accessible to a Black audience is admirable. The best of her poems, however, are thoughtful and ironic psychological studies like "The Chicago Defender Sends a Man to Little Rock," in which a Black newspaper reporter concludes, after visiting the city infamous during the Fifties for the virulence of its racism, that

The biggest news I do not dare
Telegraph to the Editor's chair:
"They are like people everywhere."[30]

Melvin B. Tolson's life as scholar, poet, journalist, and teacher was dedicated to promoting and celebrating the cultural diversity of the Black race. His M.A. thesis at Columbia University was on the Harlem Renaissance, and Harlem remained for him the emblem of Black artistic enterprise. He taught at Black schools all his life—at Wiley College, at Langston University, and at Tuskegee Institute. The very titles of his books indicate his interdisciplinary approach: *A Gallery of Harlem Portraits* (published posthumously in 1979), *Rendezvous With America* (1944), *Libretto for the Republic of Liberia* (1953), and his masterpiece, *Harlem Gallery, Book I: The Curator* (1965). From 1937 to 1944 Tolson wrote a weekly column for the *Washington Tribune* called "Caviar and Cabbage." In the September 28, 1940 entry he explained his philosophy:

An intelligent mind sees the whole, the contrasts in environment and personalities, the mountain and valleys, the good and bad, the comedy and tragedy....In every man there is the saint and the sinner, the rattlesnake and the monkey, God and the devil....Caviar and cabbage differ only in the arrangement of electrons.[31]

In 1939 Tolson's poem "Dark Symphony" won first place in the national poetry contest sponsored by the American Negro Exposition in Chicago. It subsequently appeared in *Rendezvous With America* . Each of the poem's six sections is an orchestral movement in the "symphony" of Black American history. "Allegro Moderato" celebrates the fighting spirit of men like Crispus Attucks; "Lento Grave" is a tribute to the "sorrow songs"

of slavery; "Andante Sostenuto" is a transitional inter-
lude, presaging the appearance of the "New Negro"
of the Harlem Renaissance in "Tempo Primo"; "Larghetto"
moves us through the Thirties into the futuristic vision of "Tempo di Marcia," in which the Negro marches
"out of the abysses of Illiteracy" and the "dead-ends
of Poverty" to advance "With the Peoples of the
World..."[32]

In 1947 Tolson was appointed Poet Laureate of Liberia; in honor of that nation's centennial he wrote *Libretto for the Republic of Liberia* , whose eight sections
are named for the notes of the diatonic scale. This highly
erudite work received mixed critical reviews. Tolson's
greatest—and most maligned—work was yet to come.

Harlem Gallery occupied the remaining decade-and-
a-half of his life. Of the proposed five-part epic, only
the first part saw publication before his death. Conceived on a far grander scale than Hughes's *Montage
of a Dream Deferred, Harlem Gallery, Book I: The Curator*
is a sort of *Spoon River Anthology* of Black urban life,
organized around a place—the art gallery—and following the sequence of the Greek alphabet. The portraits
of the Black artists, musicians, socialites, and low-lives
who visit the gallery are punctuated by an ongoing
dialogue between the curator of the gallery—an American mongrel of "Afroirishjewish" origin—and his al-
ter-ego, the African Dr. Nkomo. The curator defines
the Negro as "a dish in the white man's kitchen— / a
potpourri, / ...a hotchpotch of lineal ingredients"; even
a well-meaning white American will find "...himself a
Hamlet on the spot, / for, in spite of his catholic pose,
/ the Negro dish is a dish nobody knows." The Black
artist is "a flower of the gods, whose growth / is dwarfed
at an early stage" by white critics and Black critics
alike, as the "Idols of the Tribe," declaring that "We

/ have heroes!" demand that the artist "Celebrate them upon our walls!"[33]

Pressured by the snobbish demands of the Black bourgeoisie and the patronizing limits set by white critics, the Black artists in *Harlem Gallery* either perish, suffer obscurity, compromise their art, or live a schizophrenic existence

> torn between two masters,
>   God and Caesar—
> this (for Conscience),
>   The Chomolungma of disasters.[34]

When the book was published in 1965, the critics of the Black Aesthetic movement passed judgment: this "epic," with its Greek subtitles, difficult vocabulary, and learned allusions, was condemned as highbrow decadence; Tolson's eclecticism (allusions ranging from Pasternak to Xenos, from Satchmo to Yeats) was considered nothing more than an emulation of "Whitey." *Harlem Gallery* went under in a barrage of Black Militant fire. Tolson could have been describing his own fate when he wrote:

> Poor Boy Blue,
>   the Great White World
>   and the Black Bourgeosie
>   have shoved the Negro artist into
>   the white and not-white dichotomy,
> the Afroamerican dilemma in the Arts—
>   the dialectic of
>   to be or not to be
>   a Negro.[35]

Born in Detroit in 1913, Robert Hayden received his B.A. from Wayne State University and an M.A. from the University of Michigan. He was on the faculty at

Fisk and various other universities before becoming a professor at the University of Michigan, where he taught until his death in 1980. On permanent staff of the Bread-loaf Writers Conference, Hayden also served two consecutive terms as Consultant in Poetry at the Library of Congress. In a "statement of poetics" in Bernard Bell's *Modern and Contemporary Afro-American Poetry*, he wrote of his work that "I think of the writing of poems as one way of coming to grips with inner and outer realities—as a spiritual act, really, a sort of prayer for illumination perfection."[36]

Hayden's first book, *Heart-Shape in the Dust*, appeared in 1940; his last, *Collected Poems*, was published posthumously in 1985. His *oeuvre* demonstrates a life-long application of his literary expertise to the exploration of the sordid grandeur of the human soul. A follower of the Bahai faith, Hayden believed in world unity, the oneness of mankind, and the richness and diversity of individual difference. Whether writing in the persona of a retired lyncher or as the co-discoverer of the North Pole, whether re-evoking the horrors of the slave trade or describing the daily risks taken by window washers outside his office, he charged his poems with a meditative urgency.

Hayden drew deeply from folk sources; his work abounds with ballads, snatches of gospel, homages to historical figures, and affectionate elegies for everyday heroes and heroines. The ignominious death of a gospel singer is treated sympathetically in his "Mourning poem for the Queen of Sunday":

> Lord's lost Him His mockingbird,
> His fancy warbler;
> Satan sweet-talked her
> four bullets hushed her.
> Who would have thought
> she'd end that way?[37]

In "Unidentified Flying Object" a Black maid is whisked up into a flying saucer in a modern day version of the Ascension, leaving her suitor "a changed man, / not drinking nowadays and sad." Although Hayden celebrated historical figures from Crispus Attucks and Nat Turner to Jack Johnson and Paul Robeson, he'd as soon sing the tale of an ordinary "tragic mulatto" in "The Ballad of Sue Ellen Westerfield," or recount the adventures of a street urchin in Cuernavaca in "Kid."

The response Hayden elicits from his audience is interior, more a lightbulb going on upstairs than a shouted "Amen." This private vision is not introversion but rather an invitation to accept the world—even its most public face—on intimate terms. To achieve this interpenetration, Hayden travels the full trajectory of diction. His poems vary from the lush baroque of "A Ballad of Remembrance" ("the sallow vendeuse / of prepared tarnishes and jokes of nacre and ormolu") to the jumbled misspellings of a Civil War soldier's letters in "The Dream" ("I am tired some but it is war you / know and old jeff Davis muss be ketch an hung to a sour / apple tree like it says in the song"). A case in point is the poem "Middle Passage," a potpourri of different voices: a litany of ships' names, the heightened rhetoric of prayer, excerpts from ship logs, hymn lyrics, interior monologue, and the poet's own evocative, formal commentary. These together create a fascinating account of the evils of the slave trade, as "Shuttles in the rocking loom of history, / the dark ships move, the dark ships move." For his tribute to Frederick Douglass, he fashions a sonnet in two sentences, the first driven, insistent with a righteous fury:

> This man, this Douglass, this former slave, this Negro
> beaten to his knees, exiled, visioning a world
> where none is lonely, none hunted, alien...[38]

The second is brief and lilting: "fleshing his dream of the beautiful, needful thing." "Those Winter Sundays," a tender elegy to the father who rose in "the blueblack cold" to start the morning fire, ends with the exclamation: "What did I know, what did I know / Of love's austere and lonely offices?"

Hayden borrowed from a story by Gabriel Garcia Marquez to fashion an *ars poetica* in "For a Young Artist." "A naked old man / with bloodstained wings" is found in a pig sty, caught, caged, and exhibited. Repelled, yet fascinated by his inexplicable presence, "Carloads of the curious" alternately ask his blessing and torment him. Finally, in the dark with no witness save the "hawk-haunted fowl," he makes a few clumsy attempts, and then, with a "silken rustling in the air," achieves "the angle of ascent." We are not privy to the moment of ascension, just to its prelude and its completion. The poem becomes an allegory about the nature of revelation (which does not come without hard work and censure), as well as about the ultimate elusiveness of that revelation.

Like many Black poets, Hayden wrote often of his relation with the "self-destructive, self-betrayed" nation he laments in "Words in the Mourning Time." The depth of his feelings for this country may be seen in "American Journal," as an extraterrestrial visitor files this report:

> confess i am curiously drawn unmentionable to
> the americans doubt i could exist among them for
> long however psychic demands far too severe
> much violence much that repels i am attracted
> none the less their variousness their ingenuity
> their elan vital and that some thing essence
> quiddity i cannot penetrate or name[39]

Much has been made—often negatively—of the "universality" of this generation of Black poets. The most striking thing about their work, when it is seen together, is the fact that by stripping their Black characters down to their central humanity, these poets made them the common denominator. In "Astronauts" Robert Hayden describes the first earthlings to walk on the moon, who speak for the entire watching earth:

> What is it we wish them
> to find for us, as
>   we watch them on our
> screens? They loom there
>   heroic antiheroes,
> smaller than myth and
>   poignantly human.
> Why are we troubled?
>   What do we ask of these men?
> What do we ask of ourselves?[40]

THE POETICS OF RAGE

The assassination of Malcolm X in 1965 marked a turning point in Afro-American history. Malcolm's death convinced many Blacks that violence was unavoidable in the struggle for equality. There was no longer any pretense: Blacks were not part of the American dream; any portion of that pie would have to be taken by force. The cry of "Black Power!" and the belief in the political expediency of separatism had a major literary impact, producing poetry workshops in every urban center, many new journals, critics who debated the parameters of the new Black Aesthetic, and an abundance of young poets. To judge by the poets included in the many anthologies published during the Black Arts period—the years between the late Sixties and the mid-Seventies—everybody and his soul-brother were writing poems. Eugene Redmond counts literally hundreds of poets in his chapter on the period in *Drumvoices* , his critical history of Afro-American poetry. The sense of urgency which saturated their work permeated the entire Black community: The Revolution, if it was not already actually happening, seemed certainly to be just around the corner, and by embracing the Black experience and exhorting the Black community to join the Revolution, the new poetry served as an important tool for consciousness-raising. The Black Arts movement was clearly an outgrowth of the political mood of the time, yet the precipitously increased alienation of Black artists also had roots in the generation immediately preceding the Black Arts movement—in the Beat movement which came to prominence in San Francisco and New York City in the late Fifties.

The spirit of community which flourished in North Beach and Greenwich Village allowed Black writers full participation in the cultural experiment of beatification. Rejecting the mores of the gray flannel suit society, the Beats substituted their own visions of illumination and ecstasy. Strongly influenced by jazz and the musicians who created it, they valued spontaneity and individualism and deplored the rigidity and materialism of the "square world." Because jazz was such an important element of the Beat ethos, Black artists were a fundamental part of the movement. Bob Kaufman in San Francisco and LeRoi Jones in New York City grew from the Beat movement in very different directions.

Kaufman was well-established in the Beat poetry scene in San Francisco in the late Fifties; indeed, he was one of its chief architects—the term "beatnik" supposedly

originated with him. Lawrence Ferlinghetti published
two of his volumes in his City Lights series and contributed a "telegraphic preface" to his first major
collection, *Solitudes Crowded With Loneliness* (1965). Most
of Kaufman's poems were spontaneous recitations,
improvised in the manner of the great jazz musicians
to whom he often pays homage; they were committed
to print at his wife's insistence through the use of a
tape recorder. His range is wide: from humorous satire to surrealism to prophecy and protest. Standing apart
from America, he views this nation critically, as in this
passage from "Hollywood":

Five square miles of ultra-contemporary nymphomania,
Two dozen homos, to every sapiens, at last countdown,
Ugly Plymouths, swapping exhaust with red convertible Buicks[41]

Kaufman's America is inhabited in "Teevee People"
by "creeping cardboard creatures" and "Poets of the
gray universities in history suits, / Dripping false Greek
dirges from tweedy beards." Among the desires enu-
merated in "Unholy Missions" is Kaufman's wish "to
prove that Los Angeles is a practical joke played /
on us by superior beings on a humorous planet." In "Bene-
diction" he forgives American for "Nailing black Jesus
to an imported cross / Every six weeks" and for "Burning Japanese babies defensively," because

I realize how necessary it was.
Your ancestor had beautiful thoughts in his brain.
His descendants are experts in real estate.
Your generals have mushrooming visions.
Every day your people get more and more
Cars, televisions, sickness, death dreams.[43]

Kaufman proclaims himself an "Abomunist" in his

"Abomunist Manifesto," an absurd declaration of independence from the world described in "Abomnewscast...On the Hour..." as

stockpiling atomic missiles to preserve peace, end of
mankind seen if peace is declared, UN sees encouraging
sign in small war policy, works quietly for wider
participation among backward nations...[44]

Kaufman sees the present as a struggle between jazz and death. In "War Memoir" he writes, "What one-hundred-percent redblooded savage / Wastes precious time listening to jazz / With so much important killing to do?" In "Battle Report" the revolution is finally won: a city is brought down by the sound of jazz.

In 1963 Kaufman composed a poem called "Small Memoriam for Myself" and took a Buddhist vow of silence. He neither spoke publicly nor wrote for the next ten years. He broke his silence on the day of the U.S. Withdrawal from Vietnam in 1973, and a new collection of poems, *The Ancient Rain* , was published in 1981. The poems in this volume bless the world with love, but bring with that love the awful vision Kaufman sees in the title poem: "a poet spread-eagled on this bone of the world." This vision is extended in the long poem "The American Sun," printed entirely in urgent capital letters:

...THE AMERICAN SUN
BRINGS DEATH TO ALL ENEMY
EMPIRES, THE AMERICAN SUN BRINGS
DEATH BY FIRE TO ALL WHO DARE
OPPOSE THE AMERICAN SUN, EMPIRES
OF THE PAST ARE BREAKING FROM
THE CONSTANT POWER OF THE AMERICAN
SUN, THE AMERICAN SUN CHALLENGES
ALL OTHER EMPIRES AND DEMANDS

THEY RESPOND TO THE CHALLENGES
OF THE AMERICAN SUN, THOSE THAT DO
NOT RESPOND ARE TO BE BROKEN AND
BURNED...[45]

Faced with this vision, Kaufman retreated again into
silence in 1978. He died in poverty and obscurity in
1985.

The most reknowned Black Beat poet was LeRoi Jones.
Born in Newark, New Jersey, and educated at Howard
University (where he attended Sterling Brown's "un-
official" classes on jazz and was finally dismissed for
"nonconformism"), Jones began a process of self-edu-
cation: during his years in the United States Air Force
he read voraciously, and after his discharge studied at
the New School for Social Research and Columbia University, moving to Greenwich Village to join the Beat
scene.

The confessional mode of the Beat poets became a
way for Jones to sublimate pressures from a hostile
society. The title poem of his first book, *Preface to a
Twenty-Volume Suicide Note* (1961), describes a world
in which the stars leave holes in the firmament and
his daughter is portrayed as not praying, but "peek-
ing into / Her own clasped hands." In this existential
world, "Nobody sings anymore." Resignation and self-
disgust escalate to a paralysis of will, an inability to
change what he knows must be changed in "Look for
You Yesterday, Here You Come Today," a poem whose
very title indicates Jones's closeness to the blues tradition:

> terrible poems come in the mail. Descriptions of celibate
>   parties
> torn trousers: Great poets dying
> with their strophes on. & me

incapable of a simple straightforward
anger.[46]

Rootless and incapable of anger, Jones searches for
his identity in several of the poems in this book. In
"Hymn for Lanie Poo" he juxtaposes images of Africa
and America, and looks from the Gansevoort St. docks
toward the horizon

until it gets up
and comes to embrace
me. I
make believe
it is my father.
This is known
as genealogy.[47]

His unfulfilled search for identity culminates in this
book in a poem titled "Notes for a Speech," in which
Jones observes that "African blues / does not know
me," and concludes that he is "as any other sad man
here / american."

The poems of *The Dead Lecturer*, whose publication
in 1964 nearly coincided with Jones's Obie-winning play
The Dutchman (and with Bob Kaufman's vow of silence),
reflect the poet's sharpening conflicts. "I am inside
someone / who hates me," he writes in "As Agony.
As Now.":

It is human love, I live inside. A bony skeleton
you recognize as words or simple feeling.

But it has no feeling. As the metal, is hot, it is not,
given to love.

It burns the thing
inside it. And that thing
screams.[48]

The syntax is wrenched—sentences are aborted, parenthetical statements are begun but never completed—as if his song had lived through all the labor pains of language. The source of Jones's pain was his sense that he must find a way to offer his talent to the needs of the world. In "Short Speech to My Friends" he contemplates the compromise of silence, and he castigates himself in several poems for his "lies." The most important poem in the collection, however, is "I Substitute for the Dead Lecturer," the poem in which Jones kills himself to find himself and his mission.

The poem begins with his critics, who "say that I am dying. That / I have thrown / my life / away." He sees that "Cold air batters / the poor," and realizes that all he can offer is "what is, for me, / ugliest...shadows, shrieking phantoms": to be "Against all / thought, all music, all / my soft loves." The necessity for political action forces him to forsake "soft" poetry because doing so is the only wealth he has to give to the desperate. Terrified that "the flame of my sickness / will burn off my face. And leave / the bones, my stewed black skull, / an empty cage of failure," Jones kills/and silences/a portion of himself.[49] A Black man with a new name and new militancy rose from his tomb. He dropped out of the Beat scene, leaving Greenwich Village, his Jewish wife, and his white friends behind. He moved to Harlem, founded the Black Arts Repertory Theatre there and in 1966 founded Spirit House, an artist's community dedicated to bringing cultural renewal to the Black community of Newark. He was now Imamu (spiritual leader) Amiri (blessed) Baraka (prince).

The poetry of Baraka's Black Nationalist period (1965-74), written in the language of the street, appeals directly to the audience for an active response, as in "The Nation Is Like Ourselves":

> please mister liberated nigger love chil nigger
> nigger in a bellbottom bell some psychedelic wayoutness
> on YO people, even wile you freeing THE people, please
> just first free YO people...[50]

In "Black Art," from *Black Magic Poetry* (1969), the poem itself becomes a guerrilla warrior:

> Knockoff poems for dope selling wops or slick halfwhite
> politicians Airplane poems, rrrrrrrr
> rrrrrrrrrr...Setting fire and death to
> whities ass.[51]

Such poems reflect Baraka's philosophy that poems must impinge directly on the world in order to be vital. "Poems are bullshit," he says elsewhere in"Black Art," "unless they are / teeth or trees or lemons piled / on a step." This philosophy allows Baraka's poems to attack not only "whitey," but other enemies of the ideological revolution—primarily the Black middle class— as well. Many of his poems rely on the traditional device of "signifying," or playing the dozens, as when in a poem called "W.W.," he writes of a bewigged Black woman, "you look like / Miss Muffett in a runaway ugly machine," or when, in "Rockefeller is Yo Vice President, & Yo Mamma Dont Wear No Drawers" (whose very title plays the dozens), he calls Black politicians "quislings."

While Baraka's later poems are uneven and his Anti-Semitism and name-calling often embarrassing, they were written in the dark times Baraka described in "Afrikan Revolution," when Black people all over the world were "Under the yoke, the gun, the hammer, the lash," and it seemed the world had to "Change or die." His hope, expressed in "All in the Street," was that Black posterity would be able to say

> We know how hard it is to be black
> in that primitive age. But do not
> naaw...do not ever despair.
>
> We won
> We here.[52]

Whereas Baraka sees his writings as a blueprint for a new world, Etheridge Knight's poetry represents a victory over reality. Born in Corinth, Mississippi, in 1931 and educated in public schools there, Knight says of his life in *Poems from Prison* (1968) that "I died in Korea from a shrapnel wound and narcotics resurrected me. I died in 1960 from a prison sentence and poetry brought me back to life."[53] In "The Idea of Ancestry," he describes the vicious circle of crime and heroin, softened by the sustaining love of his extended family. In "The Violent Space (or when your sister sleeps around for money)," Knight uses rhyme to simulate the trapped feeling of a man who would like to help his sister out of her misery if he were not stuck so deeply in his own:

> And what do I do. I boil my tears in a twisted spoon
> And dance like an angel on the point of a needle.
> I sit counting syllables like Midas gold.
> I am not bold. I can not yet take hold of the demon
> And lift his weight from your black belly,
> So I grab the air and sing my song.
>
> (But the air can not stand my singing long.)[54]

Closer to the Black masses than Baraka, Knight uses street language and prison jargon to express longings and questions shared by the underclass. He explores a wide range of human relationships with sincerity and humility, and his work comes closer to expressing the ideals set forth in the Black Aesthetic than does that of many of his peers.

The Black Aesthetic—whose fundamental tenets were that literature must take its place in the liberation of Black Americans, that it must do so by reflecting the Black experience, that it must reject the literary standards of an oppressive society, and that it must work to promote the sense of Black self-respect and community—played a crucial part in the development of the Black Arts movement. Following Baraka's example and guided by the Black aestheticians, foremost among them Hoyt W. Fuller and Addison Gayle, Jr., Afro-American poetry enjoyed a rebirth in the late Sixties and early Seventies unrivaled by anything since the Harlem Renaissance. Among the noteworthy books published in the period were, in 1969, Don L. Lee's *Don't Cry, Scream* ; Larry Neal's *Black Boogaloo* ; and Sonia Sanchez's *Homecoming (1969)*. 1970 saw the publication of Nikki Giovanni's *Black Feeling, Black Talk, Black Judgment* ; Mari Evan's *I Am a Black Woman* ; Don L. Lee's *We Walk the Way of the New World* ; Clarence Major's *Swallow in the Lake* ; Sonia Sanchez's *We A BaddDDD People* ; and Gerald W. Barrax's *Another Kind of Rain*. Jayne Cortez's *Festivals and Funerals* was published in 1971. Poet-musician Gil Scott-Heron produced several powerful albums. The new poets, most of them university-educated, strove for "relevance" and urged their audiences toward Black unity and Black power. They rejected white critical standards and sought instead to use the verbal virtuosity of the urban Black poor to call up audience response. In order to reach the people, authors read in churches and pool halls, at rallies and on street corners. Black publishing houses were founded:

Dudley Randall began his Broadside Press in Detroit with twelve dollars, which he used to print a broadside of "The Ballad of Birmingham" by folksinger Jerry Moore. On the heels of this first broadside followed books, anthologies, literary criticism, cassette tapes, U.S. distribution of the London-based Heritage Series (featuring African authors), and an annual prize for young poets. Randall's poem, "A Different Image," from his *Cities Burning* (1968) is an eloquent description of the theme lying at the heart of the Black Aesthetic; it calls for Blacks to

> Shatter the icons of slavery and fear.
> Replace
> the leer
> of the minstrel's brunt-cork face
> with a proud, serene
> and classic bronze of Benin.[55]

The dialectics of history meant, for Black intellectuals, a dialectics of oppression. Hence, freedom fighters like Harriet Tubman, Malcolm X, and Martin Luther King, Jr., became subjects of poems. Popular folk heroes were also celebrated: Calvin Forbes and Etheridge Knight wrote about Shine, a legendary Black man who survived the sinking of the Titanic and danced afterwards in the streets of Harlem. Jazz musicians were among the folk heroes , and the structures of blues and jazz found their counterparts in the poetry. Often the oral influence was so strong that the poem needed to be performed or read aloud for the significance of its sounds to be recognized, as, for example, Don L. Lee's "Communication in Whi-te" from his 1969 volume, *Don't Cry, Scream* :

> dee dee dee dee dee wee weee eeeeee wee wee
> deweeeeee ee ee ee nig

nig nig nig nigggggggggggg cleek cleek cleek
cleeeeee cleekcleek
rip rip rip rip rip rip / rip / rip / rip / rip / ripripripriprip
pi pi pi pi pip
bom bom bom bom bom / bom / bom / bobombombom
bombombombombombombom
deathtocliikdeathtocleekdeathtocleekdeathtocleek
deathtocleekdeathtodeathto
alllllllllalllllll all lllll deathto
alllll allllallllllleeeeee
te te te te te te / te / te / te / te / te / te / tetetetetete
tetetetetetete:
the paris peace talks, 1968.[56]

The war on white America manifested itself in an
insistence on Black subjects, Black speech, political activism. Though this stance resulted in some poems of
great energy—Ted Joans's ".38" or Sonia Sanchez's "a
/ coltrane / poem" are examples--there rumbled beneath the surface a naive adherence to superficial traits.
Only a few poets of this younger generation rebelled.
Ishmael Reed's "catechism of d neoamerican hoodoo
church" offers this advice:

DO YR ART D WAY U WANT
ANYWAY U WANT
ANY WANGOL U WANT
ITZ UP TO U / WHAT WILL WORK
FOR U.[57]

"no one's going to read / or take you seriously," Al
Young warns in "A Dance for Militant Dilettantes,"
"until you start coming down on them / like the black
poet you truly are." This new Black poet, however,
turns out to be as manipulated as his accommodating
predecessor, fashioned in the forge of the times but a
pawn of the reigning literary politics. Young continues:

these honkies that put out
these books & things
they want an angry splib
a furious nigra
fresh out of some secret boot camp
with a bad book in one hand
& a molotov cocktail in the other
subject to turn up at one of their conferences
or soirees
& shake the shit out of them.[58]

So dependent became the poet on audience response that there was little freedom to explore new territory without incurring accusations of "selling out" or not being "Black enough." Veterans like Tolson and Hayden were condemned as the "white man's flunkies. Lesser stars and splashy fireworks shone briefly and sputtered; few poets of the era prevail into the Eighties.

Despite the noise made in the Sixties and Seventies, the white mainstream absorbed the Black Aesthetic without much fuss, and its militance even served the public's thirst for sensationalism. And yet that sense of pride in being Black remained. It was time now to move forward, to explore deeper.

THE SEVENTIES AND BEYOND: BLACK POETRY INTO THE PRESENT[59]

MW: Well, there's no way we can do an inclusive study of our contemporaries. It's the most difficult period to assess; the returns aren't in. Even getting into an anthology is like winning the first heat of a pre-Olympic career. You don't know until the *real* race—and that's not for a hundred years. And in the race of poets to reach that imaginary anthology in the sky, it's extremely difficult for members of the pack to determine who the front-runners are. I mean, we're a community, of sorts: although we run differently, we're reaching for the same goal.

But here's my suggestion: Let's make an imaginary anthology ourselves, an anthology of contemporary Black poets

RD: Yes, and in that communal spirit, let's *not* attempt to rank, codify, and eliminate poets. The trap of literary canonization is particularly deadly for minority writers. Black poets are often "lesser known" to the white-dominated mainstream because Caucasian ethnocentricity puts considerable obstacles between them and the information processes—the reviews, anthologies, etc., that make someone "known."

MW: Many mainstream critics are afraid they'll be setting themselves up for censure if they discuss a Black poet's book—so they don't review it.

RD: Or else they don't bother with researching those forces that have shaped Black experience, so they have no guide for entering the work. Let's have a conversation—no, a dialogue—which will allow these forces to thrive. We shouldn't play the game of pretending an objective historical focus where there is none.

MW: Let's just talk about the poets and their work. After all, they're our peers, and some of them are our friends. Why not make it clear that we're not disembodied critical voices, but Black poets discussing Black poets. Let's improvise our anthology, as if it were jazz.

RD: Michael Harper tells a marvelous story, in *TriQuarterly* , about arriving in South Africa and talking with the Black taxicab driver about American Blacks. "What language do you speak when the white people aren't around?" the driver asks. And when Harper answers "English," the driver says, "Brother, when Blacks are among themselves, don't they speak *jazz* ?" So let's "mix it up" a little, and see what the moment brings us.

MW: Amen, sister. That immediacy might dissolve the barriers between writer and audience. Bring the audience closer, as Black poets are always trying to do. Let's write "Performance-criticism," criticism that comes off the page, and becomes *voices* .

RD: There will be those, of course, who will call us irresponsible and evasive as critics...

MW: Do you think so? I hope not. Anyway, maybe we can make clear from the outset that what we're doing is very much in keeping with the Black tradition. Another positive thing about this approach might be that we can discuss as many front-runners as possible, without having to waste space describing several movements, or only discussing a handful of poets. There are many poets in this generation worthy of critical attention.

RD: I suppose a contemporary anthology would have to begin with Gwendolyn Brooks and go through Michael Harper, June Jordan...

MW: Frank Marshall Davis is still alive, living in Hawaii. And Sterling Brown died only recently.

RD: Not to forget Hayden. Then of course, the Sixties came and just blew anyone out of the water who was too quiet. Al Young—but he's branched out into novels and screenplays....

MW: Ishmael Reed started as a poet, too.

RD: Interesting that Black poets in particular are at ease moving between the genres. Alice Walker also began as a poet, and still writes poems. I don't know if she still considers herself a poet...

MW: She has a big mind and needs a big canvas. I always had a problem with the poems in *Revolutionary Petunias* —they were too small for her.

RD: Or in her first book, *Once* ...it was as if she made the poems deliberately small. You can feel them straining at the seams. June Jordan has done poetry books, but there've also been children's books, novels, and non-fiction works. She seems pretty evenhanded.

MW: I especially liked her *Who Look At Me* , that collection of graceful poems describing paintings of Black American life. She can be very elegant. And I admire the way she lives in a political, as well as a personal, world.

RD: The two worlds merge—as they should, shouldn't they?—in her latest work, like the "Poem in Defense of my Rights," for example.

MW: Yes. The Sixties' belief in the efficacy of poetry—that poems *do* something in the real, out-there world—is very much alive in her work.

RD: As it is in Audre Lorde's writing. There's that fantastic poem called "Power," where Lorde defines the difference between poetry and rhetoric as "being / ready to kill / yourself / instead of your children." In an essay she identifies herself as an heir to Malcolm and his tradition, doing her work. Naturally, the unspoken question is: "Are you doing yours?" She's another Black poet who has branched into essays and even a novel.

MW: Robert Bly recently had an article in the *New York Times Book Review* in which he says poets who write novels are compromising their muses; that if you choose to write a novel—which you do only for the money—you can never get back the true voice of your poetry. The muse will desert you.

RD: That's a terribly romantic notion, a very white American notion of a poet. In Europe, authors move between the genres much more easily. Goethe—even Rilke—would not be poets according to such a statement. There are angles of vision that can't fit in a certain genre. And that's one reason for crossing the genres.

MW: Another is audience, I think. The audience of fiction is much larger than the audience of poetry. How many people actually know that Alice Walker is also a poet? Yet another alternative is the one Ntozake Shange has chosen—getting the poetry into theatre. I think the history of *for colored girls* is a really interesting phenomenon...and the influence it had on the theatre can't yet be assessed.

RD: Theatre is a powerful medium, particularly for

poetry that still has oral presence. Which *is* so much of Black poetry.

MW: I suppose this fusion of poetry and theatre could be linked back to Langston Hughes. For example, there's Thulani Davis' libretto for the opera about Malcolm X....And I think that someone like Brenda Marie Osbey, who does portraits of a community—

RD: Yes, Osbey's *Ceremony for Minneconjoux* could readily be transported to the stage. Hers is a narrative poetry distinctly based on oral tradition. In *Ceremony*, the characters *have* to tell their story. The different angles remind me of a Black *Spoon River Anthology*.

MW: Which brings us back to the list of contemporary poets I would want to include in this anthology: Thylias Moss, Colleen McElroy, Audre Lorde, Sherley Anne Williams, Carolyn Rodgers, Quincy Troupe...

RD: Gerald Barrax, Primus St. John, Toi Derricotte, Ai...

MW: Yvonne, Gayl Jones, Ntozake Shange, Calvin Forbes, Cheryl Clarke...

RD: Cheryl Clarke's first book is called *narratives: poems in the tradition of black women.*

MW: One of the very common characteristics is, I think, that they tend to write *about* characters, viewing the characters. They're not writing soul-rendering confessions, but portraits of a community. And in a way I would say that what's been happening all along. You know, American writers joke about writing the Great American Novel. The only people I know who are trying to do that now are minority writers presenting panoramas of ethnic communities. There's Yusef Kounyakaa, whose recent book, *Copacetic*, has strong poems about New Orleans—views of New Orleans, people in New Orleans. In his newest book, *Dien Cai Dau* , is a portrait of a VietNamese girl "still burning / inside my head." Very few of these poets are turning inward. Even Ai, I think, is doing this—though her panorama isn't particularly Black—

RD: In all three of her books she does a mural of the ways in which people are cruel, or sin against one another—the panorama of evil, but she's also trying to understand that evil. It's a very dark vision but it's an absolutely necessary one.

MW: What Ai is doing is getting inside of people who hate, and understanding them from the inside. Making an anatomy of the oppressor.

RD: In *Sin*, her latest book, she slips into the skins of public heroes. Jack Kennedy's talking to Bobby in "Two Brothers," which is an anatomy of the oppressor or in this case, the very privileged—those who are accustomed to privilege and are extremely cynical about the power it brings. What's groundbreaking about Ai's work is that she's snapped the reins of propriety that have held back so many Black poets—the feeling that you have to portray the good side, that Black is beautiful and woe if anyone implies anything less. In the Sixties the narrow Party line was a survival tactic; though I think some poets felt suffocated at not being able to talk about the entire human being. From the beginning of her career, Ai addressed those nether portions of us. Perhaps the fact that she is such a mix racially— Black, Japanese, White...

MW: I think it liberates her, to a great extent. She doesn't fit into anybody's neat little categories, and that frees her from a lot of the restrictions of the Sixties. I graduated from college in 1968—it was terrible to write then. I would write something and show it around and people would say, "Well, Black people don't write about things like that." Or "That's not Black enough." The worst example of that kind of thinking was a review of a book of short stories by James Alan MacPherson. The reviewer said something like, "I haven't read this book, but the blurb on the back cover is by Ralph Ellison, and Ralph Ellison thinks it's wonderful; Ralph Ellison is an Uncle Tom, so don't read the book—it's got to be terrible."

RD: That's the epitome of the kind of arrogance / ignorance that can happen in any movement which tries to dictate exactly what one should do. When I was in college, Al Young's poems were a saving grace for me; he didn't write about just being Black—he wrote about a grandmother, an aunt, he wrote about simply being in love. Still, I was a closet poet for years because I thought I wasn't writing what I was supposed to be writing.

MW: I had a similar experience, except that my imaginary mentor was LeRoi Jones. And when he became Baraka, I was still struggling to say what I had to say, but I wanted to say it like LeRoi Jones, not Baraka. And everybody was saying, "Well, that's not Black, that's not Black." Then Baraka would come out with these scathing denunciations of practically everybody. And...I stopped writing. I didn't start writing again until the Seventies.

RD: How many people got silenced that way? I remember my first creative writing class in college. We were supposed to write a ballad. I brought in a long ballad about a lynching—obviously, I hadn't *seen* a lynching, I hadn't even read much about them—and the teacher said, "Well, this doesn't sound like you've been there. You haven't experienced this." And suddenly I was in a dilemma: I can't write about what I was supposed to write about because I haven't experienced it, so I have to write about what I know....What I find refreshing in the Eighties is that so many Black poets are talking about those aspects of life which are human, regardless of whether one is Black or white. Cheryl Clarke's second book *Living as a Lesbian* is definitely more personal. Toi Derricotte's *Natural Birth* is a powerful book dealing with both racial and sexual memory. Then there are writers going into their own minds, becoming interior—but not in a self-conscious way. Christopher Gilbert, who won the Walt Whitman prize in 1983, has several long sequences in his book *Across the Mutual Landscape*. One, "Horizontal Cosmology," is definitely influenced by jazz; but the poet admits his fear of and complacency with middle class life. At the beginning of the sixth section Gilbert says: "Looking down the empty Mason jars / in the cupboards, I forget myself. / I forget my name and its belongings, / I forget my plastic ID card / for the "Y," my Exxon card / and the square feeling it leaves in my hand." Now—those are the accoutrements of middle class life. But "my Exxon card and the square feeling it leaves in my hand..."—that "square feeling" is a bit of jazz. Bebop. I don't think a white person would have said that.

MW: It sounds a little like Leroi Jones's "Preface to a Twenty-Volume Suicide Note."

RD: It's that interior, but very cool, observation of oneself. A feeling of apartness.

MW: I wonder whether this is a middle class phenomenon? Whether one of the differences between the younger poets writing now and the poets of the Sixties is that the poets of the Sixties were striving to achieve a kind of "street voice," as if that were the *only* Black experience. Isn't Christopher Gilbert a psychotherapist?

RD: Yes.

MW: I think that has a lot to do with his ability to confront everyone's fears. One of the awkward problems we're faced with in our essay is the fact that universality has become such a bugbear in Black literary criticism. To say that somebody's work says something that's not explicitly Black opens you up to all kinds of criticism.

RD: That's the vicious circle poets like Gerald Barrax and Colleen McElroy have been caught in. The critical attention paid to their work has been way below what they deserve. Barrax can make irreverent allusions to famous lovers like Tristan and Isolde as easily as he can analyze his own loneliness. Colleen McElroy has a marvelous way of bending her voice to convey irony, sorrow, sassiness, jauntiness. In her book *Queen of the Ebony Isles* there's a passage that goes: "I am only the other side of the coin / a voice buzzing inside your head all day long." Then there's Primus St. John whose poems are mostly personal. But as he says in his book *Skins on the Earth:* "...though we do not believe it yet the interior life is a real life."

MW: One of things our generation is achieving is that we are not saying "Look at me, I'm human too"—which is what most of the generations before us had basically been saying—but: "Look, I'm human, and my humanity is the common denominator. Not that I have to be integrated into your humanity. *My* humanity is what you must find in common with *me.*"

RD: The differences only show us how diverse we all are. Audre Lorde says on the back of her book *Sister Outsider:* "I am who I am, doing what I came to do, acting upon you like a drug or a chisel, to remind you of your me-ness, as I discover you in myself."

MW: I heard Lucille Clifton a few years ago. I admire her work, for many reasons—the sense of connectedness in *Good News About the Earth*, the light and promise of her vision in *An Ordinary Woman*...and one of the things she did before her reading was to put her hands together in front of her chest, bow to the audience and say: "The god in me recognizes the god in you." Basically it's the same thing Audre Lorde is saying. It's optimistic in that it believes if we are able to reach that...me-ness within ourselves, then we know that the central core of ourselves is something benign...not something horrible. The Romantics believed if you get down to the basic center of a person, what you find is something we have in common, something positive; something that enables us to face each other with respect.

RD: The way Lucille Clifton bowed to the audience reminds me of Eastern philosophies, particularly the ecstatic poet Kabir. There is a difference between that Eastern sense of the individual, which joins us all, and

the American ideal of the Individual, which is a mas-
culine silhouette and tends to run away from the community—I mean, there are all these Deerslayers who
are always going out into the forests...In her latest book,
called *Next*, Clifton writes: "here / is california / swing-
ing from the edge / of the darkening of america / and
over there, sitting, / patient as gautama / enlightened,
in the water, / is asia."

MW: The celebrations of individuality that we tend
to see in Black poets are much closer to the Eastern
than to the Western sense...Walt Whitman, whose individuality is all-inclusive and all-embracing, being the
exception. The individuality we see in these poets is
much closer to Whitman than it is to Hemingway, for
example—-I'm thinking of Cyrus Cassells' *The Mud Actor*—that long sequence in which he almost becomes
Hiroshima. That is a somehow a kind of all-embracing
egotism...

RD: Which ultimately becomes selfless. Cyrus Cassells not only has the Hiroshima poem but those meditations on Satie, also in *The Mud Actor*, spoken through
a persona living in *fin de siecle* France. I can only think
of the German word, *Ausstrahlung*—a radiance goes
through his work.

MW: Ntozake Shange says in *for colored girls*, "I found
god in myself...& i loved her fiercely..." but I don't
really have the sense that Ntozake is a mystic in the
same way that Lucille Clifton and Cyrus Cassells seem
to be. Honest mystics. Another such mystic is Bob
Kaufman, who retreated into silence.

RD: I think his influence is coming back. If you take

the death of Malcolm X and the Watts riots as the turn-ing point, Baraka's reaction and Kaufman's are oppo-site sides of the spectrum. Baraka changed his name, killed his other self, and the anger, the rage, emerge...whereas Kaufman seemed to turn the rage in on himself.

MW: Well, I think he swallowed it, and by doing so, transformed it. There's a great humility in his vow of silence. Of course, Kaufman also has to be included in our imaginary anthology.

RD: As well as Derek Walcott, who is from the Car-ibbean; but I feel he should be included because he now resides in the U.S. He's had a profound influ-ence.

MW: But it's mostly linguistic, don't you think? Ver-bal somehow, rather than thematic. I like some of his poems very much. I have some quarrels with Walcott, but his lush language is almost overwhelming.

RD: On the other hand, his language is marvelously rhetorical. He blends his British education with the slip-page of island patois. The English syntax is wonder-fully complex, whereas the individual words in patois have much more elemental power. As you said, it al-most becomes too much, this pushing through the vines...but one gets this incredible mesh and smash of language.

MW: Those poems are so rich. Pick any lines at ran-dom: "I stood like a stone and nothing else move / but the cold sea rippling like galvanize / and the nail holes of stars in the sky roof..."

RD: Or the poem "Sea Grapes," which touches on the cultural schizophrenia of a Black poet—"The Classics can console. But not enough."

MW: When Walcott's good, he thinks through a situation, a problem, and gives you something new.

RD: Yes, though occasionally it seems as if his facility with the English language just carries him away. Probably one of his biggest pitfalls is that he writes so *well* . I thought his book *The Fortunate Traveller* was disappointing in this way; whereas I enjoyed *Midsummer*—that glaring midsummer heat in the West Indies, where time stands still—"The Empire sneers at all thought in the future tense." But I am torn: the poems are beautiful, rhetorical in a Latin way, but some of it is gorgeous simply because of the writing. Still, there are moments in which he confronts himself as a man of letters who has become too adept, who wishes he could get back and just—meet himself smack on. *The Arkansas Testament*, his latest book, accomplishes this, I think.

MW: Yes, I love that side of him. How about Michael Harper?

RD: Harper's linguistic philosophy is fascinating. He has made Black musicians—particularly Coltrane—his matrix. The phrase "a love supreme, a love supreme" has become his refrain, his tattoo. The Black musician is his emblem not only of the creative process, but of the dilemma of the Black artist. This reminds me of Melvin B. Tolson, whose *Harlem Gallery* is a philosophical discourse on the problems the Black artist faces in America. Harper has created a panorama of not-necessarily-Black characters who are very often oppressed.

MW: And very often artists. Harper is, I think , a poet's poet. His concern is really with art.

RD: With art, but also with how far art can go toward saving you, and how far it can go in helping you deal with rage, in that political sense. As he writes at the beginning *Images of Kin*:: "A friend told me he had risen above jazz. I leave him there." His poems are almost jazz orchestrations—like late Coltrane, or Miles Davis when he's in a playing mood; they'll do those kinds of riffs. You know, sometimes the ellipses in Harper are so severe that meanings hit you halfway down the street. Americans are used to that kind of technique in music, and visually, too—look at cinematography. But the ways we think, the ways we perceive language, aren't as developed. Harper teaches us how to think in this new way, on many different levels, and hold a thought almost as a chord while something else is going on. Of course, if you haven't done your homework, you're lost. You have to know your history; as he says, "Where there is no History, there is no metaphor." Both *Images of Kin* and *Healing Song for the Inner Ear* have epigraphs at the beginning of sections and poems; he doesn't put credits beneath them. Sometimes I've discovered the sources by accident, months later. It's like he's saying "This should be common knowledge, but it ain't; and you're just gonna have to figure it out."

MW: I think he's challenging us, teasing. He says: "Follow me. I make my own audience."

RD: Jay Wright is another poet who has developed along those lines. His earlier poems were more accessible; often they were describing panoramas in a life which included Black and Hispanic neighborhoods. But as for his later works...some of them have become, for me, impenetrable.

MW: I often find difficult poets intriguing: A friendly game of catch with a major league pitcher. I can see old Melvin Tolson winking at me; I can feel Michael Harper nudging me on toward understanding; they're like family. No prejudice intended: T.S. Eliot is one of my favorite uncles. But, while I love crazy ol' Ez, I don't like the contemptuous Ezra Pound I've glimpsed in some of the *Cantos*. I suspect Wright writes primarily for academics.

RD: Nevertheless. Wright can be fascinating, as in his book *The Double Invention of Komo*, which is a variation on the Dogon and Bambara initiation rites.

Let's face it—poetry in America has moved to the universities. Because we have a ready-made audience in our students and we go around giving readings, it's comfortable to tell ourselves oh, we have an audience out there because we have people sitting in a room, listening to us read. And academia "suggests" to poets that if they want merit, it's good to sound hard. The only way poetry is going to remain vital and alive is if authors remember that they are living in the world. As poets we often become fearful—because we are in the institution—of going outside. A few years back I gave a reading on a university campus, but I had also volunteered for "community service"—i.e., a reading at a local church. My audience there numbered fifteen, mostly old people who had come because the newspaper article had said I was going to discuss storytelling. I hadn't intended to do that, but that's why they were there. I was terrified. I suddenly realized I didn't know if they wanted to hear what I had to say. Thrown back on my own resources, I did talk about oral traditions, and then I read a story. And that was fine. I was astonished how many people in the audience had written at some point before life had gotten in the way. They had never received any encouragement, because most "professional" poets and writers had become university professors.

MW: I took a poetry workshop from Etheridge Knight in Minneapolis in 1977. We did workshops together, but we also went out into the community to give impromptu readings. I remember reading in hamburger restaurants and bars; Etheridge—this big Black man—would stand up and say: "O.K. y'all, we gonna read some poems."

One evening we were reading in a Minneapolis bar. There was a young Sioux man in this bar, who sat quietly, listening to us, drinking, for probably an hour. And then he said, "Would somebody read this?" He took a letter out of his pocket, handed it to a young white poet, and asked her to read it aloud. It was a letter from his wife on the reservation, asking him to come home, and saying that she would help him get away from alcohol, they could make it together. All the time we had been standing up there reading our poems, and this man had recognized somewhere—that's how I think of it—that he knew some poetry. I think that's one of the things poetry can do for people.

RD: This has a lot to do with audience response, with ways of reaching an audience. Michael Harper came to read at Arizona State University a couple of years ago. I was teaching a Black literature class at the time, and I had made my students—you know how traditionally shy Black students are of English Departments—I made them go to his talk in the afternoon. I had given them some of Harper's poems beforehand and they were pretty terrified. But one of my shyest students raised her hand right away and asked, "Would you explain this poem to me?" Now—that's one of "those" questions, though it should be perfectly legitimate. Michael said "Sure!" and began talking. His explanation lasted an hour, and when it was over he had covered a lot more territory than that one question warrented. He gave her a mini-lesson on how circumstances impinge on life.

MW: That's an important point—that the poem is life. I think critics miss that too often.

RD: Yes. Because life—well, you can't footnote it.

MW: We haven't mentioned everybody, of course. We left out Wanda Coleman. Her *Mad Dog Black Lady* has some powerful poems about Los Angeles and poverty and rage. And Pat Parker: I don't know if she has a book yet, but her lesbian-feminist poems in anthologies are very strong. Then there's Sherley Anne Williams; I like her California poems, and her Bessie Smith sequence in *Some One Sweet Angel Child* is wonderful.

RD: There's also the infectious energy of Thylias Moss' *Hosiery Seams on a Bowlegged Woman*, with its wit and arresting detail.

MW: And Carolyn Rodgers. Her book *How I Got Ovah* is so firmly rooted in tradition: "Poem for Some Black Women," "Mama's God." Or this passage from "Some Me of Beauty"—"i woke up one morning / and looked

at my self / and what I saw was / carolyn / not imani
ma jua or soul sister poetess of / the moment / I saw
a woman, human. / and black."

RD: Which reminds me of Angela Jackson, another
Chicago poet—her book *Solo in the Boxcar Third Floor
E* contains several memorable portraits of Black women.
And we left out Melvin Dixon, whose first book, *Change
of Territory*, is excellent. And there are new Black poets
appearing, poets of the Nineties, like Alizabeth Alexander and Karen Mitchell.

MW: You know, I think what the poets of our generation are doing is something more than what Langston Hughes suggested. We're not climbing The Racial
Mountain any more; we've been taken to the top of it
by the poets who came before us. Black poetry now
is...something like a rainbow. Black isn't monochromatic:
there's a whole spectrum of colors in it. As many colors as there are colors of Black faces.

RD: The rainbow after the storm of rage. A Black
Rainbow. Let's call our anthology that.

MW: Right on!

---

1. Stephen Henderson, *Understanding the New Black Poetry: Black Speech
and Black Music as Poetic References*, Wm. Morrow & Co., NY: 1973.
2. Carolyn Rodgers, "The New Black Poetry: Where It's At," *Negro
Digest*, XVII, Sept., 1969. Pp. 7-16.
3. Amiri Baraka, "Jitterbugs," *The Selected Poetry of Amiri Baraka /
LeRoi Jones*, Wm. Morrow & Co., NY: 1979. P. 93.
4. Claude McKay, *Harlem Shadows*, Harcourt, Brace & Co., NY: 1922.
P. 53.
5. *Ibid.*, p. 63

6. *Opportunity*, Nov., 1926, p. 342.

7. Countee Cullen, *Color*, Harper & Brothers, NY: 1925. P. 34.

8. James Weldon Johnson, *God's Trombonnes*, Viking, NY: 1929. Preface

9. *Ibid.*, p. 13.

10. *Ibid.*, p. 42.

11. *Ibid.*, p. 53.

12. Langston Hughes, *One-Way Ticket*, Knopf, NY: 1949. P. 35.

13. *The Nation*, June 23, 1926, p. 694.

14. *The Crisis*, June 1921, p. 71. Reprinted in *The Weary Blues*, Knopf, NY: 1926. P. 51.

15. Hughes, *One—Way Ticket*, p. 4.

16. Hughes, *Fine Clothes to the Jew*, Knopf, NY: 1927. p. 23.

17. Hughes, *A New Song*, International Workers Order, NY: 1938. P. 11.

18. Hughes, *Montage of a Dream Deferred*, Henry Holt, NY: 1951. P. 71.

19. Hughes, *Fine Clothes to the Jew*, pp. 77-78.

20. Sterling Brown, *The Collected Poems of Sterling Brown*, Harper Colophon, NY: 1983. P. 52.

21. *Ibid.*, p. 177.

22. *Ibid.*, p. 192.

23. Margaret Walker, *For My People*, Yale University Press, New Haven: 1942. Reprinted in *Negro Literature in America*, eds. James Emanuel and Theodore Gross, The Free Press, NY: 1968. P. 496.

24. Gwendolyn Brooks, *Selected Poems*, Harper & Row, NY: 1944. P. 4.

25. *Ibid.*, p. 16.

26. *Ibid.*, p. 23.

27. *Ibid.*, p. 38.

28. *Ibid.*, p. 53.

29. *Ibid.*, p. 66.

30. *Ibid.*, p. 89.

31. Melvin B. Tolson, *Caviar and Cabbage: Selected Columns by Melvin B. Tolson from the Washington Tribune, 1937-1944*, ed. Robert M. Farmsworth, University of Missouri Press, Columbia, MO: 1982. Pp. 188-189.

32. Tolson, *Rendezvous with America*, Dodd, Mead & Co., NY: 1944. P. 42.

33. *Harlem Gallery, Book I: The Curator*, Twayne, NY: 1965. P. 34.

34. *Ibid.*, p. 36.

35. *Ibid.*, p. 146.

36. Robert Hayden, "Statement on Poetics," in *Modern and Contemporary Afro-American Poetry*, ed. Bernard Bell, Allyn & Bacon, Boston: 1972. P. 175.

37. Hayden, *Selected Poems*, October House, NY: 1966. P. 50.

38. *Ibid.*, p. 78.

39. Hayden, *American Journal*, Effendi Press, Taunton, MA: 1978. P. 37.

40. *Ibid.*, p. 78.

41. Bob Kaufman, *Solitudes Crowded With Loneliness*, New Directions, NY: 1965. P. 24.

42. *Ibid.*, p. 50.

43. *Ibid.*, p. 9.

44. *Ibid.*, p. 87.

45. Kaufman, *The Ancient Rain: Poems 1956-1978*, New Directions, NY: 1981. P. 61.

46. LeRoi Jones, *Preface to a Twenty -Volume Suicide Note*, Corinth, NY: 1961. P. 15.

47. *Ibid.*, p. 9.

48. Jones, *The Dead Lecturer*, Grove Press, NY: 1964. P. 15.

49. *Ibid.*, p. 59.

50. Amiri Baraka, *Selected Poetry of Amiri Baraka / LeRoi Jones*, p. 191.

51. *Ibid.*, p. 106.

52. *Ibid.*, p. 214.

53. Etheridge Knight, *Poems from Prison*, Broadside Press, DEtroit: 1968. Back cover.

54. *Ibid.*, pp. 22-23.

55. Dudley Randall, *Cities Burning*, Broadside Press, Detroit: 1968. Reprinted in *The Black Poets*, ed. Dudley Randall, Bantam, NY: 1971. P. 142.

56. Don L. Lee, *Don't Cry, Scream*, Broadside Press, Detroit: 1969. Reprinted in *The Black Poets*, p. 299.

57. Ishmael Reed, *catechism of d meoamerican hoodoo church*, Paul Breman, London: 1970. Reprint in *New Black Voices*, ed. Abraham Chapman, New American Library, NY: 1972. P. 334.

58. Al Young, *Dancing*, Corinth, NY: 1969. Reprinted in *New Black Voices*, P. 368.

59. The conversation between Marilyn Waniek and Rita Dove took place in the spring of 1986; it was updated in 1990.

LANGUAGE POETS, NEW FORMALISTS AND THE TECHNIQUIZATION OF POETRY

By Lynn Emanuel

"There has never been a society—until our own—in which all representations are available equally to any observer at any time. That we are rapidly approaching such a condition (or have reached it) is the result of complex social transformations: rising literacy, increasing urbanization, and the accelerating incitement to control all things, especially the forbidden, by making them subjects of discourse." 2

That this is an age, among poets, of technique, method, formalisms (both traditional and experimental), is not only the subject of my essay, but its context. So sharp has the line of demarcation been—the various moats and defenses around each camp—that the subject has often seemed to have its own shape, its own form: a profound and secure dualism. Between them, the language poets and the new formalists have divided up the current literary scene. They have divided it into"open" poetry (i.e." New American"), the "postmodernism of resistance," and "closed" poetry ("Traditional bourgeois European and US Academy") 3, the "postmodernism of reaction."4 This is an essay about our current lust for formalisms.

My purpose has been to look at representative formulations of these arguments: recent literary culture that has passionately and consistently promoted the differences between the language poets and the new formalists. My purpose has been to ask some questions about this perceived dichotomy: to ask what seeing poetry in this way is useful for, to look not only at what is said, but at the nuance, the body language. As one "of a community of writers actively in pursuit of the art" I have chosen to view these recent innovations with equal admiration and skepticism. My true agenda has become to describe, not the differences between the formalists and language poets, but their similarities; to explore the intersections of neo-formalism and its rival, language poetry; to consider the implications of the fact that these two groups, ostensibly opposed, share common assumptions to a surprising and perhaps discomforting degree.

The question that governs this essay is " What else are we talking about when we talk about form?" What else, in the guise of conversation about "form," is being smuggled into American verse? Form is the nominal subject of this essay; the real subject is secrecy.

Three years ago at a conference on global culture at the University of Pittsburgh, Susan Sontag defended what she called "high-brow or specialized culture" because she said, "We now have a culture to which everyone has access." In contemporary poetry this interest in the high-brow or specialized has manifested itself in formalism. In a standard postmodernist move, poets—both language poets and new formalists—have taken up an adversarial stance to a dominant culture: to the hegemony of free verse. Formalism calls for, in writers, specialization and expertise and, in readers, a concomitant connoisseurship. In verse, formalism, whether traditional or experimental, has become "the collector who liberates things from the curse of being useful."5 Formalism makes poetry dear again. Here are two representative depictions of the "orthodoxy of free verse." One is by Dana Gioia in a recent essay on new formalism:

> "The new formalists put free verse poets in the ironic and unprepared position of being the *status quo*. Free verse, the creation of an older literary revolution, is now the long-established, ruling orthodoxy; formal poetry the unexpected challenge."[6]

And another is by Marjorie Perloff in a review of the language poets:

> "There are two ways of responding to this situation [of language becoming commodity].... One may, as do the bulk of 'creative writing' teachers and students in workshops across the country, turn one's back on contemporary technology and write 'personal poems' in which an individual 'I' responds to sunsets and spiders and moths flickering on windowpanes... or one can take on the very public discourses that seem so threatening and explore their poetic potential."[7]

The yoke of a single sentence barely fits around the bulk of the new formalists and the language poets. Even in their names one can find the effrontery and lack of compromise that characterize the dynamics of the current literary community. The language poets and new formalists not only stand in opposition to one another, but stand united against a common enemy: free verse. The "free verse" of the critical literature of the new formalists and language poets does not seem to mean verse based "on the irregular rhythmic cadence of the recurrence, with variations, of significant phrases, image patterns and the like." [8] The " free verse" of the late 1980s, as it is defined and, in part, created by the critical literature of the new formalist and language poets, is abstracted and stylized. It bears only a ghostly resemblance to the traditional formalistic definition found in the Princeton encyclopedia. Rather, free verse, as it is characterized in the formalists' discussions, is poetry dominated, not by a concern with formal irregularity, but by what is seen as a set of unexamined assumptions about the relation of form to "meaning," to "content." Free verse is a debased verse, common without being popular, a poetry that, simultaneously, is middle-brow, academic and culturally illiterate. It is a verse that partakes of notions of both a pop culture and a *lingua franca*.9 To oppose free verse is actually to oppose certain kinds of "content," to oppose the notion of the preeminence of "content" itself. As Marjorie Perloff writes,

> "...it may seem easy to talk into a tape recorder and then transcribe one's words, avoiding all margins and leaving blank spaces between word groups [as the poet David Antin does]. Yet we don't in fact do it. For what is really 'easy' in the context of the present is to write little epiphany poems in free verse, detailing a 'meaningful' experience . I am walking, let us say, in the snow, and I notice strange footprints: I am reminded of the day when....*That*, I would posit, is *easy*. And 'they' do 'do it' in a thousand dreary little magazines and chapbooks."10

and Dana Gioia,

> "... the real issues presented by American poetry in the 'Eighties will become clearer: the debasement of poetic language; the prolixity of the lyric; the bankruptcy of the confessional mode; the inability to establish a meaningful aesthetic for new poetic narrative...The revival of traditional forms will be seen then as only one response to this troubling situation. There will undoubtedly be others."11

Behind the contradictory and mutually exclusive claims made for form on the part of both schools, is a shared assumption: form divides. An investment in formalism is an investment in dualism. Form not only separates the new formalist and language poetry from free verse, but it also makes possible division of poems into traditional dualities: form and content. As we can see in the quotations above, content is not exactly "in" form, but it is acted upon, transformed, transfigured, or eluded by form. In Perloff, for instance, the slosh of "epiphany" and "'meaningful' experiences," "unifying wholeness or fixed meanings"12 (as those things are represented by the walk on a snowy day), comes up hard against the technical, structural, formal: the "margins," "blank spaces," "word groups." In Gioia's description, the duality can be detected in the structure of his clauses, each of which is balanced so that the "troubling situation" in American poetry is described not by the nominal but by the adjectival. The "troubling situation" lies not in the enduring nominal "stuff" of poetry—"poetic language," "the lyric," or "the confessional mode" per se—but in their over use ("debasement"), their overabundance ("prolixity"), their outmodedness ("bankruptcy"), all of which would be rectified by traditional form. Traditional form is a kind of crucible in which the materials of poetry have their impurities burned off. This is an older technology, craft as opposed to the high tech processes suggested by Perloff.

In a McLuhanesque move these poets and critics argue that "the medium in which a representation is made produces the deepest effects irrespective of what is being represented."13 Formal poetry is its own sort of medium, so is free verse. In discussing form we are discussing not what is represented, not "content," but medium. We look for the "effects" inherent in all free verse, just as we look for the "effects" inherent in all verse concerned with formalisms.

Here is Barrett Watten from his book of essays on

language poetry, *Total Syntax,*

"I want to make a distinction between two different ways of looking at writing. The first is from the point of view of technique...And I want to oppose that to what the [Russian] Formalists called the 'subjective, aesthetic approach,' in which writing takes its basic values from psychology or biography...I also want to make a claim for technique as the most dynamic approach to writing."14

Here is Dana Gioia,

"Like the new tonal composers, the young poets now working in form reject the split between their art and its traditional audience. They seek to reaffirm poetry's broader cultural role and restore its parity with fiction and drama. One critic has already linked the revival of form with the return to narrative and grouped these new writers as an 'expansive movement' dedicated to reversing poetry's declining importance to the culture. These young poets seek to engage their audience not by simplifying their work but by making it more relevant and accessible. They are also "expansive" in that they have expanded their technical and thematic concerns beyond the confines of the short, autobiographical free verse lyric which so dominates contemporary poetry."15

Against the terminology of psychology or biography (in the language poets) and confessionalism (in the new formalists) stands "technique." In "expansive" and "dynamic" one sees a bulwark against the wastes of past infatuation with the self and the mistakes of the past. Form is astringent. To paraphrase Blake, form braces. The title of the recent, popular anthology of neo-formalists edited by Philip Dacey and David Jauss, *Strong Measures,* illustrates this. "Strong Measures" describes not only the work of the poets in the anthology, but, as Richard Wilbur points out in his introduction to the volume, puns on the phrophylactic sense of the idiom "to take strong measures against." At first reading, the language poets and the new formalists seem to argue about what form is and, in addition, to argue within their groups about how "formal" form is. The issue, however, of what qualifies as formal appears to be, for both camps, not so much an issue of identity, but of intensity or degree. The new technicians of poetry seem not so much interested in what the *sine qua non* of form is, but at what *point* a poem moves into the *category* of the formal. The question is not what is it, but how purely it is what it is. The question may not even be *"what"* is form, but *"where"* is form? Where in a poem does it seem to reside? "Form" is "in" certain aspects of a poem more than it is "in" others.

Here, again, is Dana Gioia:

"One of the more interesting developments of the last five years has been the emergence of pseudo-formal verse....Pseudo-formal verse bears the same relationship to formal poetry as the storefronts on a Hollywood backlot do to a real city street. They both look vaguely the same from a distance. In pseudo-formal verse the lines run to more or less the same length on the page. Stanzas are neatly symmetrical. The syllable count is roughly regular line by line, and there may even be a few rhymes thrown in, usually in an irregular pattern."16

And here are Dacey and Jauss:

"In our opinion, the structure of a poem as a whole (i.e., the pattern of its stanzas, rhyme scheme, and so forth) is a more important factor in determining whether or not a poem is formal than the structure of a line (i.e., the pattern of its rhythm)."17

Dana Gioia looks for form primarily in the line. Jauss

and Dacey seem to have in mind exactly the kind of poem Gioia rules out. For Jauss and Dacey, form shows itself in "the structure of a poem as a whole," rather than strictly in meter. But for all of the formalists, form is structure or pattern, whether it is the strict pattern of meter, or the more general pattern of the poem as a whole. Form is what Richard Wilbur calls paradigm.

This has not always been the case. In his introduction to Jauss and Dacey's anthology, Wilbur discusses the exceptions taken to sonnets some twenty years ago. Wilbur says that what was objected to at that time was the "vision" of traditional formalists. In this account, form is not paradigm, but lexicon.

"Both attractions and rejections, in art, have always involved more than form. I think, for example, of certain poets who, a few decades back, made war upon 'the sonnet.' These militants were not, actually, objecting to a fourteen-line paradigm having a number of possible rhyme-schemes. Their true objection was to how that form (and others) was being used by a group of accomplished and well-known lyricists, who dealt perhaps too exclusively in passionate love, natural beauty, and a vocabulary of breathless words like 'riant.' *The issue was not merely form but also, and far more importantly, vision and lexicon*" (italics mine).18

Interestingly, Dana Gioia, in describing the future of new formalist poetry, tacitly upholds the traditional objections to traditional formal verse.

"This assessment does not maintain that metrical innovation is necessary to write good poetry, that successful poetic translation must always follow the verse forms of the original or that prose is an impossible medium for poetry. It merely examines some current literary trends and speculates on both their origins and consequences. *It also suggests that the recent dearth of*

formal poetry opens interesting possibilities for young poets
to match an unexploited contemporary idiom with tradi-
tional or experimental forms" (italics mine).19

In Gioia's description, the poet's function is to "match"
the lexicon of the present to the form of the past (tradition) or the future (experimental): a contemporary
vision or lexicon (to use Wilbur's words) in a paradigm of the past or future . The notion of temporality
implied here is fascinating. "Within" the poem the present mingles with the past and future. What is equally
interesting is the notion of inherency: certain *times* are
in certain aspects of the poem. The present, the contemporary, resides in "idiom," (or "lexicon"), while both
"tradition" (the past) and the "experimental" (the avant-
garde, the future) reside in form (or "paradigm"). In
new formalist poetry, lexicon and paradigm are separate yet equal; each is enclosed within the poem and
yet segregated from the other. It is crucial to the project of the new formalist poem that lexicon and paradigm be distinct from each other. This separation *is*
the new formalist poem, just as the postmodernist building is the skyscraper with the Chippendale pediment.
The past is only supposed to rub shoulders with idiom—which should stay fresh, current, up-to-date.

This duality is not always expressed in terms of temporality. Sometimes the duality is expressed in terms
of mind and body, head or heart. Molly Peacock talks
about a "dreadful dualism" that said to her "either
be...quickened by true emotion, *or* be...all technique and
no guts." In a reversal of Adrienne Rich, who has called
form the "asbestos glove" that protects the poet from
the heat of subject, Peacock sees form as an enabling,
liberating device. However, at the same time that she
defines form as a means of overcoming dualities, Peacock also describes the function of form in one of her

own poems as matching the structure "large and worldly" to the content "small and private..."20

Among the language poets, as well, the traditional dualities between form and content, paradigm and lexicon stand, in spite of the fact that there is more bickering, more strife between lexicon and paradigm. These dualities are put to work to abrade the "transparency of language."21Here is a section from Bruce Andrews' poem "Funnels."22

an armada

whose pollen will not mate at all

                        the animal grace it's everywhere

                    always a bridesmaid never a bride

float and fade

                        old awful

                    are fulfilled

mild-voiced immediately to one over the tube on hook of

    the little nations

                        me own hook

And here are three different readings of it. First, one by Barrett Watten:

> "One might assume that [Andrew's] work is involved with the surface characteristics of language; so "an armada" has one referent and "whose pollen will not mate at all" has another. The degree of connection is given by the spatial arrangements on the page ...
> "The effect of this [poem] on a listener involves what the

[Russian] Formalists called 'rhythm as a constructive device.' The phrases are units. The poem goes: unit...unit...unit. After a while a point of balance in the phrase begins to be heard; it takes on a meaning of its own. At first, one is not particularly hearing the words due to their referential shifts; it takes work to get from one isolated plane of reference to another at the speed of reading out loud. But what actually happens is that the rhythmic parallels turn into a meaning-structuring device. After ten minutes of this the phrases start to assume a rhythmic point of balance; the words take on weight in relation to that."

The second by Robert Grenier:

"[William Carlos] Williams identified with the phrase in his variable foot. Although it seems more associational— you could have a variance in the possible number of syllables included in roughly parallel time units, as one line follows another down the page. So what this seems to be doing in part is dissociating that form of the variable foot from specific statement..."

And the third by Bob Perelman:

"[Andrews] seems to be, especially in this work, always going back and forth between very familiar language and very unfamiliar language. It's defamiliarization. So 'always a bridesmaid never a bride.' When he comes to that it clicks in immediately; that's just a cliche, and he hears it in this easy intimacy with no dissonance. But after a while of hearing that in a disjunctive context, 'always a bridesmaid never a bride' sounds just the same as 'not as deviant enough.' All of a sudden the nonsyntactic or unusual phrases take on the same weight as the cliches. By playing back and forth between the familiar and the unfamiliar, he makes you familiar with the unfamiliar."

Within each individual reading, as well as within the group, the conventional dualities persist. The originality of Andrews' poem, as Robert Grenier points out, is not that it transcends such categories as form and content with their traditional functions, but that it stands the usual relation between them on its head. Andrews "dissociat[es] that form of the variable foot from specific statement." In fact, it is possible from all three readings to draw up the standard ledger and enter in one column the items of paradigm—"foot," "phrase," "syllabic count," and"spatial arrangement" and, in another column, the items of lexicon—"specific statement, "referent," "cliches" or "unusual phrases."

"But is it poetry ?" Marjorie Perloff, in her review of the L=A=N=G=U=A=G=E poets in the May/June, 1984 issue of *The American Poetry Review*, asks a question about the intersection of classification and audience.

One may, as do the bulk of 'creative writing' teachers and students in workshops across the country, turn one's back on contemporary technology and write 'personal poems' in which an individual 'I' responds to sunsets and spiders and moths flickering on windowpanes...

All these revivals of traditional technique (whether linked or not to traditional aesthetics) both reject the specialization and intellectualization of the arts in the academy over the past forty years."

If free verse, the "art" of the academicians, the middlebrow, the new Philistines, is at once too common and too specialized, then formalists—both language poets and new formalists—are caught in a double bind. They must make a bid for "true" mass popularity, as well as for "true" erudition ("an intangible currency, but one that has the virtue of scarcity ..."), 23 while, at the same time, avoiding the academy. Ideally, poetry invested in formalism must be either so boisterously common or of a difficulty so exquisite and off-putting that it will confound the MFAs.

The problem of audience is the problem of identity. To ask "But is it poetry?" is to ask for whom, exactly, the poem exists. The problem of audience poses, for both language poets and new formalists alike, the problem of accessibility. In their reading, accessibility is hazardous. It compromises the very identity of innovative poetry. Formalist poetry must defy the criteria by which readers of poetry currently recognize and appreciate poetry because, most often, so the argument goes, that poetry is free verse. These poets must make evident the fact that the difficulties and problems of language poetry or of new formalist poetry are special, precise and intended. It must be insured that a language poem, for instance, will not be mistaken for merely a more obscure, more difficult free verse poem. If poets cannot expect universal recognition of their intentions, they can at least insure a partial recognition on the part of the *cognoscenti*. In order to protect poetry from exploitation, these new radicals must "code" their work. They must not only invent multiple audiences (those in the know and those not), but multiple texts. A recent article on avant-garde photographers (including Sherrie Levine, who presents as "her own" work by such masters as Walker Evans) illustrates nicely how this is done in photography .

"...looking at a Sherrie Levine copy of a Walker Evans, we are to imagine the experiences of three different gallery goers. The first viewer, unfamiliar with Walker Evans, assumes that Levine is a documentarian. The second viewer recognizes the image as a famous one by Evans, and therefore notes that Levine's photograph is a copy, but is hazy about how to react. The third viewer, a sophisticate who has read Roland Barthes, instantly understands Levine's commentary on the strategy by which Walker Evans conventionalized and mythologized everyday scenes so that they can be considered 'Truth.' Thus Levine's appropriated images are to be considered coded messages, to be interpreted only by a knowledgeable audience."24

It is easy to plug into this model "readers" instead of "viewers." The first reader of a language poem, for instance, unfamiliar with contemporary free verse, assumes that the language poem is simply difficult poetry. The second reader recognizes the poem as free verse in the traditional sense ("based on an irregular rhythmic cadence") but also notices that the poem is not exactly narrative, imagistic, or lyrical in the way of other free verse and is "hazy about how to react." The third reader, a sophisticate who has read contemporary literary criticism and, perhaps, even other language poets, "instantly understands" what kind of poetry this is.

On the surface, at least, the problem the new formalist poets seem to face is the opposite of the language poets'. Traditional form is accessible, but its accessibility is a great hazard. It must be protected from academic, careerist manipulations. One cannot imagine, for new formalist poetry, quite the same spectrum of reader responses as described above. When it comes to new formalist poetry, the problem is that cheap copies of the real thing are being knocked off at an alarming rate. Here, again, is Dana Gioia on a pseudo-formalist poetry.

"...line lengths seem determined mainly by their typographic width...The apparently regular line breaks fall without any real rhythmic relation either to the meter or the syntax. As Truman Capote once said, 'That's not writing—it's typing.' There is no rhythmic integrity, only incompatible, provisional judgements shifting pointlessly line by line. The resulting poems remind me of a standard gag in improvisational comedy where the performers pretend to speak a foreign language by imitating its approximate sound. Making noises that resemble Swedish, Russian, Italian or French, they hold impassioned conversations on the stage. What makes it all so funny is that the actors, *as everyone in the audience knows*, are only mouthing nonsense (italics mine)."25

Notwithstanding appeals to the popular culture of stand-up comedy, I would point out that what is being described here is, as much as any experimental poetry, a poetry in code. Not everyone in the audience *would* know if a poem were genuinely formalist or merely pseudo-formalist. In fact, in this account, pseudo-formalism can exist precisely because audiences can be fooled, because readers are *not* being able to discern the real thing from an imitation. According to this account, true new formalist poetry (not the backlot, but the real city street), like true language poetry, is a rare and expensive commodity. It takes an expert to know that "pseudo-formalism" is not writing, but typing; it takes a Truman Capote, a member, as Barrett Watten would describe it, "of a community of writers actively in pursuit of the art."

"Each of these essays was given originally as a talk to a community of writers, and each was addressed to a collective state of mind at a particular time. Each was intended, by its own argument, to make its way out of a situation in the total present in such a way that there was no going back, building a space to work in out of what were only nebulous imaginings at one time. This characterization of the critical project is very far from traditional critical thinking. Rather than arguing from texts to interpretation, I wanted to extend an argument by virtue of the disjunction between previous methods and as yet un-discussed literary facts. This is the kind of thinking that could only have been done in front of a community of writers actively in pursuit of the art."26

In his introduction to *"Language" Poetries: An Anthol-ogy*, Douglas Messerli addresses the question of audi-ence when he talks about Watten's "exploded self, a self that is subsumed in the language theory he treats." And then goes on to add:

> "And in this sense, there is a presumptive quality—in the best sense of the meaning—in most of Watten's critical writing: as a 'kind of thinking...done in front of a commu-nity of writers,' Watten's critical pieces presume and so-licit a certain range of shared values."27

To skirt the great middle ground of academic free verse, the innovators—new formalists and language poets alike—divide the poem into two texts: one revealed to a popular audience, the other to an audience of spe-cialists; one low-brow, one high-brow; one profane, one sacred; one for the consumer of mass produced goods, one for the connoisseur, the collector.

Not that this is bad. Adorno's collector, who liber-ates things from the curse of being useful, is an adver-sary of the dominant culture and a praiseworthy model for our current obsession with technique. Form can withhold poetry from the utility of mass culture; it can challenge the "now long-established, ruling orthodoxy." It can make poetry, again, into a language of subver-sion. Form can be a kind of fulcrum for moving the vast, inert mass of dominant culture.

Problems arise, however, when the double nature of the text is unrecognized and unacknowledged as a strate-gem. The problem arises when a poem's codedness, its inaccessiblity, its difficulty, is attributed to the audience's "illiteracy," the audience's Philistinism, rather than being understood as a deliberate strategy for subversion. The definition of a new formalist or language poem is: that poem which must, as one of its functions, *create* an audience for whom a poem will be out of reach.

The question "How radical is this poetry?" can be addressed by asking "How orthodox is free verse?" In a revealing account of the intersections of traditional formalism and recent literary history, Gioia hints at the darker, more troubling side of our obsession with form: its tenuous, ephemeral, even reactionary nature. Although in his account Gioia intends to emphasize the two generations that abandoned form, he cannot do so without firmly enclosing free verse within the parentheses of formalisms. After all, even the careers of Louis Simpson and Adrienne Rich—practitioners of high free verse—began with form:

> "Two generations now of younger writers have largely ignored rhyme and meter, and most of the older poets who worked originally in form (such as Louis Simpson and Adrienne Rich), have abandoned it entirely for more than a quarter of a century."

If you add to this account contemporaries of Simpson and Rich, Howard Nemerov, Richard Wilbur, Paul Blackburn and Lawrence Ferlinghetti, who have been solely or primarily interested in experimental or traditional form, then the broad outlines of recent literary history show, even more conclusively, and with few exceptions, that American poets, including the advocates of formalism, are doing now what they have always done. They are writing in traditional or experimental forms. If this is so, then the work of both kinds of formalists becomes not one of the creation or even of the recovery of new techniques, or of technique. Rather it merely seems to be a question of emphasis: of the reclassifying, according to long standing categories, not so much of poetry, as much as of poets. Given Gioia's account of his own practices, one might say that the definition of a new formalist poet begins to depend on questions of quantity.

> "In my own poetry I have always worked in both fixed and open forms. Each mode opened up possibilities of style, subject, music, and development the other did not suggest, at least at the moment....I find it puzzling therefore that so many poets see these modes as opposing aesthetics rather than as complimentary techniques. Why shouldn't a poet explore the full resources the English language offers?"28

How much formal poetry must one write before one moves out of the category of free verse writer into the category of new formalist? At what point does one become a new formalist? The issue begins to seem to be one, not of new kinds of knowledge, but of the relation of reader and writer to already existing knowledge, not what *is* form but *who* "uses" it. To quote from Sontag's "The Pornographic Imagination":

> "What's really at stake? A concern about the uses of knowledge itself. There's a sense in which all knowledge is dangerous...we must ask what justifies the reckless unlimited confidence we have in the present mass availability ...of knowledge...".29

The new museums of language need someone to keep out. Both sides have chosen those who are themselves accused of making poetry "specialized," the bulk of 'creative writing' teachers and students in workshops across the country," academies and their students.

> "How then do these promising authors, most of whom not only have graduate training in writing or literature but also work as professional teachers of writing, not hear the confusing rhythms of their own verse? How can they believe their expertise in a style whose basic principles they so obviously misunderstand? That these writers by virtue of their training and position represent America's poetic intelligentsia makes their performance deeply unnerving— rather like hearing a conservatory trained pianist rapturously play the notes of a Chopin waltz in 2/4 time."30

These writers are at once over-trained and ignorant, schooled yet uneducated, old-fashioned, out-of-date, with no sense of the historical. They are numerous and yet they have none of the virtues of the common. Like the movies' version of the young Helen Keller, they have learned to behave, but not to understand. They are a new under-class. And yet this is a class that defies the usual criteria by which classes are defined. This is not an under-class by virtue of race, ethnicity, gender or socio-economics. This under-class has swollen to include the privileged middle-class which sits safely segregated within the ghetto of the academy, or at least within certain academies.

And yet, it is as easy to imagine an ignorance and lack of sophistication that one could achieve on one's own, without the help of the academy, as it is possible to imagine succumbing to weariness or fear outside the walls of the academy so that one turns "one's back on contemporary technology and write[s] 'personal poems' in which an individual 'I' responds to sunsets and spiders and moths flickering on windowpanes." The formalists' solution is both elitist and utopian: a world, (perhaps "the real world"), or the right kind of school, in which ignorance does not exist, where true art and thinking thrive and people will learn to play Chopin as they should.

Language poets and new formalists must move from the issues of art, what is collected, withheld, made special, to considerations of audience, who will be walled out from these technologies, these new museums of language. I began this essay with Walter Benjamin and Theodor Adorno. I began with the notion of connoisseurship as a praiseworthy model for taking a stance against free verse. The model is a radical one, shared by both language poets and new formalists. They share common strategies for witholding and specializing poetry, along with both the advantages and disadvantages of these strategies; they share common notions of form and content, certain notions of audience, and the relation of language to audience. It could be argued that, beneath their ostensible differences, the language poets and the new formalists have much more in common than not.

And if this is true, then the project of the new formalists and language poets seems to be far less radical than it is nostalgic. It involves, as I mentioned above, not the recovery of traditional forms or the creation of new ones, but merely the classification or reclassification of poetry according to standard categories. In this reading, the project of these modern classifiers is taxonomic, curatorial, not one of invention or recovery, but one of emphasis. They are not concerned with *what* form is but with *who* uses it, not with definition, but with pedigree. What seems really to be at stake, to paraphrase Susan Sontag, is a concern about the availability of knowledge itself. If we are doing now what we have always done, one possible and disturbing implication of this situation is that all the strife and bickering of the current literary wars masks a basic disinclination to alter American poetry. Beneath the rhetoric of innovation lies an investment in the status quo. In this reading the project of the language poets and new formalists is not to renovate the ghetto of free verse but to free it for the subdivisions of technique.

---

1 This awkward but useful neologism is used by the editors of *Aesthetics and Politics* in their introduction to an exchange of letters between Theodor Adorno and Walter Benjamin. *Aesthetics and Politics*(London: New Left Books, 1977), p. 106.

2 *The Secret Museum: Pornography in Modern Culture*, Walter Kendrick (New York: Viking, 1987), p. 33.

3 The descriptions in parentheses are Amiri Baraka's from his essay, "The Poetry of Urgent Necessity," *Poetry East*, Nos. 20 and 21 (Fall 1986), p. 34.

4 *The Anti -Aesthetic: Essays on Postmodern Culture*, ed. Hal Foster (Port Townsend, WA: Bay Press, 1983), pp. xi-xii. Even now, of course, there are standard positions to take on postmodernism: one may support postmodernism as populist and attack modernism as elitist or, conversely, support modernism as elitist—as culture proper— and attack postmodernism as mere kitsch. Such views reflect one thing:...In cultural politics today, a basic opposition exists between a postmodernism which seeks to deconstruct modernism and resist the status quo and a postmodernism which repudiates the former to celebrate the latter: a postmodernism of resistance and a postmodernism of reaction.

5 *Charles Baudelaire: A Lyric Poet in the Era of High Capitalism*, trans. Harry Zohn (London, Verso Editions, 1983), pp. 113-114.

6 "Notes on the New Formalism and the Revival of Traditional Forms in Poetry," *The Hudson Review*, Vol 40, No 3, p. 395.

7 "The Word As Such: L=A=N=G=U=A=G=E Poetry in The Eighties," *The American Poetry Review*, Vol 13, No 3 (May/June 1984), p. 21.

8 *The Princeton Encyclopedia of Poetry and Poetics*, ed. Alex Preminger (Princeton, NJ: Princeton University Press, 1974), p. 288.

9 To say that the language and neo-formalist poets are united by the common enemy of free verse is to have already entered a labyrinth of complications. For instance, new formalists would call much language poetry free verse. See below, footnote 23.

10 *The Poetics of Indeterminacy: Rimbaud to Cage* (Princeton, NJ: Prin-

ceton University Press, 1981), p. 292.

11 Gioia, op. cit., p. 408.

12 "Breaking All the Rules,"*The New York Times Magazine*, June 12, 1988, p. 43.

13 Kendrick, op. cit., p. 221.

14 *Total Syntax*, Barrett Watten, (Carbondale, IL: Southern Illinois University Press, 1985), p. 1.

15 Gioia, op. cit., pp. 403-404.

16 Ibid, p. 404.

17 *Strong Measures: Contemporary American Poetry in Traditional Forms*, eds. Philip Dacey and David Jauss (New York: Harper & Row, 1986), p. 9.

18 Ibid, p. xx. In a recent issue of *Paper Air*, (Vol 3, No 3) a magazine devoted to avant-garde poetry, including language poetry, one can find in a long poem by the British poet, Allen Fisher, the following lines:

The imaginary takes over from laughter,
in is a joy without words, a riant spaciousness
become temporal.
The demonstrative points to an enunciation,
it is a complex shifter straddling the fold of
naming it, and the autonomy of the subject.

19 Gioia, op. cit., p. 402.

20 "What the Mockingbird Said," *Poetry East*, op.cit, pp. 110-113. The new formalists are not the only ones to make a distinction between technique and "guts." The language poets, too, write about this duality. Here is Barrett Watten in *Total Syntax:* There has been a tremendous sophistication of technique among certain writers I want to deal with....Technique has assumed many of the constructive qualities that the [Russian] Formalists saw as *literaturnost*. But there is almost a block at this point—a number of writers have thrown themselves into technique with such incredible force that getting beyond that technique, expanding its range, becomes a problem. In some cases technique has been proposed as a static value toward the production of one kind of text. The Formalists' position was formed against the background of many different kinds of writing. And it assumed a social context for this position that now seems intrinsic to their method. Starting from the point of view of technique did not limit discussion to technique but led to a way of seeing what was most active in writing .

21 *The American Poetry Review* , pp. 20-21.

22 Watten, op. cit., pp. 17-19. It is worth mentioning that the "spatial arrangement" of this poem is, according to Gioia's essay, one of

the earmarks of free verse.

23 Kendrick, op. cit., p. 15.

24 "The Self-Reflexive Camera,"*Boston Review*,Vol XI, no 2 (April 1986), p. 13.

25 Gioia op.cit., p. 406. Notice the double meaning of mass culture. Hollywood and nightclub comedy are employed to represent both "bad"mass culture and "good" mass culture, that which is fake, phony, debased, and that which is common, shared, "gotten" by everyone.

The worker writer movement in England provides an interesting addendum to the new formalist claim. A loose, nationwide network of writing workshops organized by blue collar workers, the Federation of Worker Writers and Community Publishers is a grassroots movement devoted to social activism and the writing and publishing of their members in order "to register the fact that the working class, the majority of the population, are still, in Tillie Olsen's words, 'marginal to the culture'." Although the subjects of the poems are frequently gritty, the form is often in traditional rhyme and meter. It is interesting to speculate on what the new formalists make of this blue collar, frequently socialist poetry in which traditional form is often strictly used. Here is an example from a chapbook, by Joe Smythe. *Come and Get Me* (Manchester, Commonword, 1979), p. 16:

Lyricists

Jack the Liar was carved by a jock
For telling the truth about his cock,
One woman of many and boasting, too,
Let Jack the Liar's truth be learning you.

Jimmy from Leeds got seven years stir
For rape and abduction of a lady Mayor
Who kept him in bed for sixty days,
When they were found blamed The Laws delays.

Rosie Sweetarse who whored when she could
Knew that her ponce was up to no good
When he took her to Bradford for a day by the sea,
Morning till night she ground out stiff curry.

Whatever happens it's happened before
To braggart and crook and ramrodded whore.
Nothing like this never happened with you?
Make way for a saint and Jack The Liar Two.

For making me aware of the worker writer movement and for providing me with their poetry, I am grateful to my colleague, Nick Coles, at the University of Pittsburgh.

26 Watten, op. cit., p. ix.

27 *"Language" Poetries: An Anthology*, ed, and intro. Douglas Messerli (New York: New Directions, 1987), p. 6.

28 Gioia, op. cit., pp. 400-408.

29 Kendrick, op. cit., p. 224.

30 Gioia, op. cit., p. 407.

READING THE NEW FORMALISTS

By Robert McPhillips

I

American Poetry in the 1980s is undergoing an unexpected revolution. After decades of free verse dominance, there has been an unanticipated return to form among many younger poets. Despite much publicity, the significance of this revolution has not yet been properly assessed. Rather, it has been confused by polemics. Since the rise of the Beat and Confessional poets in the late 50s, the common assumption of the literary establishment has been that meter and rhyme were outmoded techniques for innovative contemporary poetry. While a few older poets like James Merrill and Richard Wilbur continued working in form despite literary fashion, younger poets, by and large, no longer found it profitable to master traditional metrics. Instead, they took it for granted that each poet achieved a personal voice only by creating his or her own idiosyncratic, "organic" forms. By the late 60s, this ideology of "open" forms was further fueled by a heightened political activism on university campuses. For many young poets, poetry became a way to assert their personal identities against a discredited version of an elitist past. The use of "open" forms thereby took on a new political significance. The complete success of this aesthetic is demonstrated by the anthologies of the past twenty years, since anthologies, by their nature, attempt to define a canon. Daniel Halpern's *The New American Poetry Anthology* (1975), for instance, includes over three hundred poems by seventy six younger poets. Of these, only two are in traditional forms, a villanelle and a sestina. Other anthologies present similar pictures. For young poets to write in traditional forms, it had become ideologically as well as aesthetically unfashionable.

In the past few years the established aesthetic of free verse has been challenged. This swerve actually began in the late 70s with the appearance of first books written primarily in form. But the debuts of such poets as Robert B. Shaw, Charles Martin, and Timothy Steele went largely unmarked by the New York literary establishment because they were published by university presses. The first widespread notice of a radical shift in sensibility was the journalistic sensation in 1982 over Brad Leithauser's first volume, *Hundreds of Fireflies*, the first collection of formal poems by a younger poet published in years by a major New York press. This book was festooned with glowing blurbs from such established formal poets as Merrill, Wilbur and Anthony Hecht who probably recognized an aesthetic in Leithauser's poetry vaguely similar to their own elegant work. Their support was promptly echoed by the New York critics, and eventually even by Helen Vendler, who finally realized that something new was afoot. Critics soon began remarking on how much formal verse had been appearing in literary journals over the previous few years, and this trend was quickly dubbed the New Formalism.

Since Leithauser's election as what Tom Disch in *The Nation* called "the prom king of American poetry," there have been a number of important first volumes by poets working to a greater or lesser extent in form, most notably Amy Clampitt, Gjertrud Schnackenberg, Mary Jo Salter and Dana Gioia. Lately Vikram Seth's *The Golden Gate*, a novel written in Pushkin's *Eugene Onegin* stanza,

and James Cummins's *The Whole Truth,* a detective story
told in sestinas, have been published. Meanwhile several new anthologies have appeared—among them *Strong
Measures* (1986), edited by Philip Dacey and David Jauss,
and *Ecstatic Occasions, Expedient Forms* (1987), edited
by David Lehman—which demonstrate the renewed
interest in poetic form.

However obvious, then, that there has been a significant aesthetic shift in recent American poetry, much
confusion still exists about the nature of the New Formalism. Part of this confusion remains ideological. The
seriousness of this new aesthetic is most clearly demonstrated by the impassioned attacks made upon it by
the advocates of free verse. Ariel Dawson dismisses
the revival of form through recourse to pop-sociology
in her essay in the *AWP Newsletter,* "The Yuppie Poet."
She argues that "the popularity of formalism is related
to the desire to shape the poem into an acceptable product," insisting, further, that "the reemergence of formalism is perfectly harmonious with the yuppie knack
for resurrecting elitist traditions."

Diane Wakoski's attack on the revival of form in the
American Book Review was even more vehemently ideological. In "The New Conservatism in American Poetry," she assumed the hysterical tones of a witch hunt,
proclaiming John Hollander to be no less than the "devil"
himself for criticizing free verse. After a long personal
attack on Hollander, Wakoski listed his chief sins as
"denouncing, basically, the free verse revolution, denouncing the poetry which is the fulfillment of the
Whitman heritage, making defensive jokes about ill-
educated, slovenly writers of poetry who have been
teaching college poetry classes for the past decade, al-
lowing their students to write drivel and go out into
the world, illiterate of poetry." (One might speculate

why Wakoski feels threatened by such a statement which seems more sane than Satanic.) Finally, Wakoski reduced her ideological attack to literary jingoism when, in insisting on the centrality of Whitman and Williams to our tradition, she claimed that to write in traditional forms was un-American. Reducing her vision of American poetry to one tradition—not incidentally her own— she then specifically banished Robert Frost and T.S. Eliot from the American canon as "Europeans." As Dana Gioia remarked in response to Wakoski, this search "for the new American voice" by rejecting all schools but her own "seems curiously reminiscent in tone and content to the quest for pure Germanic culture led by the late Joseph Goebbels." Instead, he proposed "the radical notion that American poetry is whatever poetry happens to be written by Americans."

Clearly the nature of the response that the New Formalism has evoked from some fervid champions of free verse suggests the movement's potency. Perhaps what is most significant about this response is that it has, in its ideological zeal, failed to perform the primary function of responsible criticism: to closely examine and evaluate individual texts. Dawson's yuppie and Wakoski's conservative poets exist purely as abstractions. Both critics automatically equate politics with aesthetics and argue from political rather than from aesthetic grounds, reducing the revival of meter and rhyme in all of its diverse manifestations to mere reflections of a reactionary political ideology.

A close reading of poets working in form demonstrates the difficulty of equating versification with politics. The subject matter of much New Formalist poetry is specifically at odds with such an interpretation. The political vision of Vikram Seth's *The Golden Gate* is both pro-gay and anti-nuke. Marilyn Hacker is an outspoken lesbian who sees no contradiction between her use of meter and rhyme, of vilanelles and sonnets, and the feminist content of much of her poetry. Similarly, Molly Peacock has argued, in both *Ecstatic Occasions, Expedient Forms* and in *Poetry East*, that writing in form has, paradoxically, freed her to explore such delicate subjects as masturbation and abortion.

The real problem, then, with most of the attacks on the New Formalism has been a failure to confront the poetry directly. Ideology has prevented critics from making many concrete aesthetic judgements of New Formalist poems. Perhaps sensing a threat to their own power within the literary establishment, the defenders of free verse wish to dismiss the movement categorically. In the process, they have failed both to provide an overview of the movement and to make distinctions among the numerous poets writing in form. It is time that an overview which makes such fundamental distinctions is given.

The emergence of the New Formalism is not some instantaneous occurrence paralleling current political trends. The revival of interest among young poets in the aesthetic possibilities that formal verse opened up began in the 70s and centered largely around three universities, Harvard, Stanford and Brandeis. If Robert Lowell was the more famous presence at Harvard, the most influential figure among aspiring poets in the 70s may actually have been the classicist and poet, Robert Fitzgerald, whose students included Brad Leithauser, Mary Jo Salter, Katha Pollitt, Robert B. Shaw and Dana Gioia. At Stanford and Brandeis the main influences were poet-critics Yvor Winters and J. V. Cunningham, whose insistence on tight metric control can be seen in such young poets as Timothy Steele and, indirectly, in Calcutta-born Vikram Seth. For these poets a return to form provided a fresh angle from which to convey personal experiences as well to escape from the obsessively private concerns of the confessional free verse poem. The traditional techniques of formal poetry also set up new linguistic risks for them, challenging the imagination in ways that free verse, by and large, had ceased to do.

This return to traditional form by contemporary poets is not without its aesthetic traps. Writing in meter and rhyme requires a level of technical skill beyond the grasp of many poets whose incompetence often leads them to cheat with meter. The result has been a recent proliferation of what Dana Gioia, in his essay in *The Hudson Review*, "Notes on the New Formalism," identifies as the "pseudo-formal poem." The pseudo-formal poem may have the look on the page of conforming to regular stanzas and may rhyme here and there. But it never successfully creates a regular metric pattern strong enough to become the basis for the metrical substitutions which provide tension in many formal poems. Such poems flaunt a technique they do not truly possess and exploit the contemporary reader's uncertain knowledge of metrics. A related problem is a poet's overvaluation of form at the expense of a poem's emotional impact. Too strict an adherence to metrical regularity along the lines advocated by Yvor Winters can make a poem seem overly contrived and monotonous. The abundance, on the one hand, of sloppy formal verse and, on the other, of a mechanical execution of form, fuels justifiable aesthetic criticism of the New Formalism. But this is not the primary kind of criticism being leveled at the New Formalists by the ideological defenders of free verse.

Ultimately, it is necessary to judge a new literary movement by the quality of the work it produces. Thus far, the critics of the New Formalism have failed to evaluate the quality of the poetry it has produced and to distinguish the mediocre from the more accomplished poets connected with the movement. This is partly the result of the hasty attempt to dismiss the New Formalism as politically reactionary without carefully examining individual poets. But part of the confusion also comes from the imbalanced attention given to a few poets published by prominent New York houses, especially Knopf. Critics have allowed a few publicists and editors to dictate literary taste as if they were disinterested judges of what is most vital in contemporary poetry. The most blatant result of this New York bias has been Brad Leithauser's premature designation as a major poet.

This media coup has done much to distort the general reader's perception of the New Formalism. For this reason, it is important to examine the actual achievement of Brad Leithauser in relation to his more gifted but lesser known contemporaries connected with the revival of form: Timothy Steele, Charles Martin, Gjertrud Schnackenberg and Dana Gioia. This examination will suggest the range of the achievement of the New Formalists and the ways in which they are bringing renewed vigor into contemporary poetry. Most importantly, a close reading of the best of the New Formalists should help to shift the level of critical debate from the vague and ideological to the specific and aesthetic.

II

Anyone even casually aware of the New Formalism is likely to recognize Brad Leithauser's name. As a result of the inordinate amount of attention *Hundreds of*

Fireflies generated, Leithauser was the recipient of several literary prizes, including a MacArthur Fellowship. He followed up his poetic debut with a semi-autobiographical novel, *Equal Distance* (1985). This novel's lack of narrative drive was overlooked by most critics who seemed content with the occasional lyric detail they expected from a poet's prose fiction. Quick on the heels of this widely-recognized novel, Leithauser published his second book of poems, *Cats of the Temple*, a volume that virtually mirrors his first, both in structure and subject matter, though it is a considerably slighter achievement. In *The Washington Post Book World*, Bruce Bawer dismissed it as "a slender rural travelogue of sorts, a series of coyly baroque, nature-centered studies in poetic technique." Richard Tillinghast likewise panned it in *The New York Times Book Review*, while Helen Vendler qualified her earlier praise in *The New York Review of Books*. But a few critics nonetheless awarded it glowing reviews, most notably John Gross in the daily *New York Times*, which rarely covers poetry. All told, *Cats of the Temple* received an amount of attention bestowed on few books of poetry, seeming to confirm Leithauser's status as the preeminent poet of his generation, a role, understandably, he has been quite willing to assume. He has published literary essays in numerous prominent journals, including two pieces for *The New Criterion*—"Metrical Illiteracy" and "The Confinement of Free Verse"—where he set out to define, rather narrowly, some of the principles underpinning the revival of form in the 80s. Leithauser errs in underestimating the range of genuine innovation that free verse introduced to poetry.

Leithauser is not untalented. At its best, his work provides the pleasures afforded by language used crisply to make minute observations. Here, Leithauser's model is clearly Marianne Moore. Like Moore, he frequently

chooses to focus on exotic objects—fireflies, seahorses,
Japanese art works and moss gardens—as the basis for
achieving whimsical linguistic effects. But when writing such poems in this vein as "Hundreds of Fireflies"
and "Seahorses," Leithauser's linguistic flourishes don't
seem derived from any deep experience. He is at his
best in a poem like "An Expanded Want Ad," which
is representative of Leithauser's poetic method. Here
the abbreviations in an ad for a summer cottage in
"Pig Riv" propel the poet into a vision of the landscape along the Pigeon River in his native Michigan:

> there's a good view
> of the Pigeon, a river that carries
> more than its share of sunny jewelry,
>   for days here are mostly blue,
>
>   and nights so clear
> and deep that in a roadside puddle
> you can spot the wobbly flashlight flare
>   of even a minisculer star.

What gives this poem more weight than an elegant
verbal exercise like "Seahorses" is its emotional roots
in the personal landscape of the poet's childhood. But
even at that, the author's vision is too filled with sunny
blue skies to move the reader deeply.

Leithauser finally seems more interested in using this
locale as an occasion for metrical and linguistic playfulness than in using form to evoke a sense of the
landscape's human significance. But while one can take
pleasure in the shape of the poem which simulates the
river's flow, Leithauser's technique is surprisingly sloppy.
His use of rhyme is more tentative than sure. Off rhymes
like clear/star appear randomly throughout a poem
whose regular rhyme pattern is set by such perfect rhymes
as floors/doors and view/blue. While slant rhyme can

be used powerfully, Leithauser's substitutions of off rhymes seems merely random, suggesting a struggle for mastery rather than significant variations. His technique is often as casual as his language is whimsical.

Leithauser's range, moreover, is extremely limited. His chief talent is for superficial observation. When he attempts to move beyond the elegant description of unpopulated, post-card pretty landscapes (indeed, many of his poems derive from travel) or of Mooreish exotica, he is largely unsuccessful. Thus far, he has limited his attempts to two quite different types of poems: light verse epigrams and autobiographical narratives. Both books of his poetry contain numerous epigrams which he identifies as "minims" and riddles. At their best, they are merely clever; at their worst, they are contorted and opaque. Sometimes they are merely puzzling, as in the obscurely titled and logically confusing "That Trojan Horse":

> It pretty much stinks,
> though it may be only human—
> the way Man looks at Woman
> and secretly thinks,
> You've got to believe
> it's better to give than to receive.

One recognizes Leithauser's attempt to achieve a worldly tone of cynicism, but the final couplet lacks both the necessary clarity and sting. What, precisely, does the poet "believe" is "better to give than to receive"? Leithauser's light verse reads like clumsy exercises in technique which were better left in his notebooks.

Leithauser's autobiographical narratives form the centerpieces of both his poetry collections. While these poems provide a welcome contrast to the preciosity of

his lyrics, unfortunately, like his novel, they fail both
to achieve much narrative energy and to present a fully
engaging persona. Moreover, the smugness of Leithauser's
tone becomes off-putting. One finds this conceit particularly in "Two Summer Jobs" which juxtaposes the
poet's stints as a tennis instructor for suburban-De-
troit housewives and as a law clerk. "Law Clerk, 1979"
reaches the peak of the poet's self-satisfaction when it
compares his worldly success in New York with the
quite different situation of one of his poetry-writing
rivals whom he runs into while he's "roundabouting
home through Central Park":

> He's wearing jeans and a work-shirt with a rip
> in the neck, whereas I'm caught in the trap-
> pings of a Wall Street lawyer. As we lob our
> pleasantries across the Sartorial Gap
>
> he studies me. Mark's a poet too, if you take
> the thought for the deed—but who am I to talk?

Leithauser clearly means to be lightly humorous when
he comments on the pedantically phrased "Sartorial
Gap" and when he alludes to a period of writer's block—
"but who am I to talk?"—he's attempting to struggle
through by writing parodies (many of them unfortunately presented in the poem). But what the reader
notices is the author's self-regarding sense of superi-
ority. The poem leaves little doubt that Leithauser thinks
he indeed *is* the one to talk. The reader is unlikely to
share Leithauser's glee that he can manage it all. Com-
pounding their problems of tone, these autobiographical narratives are written in sloppily irregular iambic
pentameter and are filled with awkward verbal tricks
such as "roundabouting" and clumsy line breaks like
"trap-/pings." Like their narrator, they are quite sim-

ply pedestrian.

Even at his best, Brad Leithauser's achievement hardly justifies his extravagant reputation. One palpably misses in his poetry a serious moral vision, a sense of life's complexity, a recognition of something more profound than shimmering surfaces. Because Leithauser's poems are seldom animated by a profound emotion or a complexly engaging human situation, his use of form seems finally superficial. Meter and rhyme, like the shape of some of his stanzas, are used primarily to embellish Leithauser's fanciful observations. As such, form functions in his work at best to produce minor poems of mildly pleasing artifice.

III

Like Brad Leithauser, Timothy Steele has published two books of formal verse, *Uncertainties and Rest* (1979) and *Sapphics Against Anger* (1986). Though his reputation is modest compared to Leithauser's, he is a more accomplished poet. Of the poets under consideration here, Steele is the most strongly influenced by the Winters/Cunningham Stanford school of formal verse. The Stanford style is characterized by strict adherence to traditional meters, almost always iambic, a devotion to the "plain style" of Ben Jonson, paraphrasable intellectual argument, and emphasis on reason controlling emotion. As Such, Steele's poetry is visually less exciting than Leithauser's, and his strict metricality can, at times, lull the reader with its rhythmic uniformity. He rarely surprises one. Yet on the whole, Steele's use of form is crisp and verbally precise. He uses rhyme to sharpen his perceptions, and his range is wide enough to include ideas. Indeed, he possesses a distinctly neoclassic sensibility which enables him to write clearly on any number of subjects: the landscapes of his Vermont youth and of his California adulthood, literary and historical figures, movies, philosophical ideas. He is a particularly strong love poet and, unlike Leithauser, an accomplished epigrammatist.

"The Sheets," on a first reading, seems one of Steele's slighter accomplishments, a poem perhaps too close in its imagery to Richard Wilbur's celebrated "Love Calls Us to the Things of the World." It does, however, showcase a number of Steele's strengths as a poet: his ability to evoke childhood, to capture images sharply, to weave in book-learning effortlessly without destroying the poem's delicate lyricism. The first two of the poem's stanzas present the image of sheet s blowing in the wind "against a backdrop of / A field whose grasses were a green / Intensity of light." The third stanza introduces the children observing the sheets in the wind, the memory of which recalls for the persona the modest epiphany which the poem's remaining stanzas elaborate:

> And thinking of this now recalls
> > Vassari's tale of how
>
> Young Leonardo, charmed of sight,
> Would buy in the loud marketplace
> Caged birds and set them free—thus yielding
> Back to the air which gave him light
> > Lost beauty and lost grace.
>
> So with the sheets: for as they drew
> Clear warming sunlight from the sky,
> They gave to light their rich, clean scent.
> And when, the long day nearly through
> > My cousin Anne and I

> Would take the sheets down from the line,
> We'd fold in baskets their crisp heat,
> Absorbing, as they had, the fine
> Steady exchange of earth and sky,
>   Material and sweet.

Steele doesn't focus his attention on sheets because of their exotic possibilities. Instead, he concentrates on commonplace, even drab objects, and makes them bear the weight of memory, amplifying their significance through the anecdote about Da Vinci, and transforming them into figures, "Material and sweet," of wonder as they absorb both earth and sky. Steele uses form here to strengthen memory, to deepen emotion, not merely as a foundation for verbal effects.

What is particularly pleasing about Steele's poetry is how its metrical fluency reinforces a clear, thoughtful and generous human voice. "Sapphics Against Anger" deftly displays this merging of form and voice. Steele adapts a rarely-used classical verse form, the sapphic, which normally contains three lines of eleven syllables and a fourth of five syllables, to underline his belief that anger—passion in general—must be controlled, given form:

> For what is, after all, the good life save that
> Conducted thoughtfully, and what is passion
> if not the holiest of powers, sustaining
>   Only if mastered.

This stanza forms the ethical and aesthetic core of Steele's work and can be read, as well, as one of the crucial critical statements of the New Formalist movement. Here and elsewhere, Steele reflects the New Formalist's desire to escape from the kind of extreme, frantic emotions explored in the personal lyrics of the confessional poets.

Regrettably, Steele isn't as flexible in his choice of forms as he is in the range of his subjects. There is a reactionary strain in his poetics (though not in his politics). He writes as if the Modernist movement had never occurred. One looks in vain for narrative or imagistic leaps in Steele's poetry. And, if his poetry is more philosophically sophisticated than Leithauser's, he nonetheless shares an overly benign view of human nature. He is particularly even-tempered on all occasions. Yet he works extremely well within the strict stylistic limits he imposes upon himself. His imagination is lively enough, and his intelligence human enough, to avoid the sterility that constrains other poets of the Stanford school. Steele projects a strong personal voice that is musical as well as morally and imagistically astute. He is a poet with a mature vision clearly conveyed through his skillful use of meter and rhyme.

IV

Charles Martin, like Timothy Steele, also impresses one with his intelligence, the range of his interests, the technical mastery of his verse. But whereas Steele, at his best, bears his knowledge effortlessly, Martin's poetry labors more heavily under the burden of its erudition. In Martin's case, this learning ultimately proves a strength, but it also renders his verse less immediately accessible and likable than Steele's. *Room for Error* (1978), the first of Martin's two volumes, was an impressive debut, though it went virtually unnoticed when it was published by The University of Georgia Press, and has since become almost impossible to find. His second, *Steal the Bacon*, published by Johns Hopkins, should find him a wider audience.

In *Room for Error*, it is apparent that Martin has been influenced by Pound, the central Modernist poet, whose aesthetic innovations Steele rejects. This influence is most notable in the long poem "Calvus in Ruins," a Poundian recreation of a Roman manuscript by the poet Gaius Licinius Macer Calvus, a contemporary of Catullus's of whose work only a few tantalizing fragments survive. This exuberant experiment is perhaps Martin's most interesting achievement.

While Steele's poems speak lucidly in a plain style, Martin's language tends to be denser; his meanings have to be worked through more carefully. Martin proclaims his own challenging aesthetic in "The Dance," one of four poems for Theodore Roethke: "Wild speech took place behind a formal mask." One might offer a variation on this line to summarize Steele's aesthetic as "Mild speech took shape behind a formal mask." Steele would have form mastering passion and not existing in Martin's more charged equation of the two. Much of Martin's "wild speech" in his first volume is erotic and clearly has its source in Catullus, whom Martin has translated. This influence is strongest in "Calvus in Ruins" where the language and subject matter imitated from erotic Latin poetry—in a manner recalling Pound's "Homage to Sextus Propertius"—so strongly dominate that Martin isn't afraid to abandon regular form. Instead, he plays with form, with language erasing itself—a motif that runs throughout his poems—in the instance of gaps in a disintegrating manuscript. But his tension between erotically charged language and form is also responsible for a tightly balanced and intellectually provocative lyric quite outside of Steele's range. The poem, "Satyr, Cunnilinguent: To Herman Melville," juxtaposes a scene of cunnilingus with, astonishingly enough, this meditation on *Billy Budd*:

Flesh cancels mystery:
Had Billy a young bride
As Ahab had, would he
Not have been less tongue-tied?

Might not he have been
Glib in the face of darkness?
—As you yourself, in
Some moods seem to practice

The clever, tongue-in-cheek
Art of the cunning Satyr.
How hard it is to speak
Of the things that matter.

The playing off of language with sexuality here is expertly done, Budd's sexual repression leading to his silence, his tongue-tiedness, his inability "to speak / Of the things that matter." Martin, however, manages to speak of such things through his juxtaposition of subject matter and through the tension he sets up between provocative language and precise form.

Some of this tension is lost in *Steal the Bacon*. One misses, in particular, the felicitous influence of Catullus. Martin compensates for this loss of erotic daring with a more unified volume focused on the poet's preoccupation with the origins, uses and abuses of language. This theme is announced in the book's initial poem, " Complaint of the Night Watchman," whose subject is the Tower of Babel, man's fall into language. Language is central as well to the long narrative poem, "Passages from Friday," which retells *Robinson Crusoe* from Friday's perspective. In this poem, Martin dramatizes the movement from a mythopoeic to a "civilized" discourse represented by Crusoe's eighteenth-century English, the Master's tongue, skillfully recreated by Martin. The poem is at its most ingenious when it deals with the interconnection between these discourses. Friday's acquisition of English, for instance, is counter-pointed by Crusoe's psychic disintegration. By the end of the poem, we are presented with the ambivalent image of Friday setting out to escape the island for Europe, dressing in the "Apparell" of the dead Crusoe, confused about his identity:

> for it was not I who set out, nor was it him,
> nor was it the both of us to-gether;
> I know not who it was; but, as in my Dream
> of the Night befor, when I was neither
>
> *Master* nor *Friday*, but I partook of each...

These lines suggest the range of Martin's linguistic invention even as they test language's limitations, its ability to create for one a stable identity.

Clearly, writing in form doesn't curtail Martin's diction or the complexity of his ideas. His questioning of language's limits, his concerns with the connection between the acquisition of language and the constitution of the self and with decomposed texts, align Martin with the thematics of deconstruction. This connection, though, is problematic. For, however ontologically insecure Friday might be with his newly-acquired language, Martin, in another strong poem, "E.S.L," told from the perspective of an English as Second Language teacher (Martin teaches E.S.L. in New York City), equates the ability to survive in a culture with the ability to master its language. Nevertheless, Martin's questioning of language's limits, combined with a complex sense of its possibilities, sets him apart from Leithauser and Steele. He is a more ambitious poet than either, more willing to take formal risks. One does miss, in many of his poems on domestic life in *Steal the Bacon*, the engaging personal voice that is so compelling in Steele, as well as in Schnackenberg and Gioia. But, at his best, Charles Martin uses traditional form inventively to produce a poetry of intellectual vigor and linguistic excitement.

V

Gjertrud Schnackenberg's first two volumes, *Portraits and Elegies* (1982) and *The Lamplit Answer* (1985), have received considerable attention. Although the first collection was indebted to Robert Lowell, the human feeling underlying the book, combined with a mastery of meter and rhyme and a lyric sense of ordering sequences, made it a poised and distinguished debut. The source of its inspiration is memory. This concern is rooted in the poet's love for her father, a history professor, whose death generates the volume's opening sequence of elegies, "Laughing with One Eye." It also haunts the volume's other two sections. The first of these, "Darwin in 1881," is a narrative poem reviewing Darwin's life a year before his death. If Darwin, with his devotion to making sense of the natural world, serves as an appropriate symbol for Schnackenberg's father, the poem is nonetheless more distanced than the others in the book and burdened with too much literary luggage. The final section, "19 Hadley Street," a sequence of short poems tracing the history of a Massachusetts house from the present back to the early Eighteenth century, is more successful. Here Schnackenberg's focus on quotidian details—including a man's death by cancer, plangently counterpointed by a poem describing the early days of his marriage--makes the poems' historical concerns with witchcraft and the Civil War immediately felt.

Schnackenberg's strengths are most fully displayed in "Laughing with One Eye." In this sequence, the poet's concern with form and memory grows out of the very real loss of her father. Memory, meter and form help the poet compensate for this loss even as they help to recreate her father's life in art, for Schnackenberg realizes that "death alone makes life a masterpiece," that death is the closure which finally gives life form. This sequence links twelve poems whose basic verse unit—varied frequently and pointedly—is the iambic pentameter quatrain. The poems attempt to come to terms with the father's death by circling back on incidents in the poet's shared life with him—fishing on a lake before dawn, travelling in Europe—in which death was a felt presence.

The fluidity of Schnackenberg's technique is most evident in her rendering of three dreams after her father's death that are interspersed throughout the sequence. The first of these poems titled "A Dream" shows Schnackenberg at her most impressive:

> *Death makes of your abandoned face*
> *A secret house an empty place*
> *And I come back wanting that much*
> *To ask you to come back I touch*
>
> *The door where are you it's so black*
> *The taste of smoke is smoke I back*
> *Away when creeping lines of fire*
> *Appear and travel faster higher*
>
> *Where are you and beneath the floor*
> *God turns the gas jets up they soar*
> *The way flames soar and I should run*
> *And blackness burning like the sun*

All empty underneath my hair
I start to chuckle where oh where
My brimming eyes don't understand
I press my grin against my hand

Schnackenberg expertly balances the strange logic and jagged syntax of the dream, with its shocking and irrational chuckle and grin in the final stanza, against the quickened, unpunctuated tetrameter lines and the fully regular rhymed couplets in quatrains. Schnackenberg heightens one's sense of inhabiting a dream by her smooth use of enjambment, including between stanzas. The tension she sets up between form and dream logic argues eloquently for the inventiveness of formal verse at its most skillful. This poem takes risks and triumphs gracefully.

The Lamplit Answer, a more problematic book, is more ambitious than the first. But as Schnackenberg attempts to expand her range, she seems to be straining herself beyond her natural gifts. The book contains a number of carefully written but ultimately dull longer poems. "Imaginary Prisons" is an intricately-woven but exceedingly leaden variation on Sleeping Beauty. Schnackenberg's attempts at light verse, including some overly clever—and personal—love poems are little more successful. Her self-conscious love poem, "Sonata"—which meditates on how to write a love poem in the form of a sonata with variations—fails to interest the reader in the process. Although it gives one the opportunity to see the poet grappling with form, here her colloquial tone seems glaringly incompetent in comparison to the sublimity of her language elsewhere.

But Schnackenberg's failures are more interesting than most poets' successes. And the book's many flaws are largely compensated for by its final three poems. The

last of these, "Supernatural Love," is an exquisite meditation on the beginnings of a poetic imagination. Significantly, the poem returns to the subject of the father. It juxtaposes the father's poring over a dictionary to track down the full meaning of the word "car-
nation" as his then "illiterate" four-year-old daughter
works on a needlepoint of the word "beloved," though
she's unable to read it. The dictionary definitions the
father comes up with augment the daughter's poetic
belief that carnations are "Christ's flowers": "A pink
variety of Clove, / *Carnatio*, the Latin, meaning flesh,"
the father intones. Thus, when she pricks her finger
with the needle she's using, the young poet can accommodate the father's dictionary knowledge to her
own poetic conception:

> The needle strikes my finger to the bone.
> I lift my hand, it is myself I've sewn,
> The flesh laid bare, the thread of blood my own,
>
> I lift my hand in startled agony
> And call upon his name, "Daddy daddy"—
> My father's hand touches the injury
>
> As lightly as he touched the page before,
> Where incarnation bloomed from roots that bore
> The flowers I called Christ when I was four.

Schnackenberg implies in "Supernatural Love" that
poetry, with its recourse to memory, can reunite past
and present, return the child to the lost father and to
a scene of her poetic origins, the very act of recreating
this scene transforming the writing of the poem into a
kind of "supernatural love." Schnackenberg's work to
this point is erratic, though her talent is immense. As
"A Dream " and "Supernatural Love" clearly attest,

she has already written a few of the finest poems of
her generation.

VI

Dana Gioia, a New York businessman, is perhaps
the most versatile poet associated with the New Formalist movement. He is unquestionably its most complete man of letters. In his reviews, poetry chronicles
and literary essays that have appeared regularly for
the past decade in many prominent quarterlies, especially
The Hudson Review , Gioia has established himself as
one of the most perceptive and engaged critics of contemporary poetry. In an era that celebrates "the death
of the author"—to use Roland Barthes's influential
phrase—and that spends much of its critical energy
bloodlessly deconstructing "texts," Gioia has, with unfashionable eloquence, continued to insist that poetry
derives from a distinct human voice. This devotion to
the poet as well as to poetry is reflected in his poignant memoirs of Elizabeth Bishop and John Cheever. It
is also evident in his efforts to establish Weldon Kees
as one of the central mid-century American poets, the
most notable being his editing of Kees's selected stories,
The Ceremony (1984). More recently, Gioia has published
what amounts to nothing less than the elegant manifesto of the New Formalist movement, "Notes on the
New Formalism." Here he argues persuasively the irony
that "[f]ree verse, the creation of an older literary revolution, is now the long-established, ruling orthodoxy;
formal poetry the unexpected challenge." Nowhere is
the formidability of this challenge more apparent than
in Gioia's much-anticipated first volume of poems, *Daily
Horoscope* (1986), easily the most significant debut of

the movement.

What distinguishes Gioia from the other poets under consideration here is the consistent excellence of the poems in *Daily Horoscope* and the fact that the individual poems are given deeper resonance by their careful placement within the volume's five wide-ranging yet thematically integrated sections. Gioia writes with masterful ease in poems which explore the conflicts between business and poetry, the vagaries of love and commitment, the poet's rueful sense of exile in the modern world. So strong is his ear, so innate his sense of form and strict metrical patterns that he can abandon both to write in free verse without losing the distinct clarity of phrasing and the strong musical cadences one associates with them. Gioia can also be ingeniously experimental in his use of meter and form, leading Frederick Turner to call him, in an interview in *The Southwest Review* , "the most radical, the most revolutionary" of the poets dedicated, through a return to form and narrative, to restoring poetry to a popular audience. The line breaks in "In Chandler Country" give the poem the look on the page of free verse. But in this poem Gioia experiments with the shape of a poem written in particularly intense blank verse. In so playing with the lines of the poem, Gioia can simulate the looser lines of the hard-boiled prose that is the source of the poem's language, even as, by elevating the prose to the level of blank verse, he can comment on the poetic element in Raymond Chandler's fiction.

Gioia is a poet whose stoic acceptance of the quotidian, of the necessity of living daily, does not prevent him from pressing against the limitations of the real world to discover, in *Daily Horoscope's* title sequence, that "in a moment's pause another world / reveals itself behind the ordinary." Gioia's persistent search for some transcendent order of love or beauty existing somewhere "behind the ordinary" world has yielded an unusually impressive number of delicately rendered lyrics: "The Burning Ladder," "California Hills in August," the exquisite, elegiac love poems "Parts of Summer Weather" and "The End of a Season." But perhaps Gioia's most engaging lyric is the autobiographical "Cruising with the BeachBoys." Nowhere does the poet risk the dangers of sentimentality more daringly than he does here. It is Gioia's deft use of meter and rhyme, combined with his gently ironic tone, that makes the poem so notable. This Wordsworthian lyric is generated by an apparently trivial incident in the present—in this case "one old song" of the Beach Boys heard on a car radio on a business trip that finds the poet "Miles from anywhere I've been before"—which brings back his past with great specificity and extreme emotion. Gioia's use of rhyme is particularly supple and effective, especially in the poem's final two stanzas which present him in his most vulnerable and moving voice:

> Some nights I drove down to the beach to park
> And walk along the railings of the pier.
> The water down below was cold and dark,
> The waves monotonous against the shore.
> The darkness and the mist, the midnight sea,
> The flickering lights reflected from the city—
> A perfect setting for a boy like me,
> The Cecil B. DeMille of my self-pity.
>
> I thought by now I'd left those nights behind,
> Lost like the girls that I could never get,
> Gone with the years, junked with the old T-Bird.
> But one old song, a stretch of empty road,
> Can open up a door and let them fall

Tumbling like boxes from a dusty shelf,
Tightening my throat for no reason at all
Bringing on tears shed only for myself.

The quiet tension that Gioia achieves here between the formal precision of his language and the deep emotion that tightens the persona's throat "for no reason at all" is what makes the poem work so exquisitely. It enables the poet to evoke the sensation of self-pity without succumbing to it in the manner of the confessional poets. "Cruising with the Beach Boys" represents the strongest example of the distinctive, calm, and engagingly human voice that the New Formalists most characteristically strive for, though few achieve, in their personal lyrics. This is the opposite of a lifeless artifact. In Gioia's expert hands, technique is charged with the poem's animating emotion.

Eschewing the personal voice, Gioia demonstrates his range in "The Room Upstairs," a psychologically astute dramatic monologue with a sure sense of narrative pace. The poem is spoken in the voice of an aging college professor, a bachelor who, over the years, has rented out a room in his house to students. The arrival of yet another young man provokes the professor, almost against his will, to recount the eerie tale of an earlier young boarder who died, years ago, in a climbing accident. The reminiscence develops into a hauntingly beautiful tale of necrophilic love; the passion evaded in life is consummated in a dream. The night the student dies, the sleeping professor finds himself in a room flooded with light like "the soft whiteness that you see / When heavy snow is falling in the morning." In this room the dead student appears to him and makes his appeal:

And only then I saw his skin was bruised,
Torn in places, crossed by deep red welts,
But this time everywhere—as if his veins
Had pushed up to the surface and spilled out.
And there was nothing in his body now,
Nothing but the voice that spoke to me,
And this cold white light pouring through the room.

I stared at him. His skin was bright and pale.
"Why are you doing this to me?" I asked.
 "Please, go away."
                        "But I've come back to you.
I'm cold. Just hold me. I'm so very cold."

What else could I have done but hold him there?
I took him in my arms—he was so light—
And held him in the doorway listening.
Nothing else was said or lost it seemed.
I waited there while it grew dark again,
And he grew lighter, slipping silently away
Like snow between my fingers, and was gone.

The regular iambic pentameter lines in "The Room
Upstairs" provide the calm basis from which Gioia's
narrator takes off into an extravagant, phantasmagoric
scene. The poem's metrical regularity simulates the
reserved nature of the speaker who could not have
presented such a vivid image of his homoerotic nature
except under the guise of polite decorum. Indeed, after this finely-wrought vision, the professor distances
himself from his extraordinary narrative—"That's all
there is to say. I can't explain it, / And now I'm sorry
to have bored you so"—and returns to his role as gra-
cious host, showing his new tenant to his room.

Between the polite conversation that frames the
professor's narrative, decorum has quietly but devas-
tatingly been shattered, and the reader, like the young

man addressed by the narrator, has been given access to an aspect of human experience of nightmarish beauty. In poem after poem in *Daily Horoscope* Dana Gioia uses meter and rhyme as starting points to generate deep emotion, to propel the reader from the precision of the poet's sharp observations of the quotidian into a sudden recognition of beauty and strangeness piercing, however briefly, the mundane. He performs, again and again, the duty of the truly original artist: He enables us to see the world anew. In combining the powers of form and narrative, Dana Gioia is the poet who most fully realizes the potential of the New Formalist movement.

VII

American poetry in the 80s is clearly at a crossroads. The return to rhyme and meter by a significant number of young poets has stirred considerable controversy within the literary establishment. Thus far, this ferment has been registered largely in generalized attacks by those for whom free verse represents "democratic," "American" values—despite the fact that it is hardly an exclusively American phenomenon. How cultural historians will view the significance of the New Formalists' challenge to what had become the established aesthetic of free verse remains to be seen. It is obvious, though, that the New Formalism is too formidable a movement to ignore or to dismiss offhand. At one time, it seemed liberating to be freed from the constraints of the iambic pentameter line. Such a liberation has resulted in exciting innovations and a widened range of poetic possibilities. Yet as poetry drifted closer and closer to prose, much was lost as well as gained. In reading the poetry of the best of the New Formalists, one senses not a reactionary retreat from the once radical challenge of "open" forms but instead an exhilarating recovery of much of what one had forgotten to expect from poetry: a purity of language, a clarity of cadence, a distinct musical rhythm. This renewed vitality that the New Formalists have brought to contemporary poetry will inevitably influence the direction it will take as the century draws to its close.

POETRY AND AUDIENCE

By Robert McDowell

Poets have always debated the existence, size, and importance of audience because a vision of The Reader is inseparable from what poets imagine they see when they look at themselves. As the twentieth century lumbers to its close, poets beginning to look back on it can recognize a prolonged period during which their self-esteem has disintegrated. It may well be that poets have never felt as inferior and as useless as they do today.

Their feelings are understandable. The American generations of this century have been increasingly brought up to deny the importance of poetry in daily life. Anyone who cares to can find countless examples in print to back up this assertion, but none that I have seen is quite as deliciously pithy as the recent comment made by a Philadelphia land surveyor. As I talked to him about poetry and the problems of audience, he finally cut me off.

"Yes," he said, "but poetry isn't what this country is about. Our thing is to make money. That's what we do." And he was right, even though most American poets decidedly do not.

The surveyor, in his mid-fifties, had summed up in three sentences the attitude of his generation. This attitude has provided a ready foil for American poets who have assumed an adversarial posture that has found its most explosive expression in the prophetic mode

Reprinted by permission from *Poets & Writers Magazine* (October 1988)

of Allen Ginsberg and the cryptic social criticism that flowered in the American verse of the sixties. For a short time, poetry seemed almost popular. The reading series flourished everywhere, and enrollments in poetry workshops swelled.

By the mid-seventies, however, interest in poetry seemed to be dissipating as poets turned from broad social concerns to explore more personal agendas. As the audience apparently dwindled, poets groused among themselves and generally agreed that in American writing fiction was "happening;" poetry was not. Even now when the question of audience comes up among poets and poetry's supporters, the most common response is a shrug of the shoulders followed by the claim that poetry's audience has always been small.

Though poetry sales figures and the low incomes of most poets support this view, poets are far from happy about it. I have heard, and so have you, poets complain that they are not offered six-figure contracts for new books of verse, that their poems are not attractive to book clubs or the mass-market paperback industry, that they are never adapted for television or the movies. What they complain of is true enough, but their laments do not really have anything to do with the actual audience for poetry or the problem of developing a larger audience. Their complaints do, however, give us reason to examine the poet's inferiority complex.

What is the poet measuring himself against that he feels so undervalued? If Americans have been trained to disregard the importance of poetry, then poets have been affected by such training, too. It should come as no surprise to anyone that ours is a star-worshiping culture. Celebrity is synonymous with money, and spiritual, communal, and aesthetic accomplishments are rarely admired or supported in our prevailing weather.

When poets measure their wares against the bestsellers and the products of cinema and television, they walk willingly into a downpour that will not comfort or reward them. Bitter and despairing, they take for granted the small audience they do have and cynically laugh off any proposed attempt to enlarge the audience or develop untapped ones. This is simply a modification of a self-defeating prophecy. If poets will improve their lot, they must examine the audience they do have, its strengths and weaknesses, and seriously consider what can be done to develop the vast potential audience, which is currently ignored.

What is the contemporary audience for poetry in America, and what is the potential audience?

Because it is small, I call the former the *pocket* audience. Rooted in the academy, it consists of writing workshop students, other poets, friends of poets, and a few eccentrics—the "friends" of the art. The *potential* audience for poetry, the indifferent audience, consists of everyone else who can read.

The strength of the pocket audience resides in its animated interest in the art. Members of this group read publications, attend readings and classes, and now and then even buy books. The potential audience's strength is housed in its sheer size and its ability to read at all. If people making up the potential audience ever did come to poetry, they would do just as well reading it as members of the pocket audience.

If their strengths distinctly separate these two audiences, their weaknesses reveal remarakble similarities. Members of both groups, affected by the "hurry-up offense" that is the pace of everyday life, believe in subjective response to any stimulus, even literature. Often lacking the patience, initiative, and thinking skills required to understand tradition, the pocket audience cannot tell good poems from bad while the potential audience shies away from poetry altogether, preferring prose, television, movies, and other diversions. Both audiences will most likely make embarrassing qualitative judgements. For example, few can tell the difference, in any form of writing, between sentiment (original expression of emotion, as in Yeats, Dickinson, etc.) and sentimentality (expression of emotion that is borrowed or lifted from another's life or expression, as in the work, in any age, that dominates literary publications). What both audiences seem to want most now (when they read) is writing that evokes a longing for days gone by—how it felt when the spouse left, the parent or dog died, the treasured neighborhood field was paved.

What horrible chaos have we educated ourselves into? Whereas language once corresponded, as it did in the Elizabethan age, to the entire field of human experience, today it corresponds to shrinking fields of specialization from which we cannot even agree what our common language is. The computer weenie is mute in the company of a literature professor, who in turn has little to say to his colleague from the school for business. Locked into private zones of interest, we are finding that our common language has never been so poorly reconciled with our needs, fears, and desires.

> And you, whiner, who wastes your time
> Dawdling over the remorseless earth,
> What evil, what unspeakable crime
> Have you made your life worth?

> (W. D. Snodgrass "After Experience Taught Me...,)

If our common language grows more remote, most poets are doing little to reacquaint us with it. This can be seen in the way they ignore the potential audience while smirking over their shared assumption that widely consumed poetry must be bad poetry. They embrace this notion while pointing at, and dismissing, someone like Rod McKuen. His books sell millions of copies, and he is a bad poet. But it is a mistake to assume a relationship between the popularity of a product and its quality. Yes, McKuen is a bad poet, and worse poets enjoy more critical acclaim while selling very few books. McKuen, unlike his peers, has understood the market.

The market he so thoroughly masters is almost exclusively made up of the potential audience. It is the same market worked so well by the Hallmark Card industry. Anyone who doubts that the potential audience, on occasion, desires some form of poetry should consider the sales achieved each year by McKuen, Hallmark, and other concerns of their ilk.

If we hope to improve the condition of the pocket audience while attracting its potential counterpart, thereby expanding the audience for poetry even more, some drastic shifts of focus must occur. The agents that can best bring about these shifts include the publishing industry, poets themselves, and the academy.

Occasionally, one hears the naive argument that poetry should somehow make better use of the media. Public television already offers programs, now and then, on which poets are interviewed and read their work. They do not last long, and the usual explanation for their failure is a lack of funding. Performance Poetry on video is hyped by some as attractive and effective exposure, but it only crudely imitates popular entertainment stripped of the slick production values. Other possibilities for poetry making inroads to the media do not really exist. That is not bad. The media, that great leveler, has nothing in common with art. It will do nothing to increase the audience for poetry, unless poetry apes the media's already successful and familiar products, its sitcoms and rock videos.

If any entity could increase the audience for poetry, one might easily assume that it would be publishing. but in that industry the book of poems is a marginal enterprise. Even the small press publisher, who may commence operations with the best of intentions where poetry is concerned, quickly discovers that he must rely on fiction and nonfiction titles if he will stay in business. When a book of poems does appear, a notice in a trade journal may stimulate preliminary sales; the publisher may take out ads (which do not enhance sales in the least but make the author feel good) in literary quarterlies that have been kind to the author's work; scattered reviews, if they appear, will generate some sales. But unfortunately, the majority of bookstores now practice a form of censorship by refusing to order books from any source other than major national wholesalers and the publishers in New York. This severely damages the enterprising small press and is especially crippling to the sales of poetry.

The situation would improve if publishers funneled some of the initial heavy promotion (i.e. organizing author tours, book signings and television and radio appearances) to poetry that is currently reserved for fiction and nonfiction. Unfortunately, there is no indication that publishers have the confidence and bravery to do this. When Random House brought out Vikram Seth's *The Golden Gate*, it did so in a cloth edition of thirty-five thousand copies, which enjoyed the promotion usually reserved for books of fiction that are expected to do well. To hedge its bet that the book would succeed, the publisher billed it as a "novel-in-verse." The book did well. Eeventually, it appeared on the London *Times* bestseller list. But when the trade paperback edition appeared, the book's billing was condensed to "a novel."

What does this suggest? On the one hand, it implies that a significant readership, much larger than anyone anticipated, was willing to accept story-telling in the shape of poetry—and traditional verse at that. On the other hand, it points out the reluctance with which publishers commit to and promote poetry. It is as if publishers believe that they must hoodwink an audience in order to get it to buy poetry. This timidity and cunning flies in the face of the evidence, which suggests that some poetry, at least, appeals to a larger audience.

Most poets today do not really believe this. They flatter the intelligence of their pocket audiences with sentimental snapshots, slack lines, and meandering abstractions. Frequently, they share their readers' ignorance with regard to history. The alternative need not be that our poets become businessmen, choosing Rod McKuen as their model. But they would be wise to remember the past and bring some business savvy to the task of creating a larger poetry audience. Yeats and Eliot, through their plays and criticism, greatly increased poetry's audience in their time; Eliot working in publishing, and Pound, promoting everywhere, also created audiences where none had been. These are indispensible models for contemporary poets. Poets could also help themselves, and poetry, by better understanding book publication, distribution, and marketing. It is surprising how few possess even a rudimentary knowledge of these activities that are so pertinent to the presentation and distribution of their art. In addition, they should work more closely with local arts

foundations to develop proposals for symposia, readings, conferences, and workshops that could attract larger
audiences in their communities, for larger audiences
nationally are always developed through a coalition
of smaller, regional audiences. This last claim is in keeping with the American tradition that the best regional
literature of any period always *becomes* the national
literature in retrospect.

Unfortunately, most contemporary poets spend too
little time considering their situations and responsibilities
in the world to contribute much to a community. Poorly
educated, accepting their social impotence, they cling
to their close circle of peers, keeping one desperate
eye on academic job lists and grants deadlines, and
one on some vague, vindicated seat in the lofty Dress
Circle of posterity. If poets do not tell the truth, then
few will ever listen. Telling the truth requires that
one know it first; living it helps, but little of that goes
on today because too many poets supported by universities have erected insulated lifestyles.

If poets hope to improve their pocket audience and
draw new readers from the potential audience, they
might consider getting out of the university and working elsewhere after, at most, a five-year stint. Perhaps
an organization modeled after the Peace Corps—Poets'
Corp?—should be formed to drag poets out of themselves and periodically put them to work where the
experience would benefit both themselves and the
community.

Poets can also work to overcome the now popular
timidity that keeps most from engaging in public argument about poetry. isagreement enjoys an honored
tradition in literature. The arguments of someone like
Ezra Pound serve the two-fold purpose of preserving
poetry's traditions by reassessing them and advancing

the art by introducing and debating current work. Of course, many poets would have to become better readers themselves to carry out such a project, but there are poets with the tools who are unwilling to use them. This is yet another glaring manifestation of decades of insular inferiority. Rather than stimulate audience by grappling with the art as it evolves, many pots prefer to remain silent, fearing controversy that might endanger the invitation they hope to receive to the conference, the reading they are counting on at the university, or the publication in the magazine that seems almost ready to accept their work. Often, it seems that poets spend more time on rituals of petty courtship than on writing and analyzing poetry. No doubt this will change. It must.

Meanwhile, poets can also appeal to a larger audience through the poetry they write. Poetry, at its best, has always been a storyteller's art. But most of the poetry published in this country since 1950 has not been written by storytellers (we might extend this to most of the poetry *ever* published in this country, but then no one remembers it anyway). Most of the poems written in the popular forms of the last forty years— the lyric, meditation, the essay-in-verse—have been created by writers who accept the inaccurate assumption that the good storyteller, the writer speaking directly to others, works best in prose. Most have forgotten, or never knew, that the lyric and meditation are most memorable as the lament or celebration, the reflection or speculation, of a character in an atmosphere of dramatic crisis. Most have never known that the essay-in-verse cannot work because an essay presents and explores concepts, not characters. Thus, most of our poetry reminds me of this passage by Charles Newman, author of *The Post-Modern Aura*. Newman was focusing on contemporary fiction, but his comments also zero in on the dominant attitude in contemporary poetry:

> "It is nevertheless the strategy of many Post-Modern works to memorialize in every sentence that what is going on is filtered, the product of a sensibility which requires your duration; indeed it is the central premise of such work constantly to remind you, lest you have somehow forgotten, just who is in charge. This is quite different from the traditional omniscient narrator, who, through his proforma power effectively makes the reader forget he is being manipulated-the amnesia we call 'getting swept up in the story'."

Perhaps what we need to attract a larger audience are stories in poetry that are worth getting swept up in, and poets who can tell them. There are precedents for such books: Edwin Arlington Robinson's epics in the twenties, and the verse dramas of his peer, William Vaughn Moody; many of Frost's collections; the entire body of work of Robinson Jeffers; George Keithley's *The Donner Party* in the seventies. All of these authors who endeavored to tell stories in poetry found large audiences outside the pocket, or academic audience.

Obviously, building a larger audience would be greatly facilitated by meaningful contributions in education. But poetry is'nt taught at any level of the current American system with any degree of consistent success. It is not even outrageous today to suggest that our ability to read poetry has been bred out of us. Students spend twelve years in the grammar schools and high schools, yet when they come to college, if they come at all, how well prepared are they? Do they read and think well? If they enter the work force rather than continuing their education, do they value reading, language, thought?

This is not a situation in which the teacher appears in a flattering light. How many, at any level, effectively present poetry to their students? How many work to improve their understanding by reading the criticism of poetry (much of the best of it written by poets) and the poetry itself as they would read anything else—one word at a time? If teachers did, they would bring more to the classroom dance. Unfortunately, the size of the potential audience and the limitations of the pocket audience suggest that such efforts are not being made on a large scale.

In my own teaching experience (eight years at the university level), I began many semesters by asking non creative-writing students to respond to the questions *Do you read poetry? Why/Why not?* Most claimed that they had never read poetry on their own. They remembered a brief exposure in high school, which consisted of having to read one or two poems and write about them; a few students remembered memorizing a poem for recitation before the class. Most believed that poetry is made up of "hidden meanings" that are difficult to understand. Many asserted that poetry was off-putting because it rhymed. A few (very few) insisted that they read poetry because they liked reading about love and enjoyed the serene feeling that the reading act created in them. But all of the students agreed that when they wanted to read "the real thing" they preferred prose. I hasten to add that the prose that most of them preferred is found in the magazines and paperbacks of the supermarket check-out lines.

This example suggests that the young American student, whether preparing to enter the academy or the work force, is hardly learned. In the eighties and even now, the goal of almost all education is singular: Earning Power. Students perceive reading only as a text assigned in school. Having no sense of history, they see no connection between what they read and the lives they are living. Few have ever thought that enhancing their command of language would enhance the quality of their thought, and those who do so think of it whimsically, as the workaholic speculates on the world cruise he will never find the time to take.

It is, of course, popular to blame the academy for a semi-literate culture that is rapidly losing touch with its poetry. Some critics, writers, and professors, too, have for years attacked the mediocre humanities programs of our universities. But the popularity of the lament does not negate the truth of it. The faculties of most writing and literature programs are complacent with a tenure system that rewards past performance and ignores the later decline of creative and scholarly achievement. Even most poets who teach succumb to this system, lobbying for more and more release time and sleepwalking through their classes.

The academy always seems to lag at least a decade behind what is happening in poetry. Thus writing and literature students suffer, emerging with distorted views on the state of poetry, views that are already outdated the moment they drive off campus with degrees in hand and destined, in many cases, to lead classes of their own.

Fortunately, many readers of poetry did not learn to read in the academy. The best of them either developed good reading habits early, at home, or quickly discovered that poetry would yield more if they used their classroom experience as a springboard from which they could vault headlong into their own struggling, significant discoveries. These readers of poetry, and potential readers like them, make up the best hope for a larger audience. Still, it is unfortunate that our system of education has contributed so little to their development.

If American culture is ever to grow out of its prolonged adolescence, we must learn to value poetry and nurture it. In order for this to occur, publishers and bookstore owners must wake up, becoming more imaginative and flexible. Poets must rejoin the world and accept the responsibility, as many through the centuries have, for telling its stories. Methods of teaching poetry in our schools must undergo radical improvement. If all of this takes place, we will find the climate for poetry merging harmoniously with the weather of our everyday lives. Then the need to discuss enlarging poetry's audience will be unnecessary. As we careen toward century's end, we can wish for that. We can work for it, too.

"MIGHTY POETS
IN THEIR MISERY DEAD":
A POLEMIC ON THE
CONTEMPORARY POETIC SCENE

By Frederick Turner

Note: (*This essay was written in the early seventies and not published until 1980. Some of its strictures on contemporary poetry
no longer apply, as several poets began to take directions recom-
mended in the essay after its publication.*)

One of the peculiarities of our present literary age is
that future times will find it remarkably difficult to
say of us that "history proved us wrong". The reason
for this is that we take so few real stands on the literary quality of contemporary works. We tolerate almost
any point of view, mindful of those many episodes in
past literary history when strong stands were taken
and duly reversed by posterity.

If there is one crime greater than being wrong, it is
surely that of being incapable of any opinion. Here,
then, is an opinion: that no truly great poetry has been
written in English since the Second World War. There
has been much good poetry, and enormous quantities
of competent poetry: but no Dantes, no Chaucers, no
Shakespeares, no Miltons; not even the equivalent of a
Wordsworth or Eliot. The immediate reply to such a
charge would be that of course there is major poetry,
but we cannot recognize it as such yet. But we are in
no position today to distrust our own judgment, and
we are in positive need of judgment. In literary mat-

First published in *The Missouri Review*, vol. 4, number 1, Fall 1980

ters confidence constitutes a large proportion of rightness; we can indeed be confident and wrong, but there is no way of being unconfident and right.

Rightly or wrongly, I am going to suggest that there are only two chief theories of literary art, and that all other theories can be reduced to one or the other, or contain elements of both. These two theories are the mimetic theory and the poietic theory. The former has had much the best of it, for its basic tents can be easily mapped onto closed philosophic systems, and it provides images of the artist (with his palette, smock, and easel, as it were, set up before a splendid landscape, building, or personage) that are easily assimilated by non-artist and not unflattering to the artist, for it apparently provides him with something objectively valid to do.

A mimetic theory essentially presents the artist as imitating, demonstrating, representing, or counterfeiting—what is so imitated, etc., is not immediately at issue. A work of art, according to this theory, can be praised for its truth, its accuracy, the keenness of its observation, its insight into the human psyche or condition.

A poetic theory, on the other hand, presents the artist as involved in a new creative event, the spontaneous generation of a new part of the world. The artwork cannot be praised for its truth or accuracy, is indeed not so much praised as accepted as a piece of reality.

To my first heresy, of dividing all theories of literary art into two, I am adding a second, which is that only the poietic theory gives a fully adequate account of art, and a third, that it makes a real difference, not only in the type of art that is produced in a given period or tradition, but even in its quality, whether a

poietic or a mimetic theory is generally accepted at
this time. Artists can be liberated or confined by theory; an "artist" who is not conscious enough of what
he is doing to have a theory about it, cannot be called
an artist; an artist who deliberately adopts no theory
is simply adopting a more sophisticated theory, with
its own very abstract assumptions about the nature of
theory, intention, and art.

It is easy to describe the mimetic fallacy. Reality is
in itself generative, creative, processual, "poietic": new
things happen every second everywhere. A genuine
work of art, which is always itself poietic, even when
it is confined by a mimetic theory, is a part, and an
important part, of this process. However, if we conceptually divide art from the creativeness of the universe, and if we become accustomed to this division,
then it is easy to be astonished by how well art has
imitated reality, and to formulate a theory on that basis. The real world is most real when it is most creative and self-generative; and art is the most creative
and self-generative part of the real world. Mimetic theory mistakes this reality for realism. To put all this
more simply and less accurately, one by-product of
successful poiesis is mimesis, but the by-product cannot occur in any other way. Pity the person who takes
the by-product for the purpose and end of art, and
tries to achieve it directly!

The artwork is a part of reality and has its own powerful vote in the future constitution of the world. It
can so influence the language and perceptual world of
its culture as to bring about, finally, a cultural judgment, which then becomes true, of the artwork's marvellous accuracy. More's *Utopia* helped to bring about
the present-day political regimes that so closely resemble
it; so More becomes a prophet when in fact his proph-

ecy is not only self-fulfilling, but not a prophecy at all until it is fulfilled. Life imitates art. On a less paradoxical level, it took us three or four hundred years to see how "accurate" some of Shakespeare's characters are, and more for some of Chaucer's; but the influence on our culture of Chaucer and Shakespeare over all those years is not a mere coincidence. Great art creates its own cultural context.

Metaphorically, and more than metaphorically speaking, a work of art is in its generativeness always at the at the edge of its language-culture-universe system, and it partly constitutes that edge. It is therefore a perfectly reflective surface; it "holds the mirror up to nature"! As the interface between everything and nothing, its refractive index is so great that no fraction of what strikes it is lost, but all is given back. But it can only reflect in this way because it keeps pace with the expansion of the universe, and there is nothing behind it. If an artist takes care of the invention, the realism will take care of itself.

A poietic theory, unlike a mimetic theory, cannot tell one exactly how to invent. But this seems to me more a recommendation of a theory than a defect in it.

Artistic attempts to imitate reality always fail, because the cart has been put before the horse; such attempts always represent what has already ceased to be, the moment it has given up its presentness by being seen; and all that is left is an unnaturally rigid, awkward and frozen tableau or map.

The most "accurate" mimesis, one which eliminated all the blur of motion in what it represented, all the distractions of ambiguity and distortions of change, would of course be a complete blank. If this aspect of mimesis, this nihilistic impulse, becomes a trend in art, it often expresses itself with terrifying power in the char-

acteristic genre of certain mimetic traditions, the suicide poem. The major justification of the suicide poem
is that it purports quintessentially to be the truth. But
I propose that the central quality of art is not psychological truth, or even philosophical or social truth but
poesis, the extent to which art expands the boundaries
of the world. Nor can that central quality be identified
as logical or formal structure, which are the rational
equivalents of the former more empirical demands for
truth. There *is* a poetic truth, but that truth is the ac-
colade of successful fiction: the fiction is so powerful
it *becomes* true.

One of my contentions in this essay is that just as
"classical" mimetic theory acted as a brake on the poetry of the eighteenth century, so a new version, "modern"
mimesis, is doing the same thing to ours.

What are the symptoms of our malaise? Since the
war there has been in English no major narrative poetry; no philosophical poetry; no major religious poetry; no poetry with invented human characters in it;
no important satirical poetry, nothing remotely approaching epic poetry; no verse drama; very little metrical
virtuosity; no truly *learned* poetry, that is, poetry which
can rival in its knowledge of its subject the expertise
of academic specialists; no important allegorical poetry; no great tragic or comic poetry; no major *popular*
poetry worth mentioning; no heroic poetry; and no major
poetic *fantasy*, in the sense of a poem which delights
in its own fictional world for its own sake.

These charges may be disputed severally; and it would
be a good thing if they were. But a more powerful
counter than an argument about the merits of specific
works would be this: the list I have given is a list of
traditional forms and expectations, and we should not
demand of an age as unique as ours that it satisfy the

criteria of the past.

Two replies can be made to this argument; one is that the hallmark of a great literary age is its confident seizing unto itself the genres of the past, as for instance Virgil taking over the epic, Dante taking over the Virgilian descent into Hell, and Milton reworking the whole epic tradition; the great Elizabethan verse drama was a conscious appropriation of the forms of Seneca and Plautus. Milton's *Lycidas* and Wordsworth's *Michael* are readaptations of the pastoral genre. A great genre is not a set of rules but a bundle of stored energy that can be used in many ways. Vast changes in cultural perspective took place between Homer and Milton; this did not prevent the epic from rising again in *Paradise Lost*. Every great work of art transforms and even contradicts its genre; that is what makes it great. And the "stored energy" of a genre is the set of expectations and forms it contains, to be satisfied or deliberately violated. There is no reason why a truly great writer, unembarrassed by a crippling theory of art, should not be able to take up once again the ancient forms and make them speak, as Shakespeare and Milton did, to his or her own age.

The second reply is this: indeed, the charge that the traditional forms of poetry have no great modern exponents would be pointless if great poetic innovations were taking place in response to the challenge of the new age. Unfortunately this is simply not the case. Anglo-Saxon poetry has systematically ignored the enormously exciting developments in thought and action that have gone on around it. There is no major poem dealing with the central political conflict of our time, between liberal capitalism and totalitarian communism; hardly a poem that even shows an understanding of relativity or quantum theory, let alone treats them in a poetically embracing way; nothing that deals with the moral, aesthetic and philosophical questions raised by the new developments in biology that promise that most ancient of poetic fantasies, artificial life; nothing that confronts the philosophical issues raised by Wittgenstein and the linguistic philosophers on one hand, or the phenomenologists on the other. The great advances in the understanding of language which resulted from contextual linguistics and the study of generative grammar have had little or no effect on poetry—indeed the modern insistence on poetic economy, which leaves out syntagmata and syntax from poetry as much as possible, directly contradicts what we have learnt from the linguists, which is that grammar is not merely a way of arranging words, that can be improved on in poetry, but is the essence of language itself; contemporary "concrete" poetry, which is itself no innovation, similarly eviscerates language. Though there is plenty of talk about a "new metrics" and "projective verse," the talk is generally more interesting than the actual rhythmic effects (or rather, lack of rhythmic effect) they produce. The emperor too often has no clothes. Again, there has been hardly any poetic response to the great technological adventures of our times; the exploration of the moon and the planets, the ocean-bottoms, the remote places of the earth, the new understanding of the world of animals, the conquest of natural barriers that once seemed insuperable. What response there has been is usually rather snide or embarrassed. It is arguable that many contemporary nature poets are responding to scientific discoveries in the area of ecology, but their poetry is too often a warmed-over Romanticism without the philosophic interest of much Romantic poetry, displaying not so much an understanding of the facts of biology as a sentimental desire to escape the challenges of human culture.

A more thorough analysis of what kinds of poetry contemporary poets do write today is obviously necessary. The stock postwar poem is a relatively short lyric of between a hundred and four hundred words (enough to fit a single sheet of typewriting paper) divided into about twenty lines. A few are somewhat shorter or somewhat longer. To some extent these physical dimensions are a response to the technology of publication (magazines and collections of poems vaguely and often retrospectively organized around a theme). In subject matter, many deal with personal and subjective matters in a manner which ranges from the detached and the whimsical to the starkly confessional. Perhaps this is the largest group. A similar body of poems, rather hard to distinguish from the first, deals with family and domestic incidents of one kind or another. A very large number of poems are essentially descriptions of nature, ranging from meditations in which objects of the poet's perception are merely the puppets of his more personal thought, to attempts at an entirely "objective" rendering in words of the processes of the outside world. Such latter poems are often defiantly ideological in purpose, however, in that they implicitly or explicitly reject the value of human consciousness, culture, and society, and opt for the "primal" forces and truths of the "way things are." Another fairly large category is the love poem— which is usually an elaborate, and often interestingly ingenious attempt to ward off any accusation of sentimentality in advance. There are also a number of overtly ideological poems which condemn war, lament modern developments in technology and socio-economic organization, praise primitive, ancient or foreign cultures, and attack the "values of the middle class." There have been almost no poems at all taking the opposite positions to those I have described. Most recently the reigning poetic ideology has defined itself in opposition to the despoiling of the ecology and the preservation of traditional sexual roles. Another smaller category can be described as "surrealistic"; here the object of attack is rational and linear thought, and more or less random or arbitrary images are juxtaposed. A few poems (and these are often among the strongest) attempt by fairly simple reversals of ancient myths to create a new mythology.

Much fine poetry has been written along almost all of these lines. However, the paucity of range should already be apparent; and if we turn to the basic canons of postwar poetic taste the limitations will become even more evident.

The very word "canons" gives the game away. For part of our contemporary image of poetry is that it has no canons and that it is essentially "innovative" and "experimental," that in contemporary poetry we have outgrown the myopic standards of the past and that our poetry is, must be, revolutionary. Alas, it would be closer to the truth to say that contemporary poetic taste is one of the most rigid and mandarin in history, vying for that distinction with the taste of the Augustans in the eighteenth century. One of the reasons why nobody has attacked the contemporary canons is that very barrier of mystification which is set up by those claims of innovativeness, "openness," and revolution. The most difficult theory to demolish is the theory which asserts that it is no theory at all, but simply the taking of things as they are; its author need not even descend into the arena of argument.

In fact this last observation leads us conveniently into the major rule of contemporary poetic taste: in the formulation of William Carlos Williams, "No Ideas

But In Things"—a highly abstract idea in itself. Poetry must express itself only in particulars, concrete details, sensory images. In creative-writing schools, reviews, and anthologies this doctrine has been hammered home again and again. It is a little ironic to reflect that only two hundred years ago Dr. Johnson wrote:

> The business of a poet. . .is to examine not the individual, but the species; to remark general properties and large appearances; he does not number the streaks of the tulip, or describe the different shades in the verdure of the forest.

The irony is not that Johnson was wrong and our contemporary arbiters of taste are right; nor that since good poetry has been written under both rubrics, both theories are simply irrelevant, mere fashions like farthingales or bell-bottoms, though this is closer to the truth. Nor is it even that Johnson's marvellous prose *does* evoke the streaks of the tulip, whilst contemporary poetic theorizers use a jargon of impenetrable abstraction, with words like "objective," "field," "projective," "concrete," and so on, or this one from W. S. Merwin:

> A poetic form: the setting down of a way of hearing how poetry happens in words. The words themselves do not make it. At the same time it is a testimony of a way of hearing how life happens in time. But time does not make it.

It is not the abstractness of this passage that I object to, but its impenetrability. And nobody can claim that this is atypical.

The irony is that we are locked into a vocabulary, audience, tone, stereotype of the poet, notion of form, and range of genres as narrow as or even narrower than those of Dr. Johnson's, and we don't even know it. The Augustans had at least the advantage of being consistent in their adherence to a strict and limited register of "poetic" words: they did it quite consciously, and in pursuit of a cultural elegance that has some real imaginative blood in it. They outlawed "learned" words, the kind Donne used; low and common words; technical and obscure words; and the incoherent language of passion. For them details and appearances, the transiences of perception that are so brilliantly rendered in, say, the Sylphs of the *Rape of the Lock,* are only used as *examples* of corruption and frivolity.

We choose, in the same way, to outlaw the opposite class of words: those that express abstract ideas, general categories, formal and ceremonial occasions; words we use every day, cliches and adages, the language of opinion, argument, and commonsense.

Similarly, a large part of the Augustan poetic ideal was "smoothness," which is why they placed Waller on a par with Milton; and "smoothness" is largely a matter of preserving through a scrupulous and difficult meter a grammar and syntax that is unbroken, unambiguous, complex, and perfect. Grammatical incoherence in Augustan poetry is, like detail, a deliberate evocation of an unpoetic disharmony.

We do the opposite: our contemporary taste dictates the reduction of grammar to its most inchoate and ambiguous, the removal of syntagmata and the systematic attempt to avoid the sound that a subordinate clause or accusative absolute makes when we speak it aloud. The latter are for *us* the unpoetic, the "prosaic."

The Augustans wrote for an audience (not entirely an *actual* one) which was conceived of as cultured, aristocratic, economically unembarrassed, and tacitly agreed on the virtues of social and moral order, decency, and commonsense.

Our poets profess (as our taste dictates they should)

to be writing for everyone—poetry for the migrant worker, the taxi-driver, the school child, the miner included. Hence the lavishly-funded state programs for poetry in the schools, regional poetry centers, poetry and jazz (just when jazz ceased to be a popular form, alas), poetry in pubs and shopping-centers, "dial-a-poem" or poster-poems displayed in public transport. We have been taken in by our own rhetoric. Actually the real audience for poetry is the self-doubting and sometimes self-despising middle class against which so much of it is ideologically aimed; and its effect is sometimes that delicious masochistic twinge which is the peculiar invention of the affluent second half of the twentieth century—"How alienated I am from my true sexual/cultural/natural roots, and how guilty I am for helping to destroy them." The class that our poets write for is just as limited as the audience of the Augustans, though unlike them we deny it. Moreover, the middle class has *always* despised itself, always hankered after aristocratic hauteur or proletarian or peasant vigor; the more our poets excoriate the middle class, the more surely they prove themselves to be in and of it.

The conventional Augustan tone was so internally coherent it is difficult to name; public, ironic, sometimes malicious, convinced of its own sufficiency of judgment, appealing to a consensus of civilized beings and fundamentally, with a sort of bitter sigh, asserting in a venal world the stoic values of decency, endurance and incorruptibility.

The conventional tone of our poetry is just as strictly defined. To put it unkindly, it is a sort of tough coyness which we like to think of as irony; and a hushed, desperate attempt to sound tender. There are other elements: the conscious sense of belonging to a movement (the Black Poets, the Beats, the Black Mountain School; in England, the Movement itself, the Liverpool

Poets; or *not* belonging to a movement; the sense, in confessional poetry, of shocking less experienced and enduring souls with a terrible frankness; the detachedness, or involvedness, of the poet (remarkably resembling each other); and above all an *enlistment* of the reader against an imagined status quo (which is often, in fact, fondly supportive of the rebellious poet).

The relationship between public and private is also just as restrictive (though completely reversed) as those of the Augustans. Augustan poetry is full of opinions, polemic, convictions; but (except in the deepest sense, where it is, perhaps, though unconsciously, the most psychologically revealing of any poetry) it rigorously excludes the inner feelings, struggles, self-doubts and self-hatreds of the poet. What had the private Dryden or Pope to do with his actual *work*? Even their domestic verse epistles give nothing away to a reader who craves an answering voice to his own existential and psycho-sexual inadequacies.

As for our poetry, we pride ourselves on our "honesty," on the extent that we out-confess other poets, and lacerate ourselves more thoroughly than the next. Plath and Sexton played a sort of poetic version of "chicken," with its usual results. But any hint of a poet's public *opinions, convictions,* or polemic in support of them is labeled unpoetic or dishonest; as if we really spent all our time agonizing, and none of it, say, reading the newspaper, gossiping, arguing about local rights and wrongs, or acting on the basis of principle; or as if the latter were merely a public disguise for the former. The result is a strange metamorphosis: the most private thing in contemporary poetry is what the poet thinks, while the most public is what he feels. If the unconscious is made conscious, the conscious becomes unconscious. Dig into an Augustan poem and one can find fantastic anal-sexual perversions; dig into a modern confessional poem and one will find the opinion section of *The New York Times*.

There is one exception to the preceding description: and that is certain public issues which are accepted as so safely shocking that we need not fear the accusation of dishonesty in writing poetry about them, "obviously" we all feel organically connected to them. Examples are Ecology, the plight of the Blacks, Indians, and Women. The predicament of a hypothetical public poet who found these issues boring and misconceived would be unenviable; he or she would have to face being thought of as a moral monster, or else keep his or her mouth shut entirely. On the other hand, someone who thought about those issues seriously would similarly have no poetic forum in contemporary taste to argue out the prose and cons, since argument requires coherent and complex syntax, and the latter is more or less forbidden.

The *formal* demands of current poetic taste are similarly as limited as those of the Augustans. Indeed, it is here that their kinship and oppositeness may most clearly be seen. The great meter of the Augustans was the heroic couplet: the most closed of all poetic forms. The couplet demands absolute clarity of thought, and more important, clarity of relevance. One has to know—the form *makes* the poet know—exactly what is being said, what point one is at in the argument, what is the point of the argument, what has just been said and what is next going to be said. More than this, the couplet is so artificial a form that the only possible voice the poet can use is a *mask* of greater or lesser formality, a fictional self corresponding to the metrical fiction.

The "open" forms characteristic of our last few decades are even more constricting, however. There is only *one* voice a poet can ever use in an open form. His own.

All the masks are denied to the modern poet, for
instead of having at his disposal the rhythms and tones
of other eras, and a repertoire of contemporary poetic
stances, he has only one, which is his own. "Honesty"
in its cant sense is the tritest of all masks; and *true*
honesty the final and most artificial of all the creations of a great poet. In a sense the contemporary poet
does not have even his own voice, for the regular and
even unconscious elision of syntagmata in contemporary poetry breaks down many of those little lifts, runs
and drops that make a human voice. The poet's predicament is somewhat like that of the pre-Petrarchan
poets of the early sixteenth century in England, the
"leaden" poets, experimenters like ourselves, doomed,
because of the lack of the metrical fictions later brought
over by Wyatt and Surrey and perfected by Sidney, to
wildly strained but always recognizable versions of their
own voice. Gascoigne is a good example—it is significant that he has recently been most unjustly admired.

Part of the problem is that if one says in a poem
simply what one thinks is one's own voice, unassisted
by meter, it usually sounds obvious or silly. Taking
out words like "the" "but" "so" "if," etc., makes it sound
a little less silly but rather hard to understand. In a
further attempt at making it interesting, our hypothetical poet (alas, not hypothetical enough), simply com-
plicates—inserting odd paraphrases, far-fetched syno-
nyms, and purely private associations. The poem loses
its obviousness and apparent silliness. but has become
impenetrably obscure, and nobody except poetry editors, critics, and other poets, who have a taste for this
sort of thing, is interested in reading it. Now meaning, it seems to me, exists on the border between sense
and nonsense. If run-of-the-mill Augustan poetry is mere
sense given a bounce by meter, the ordinary poetry of
our age is nonsense which pretends to sense. Meter in

poetry helps to provide the boundary between sense and nonsense, by expanding our tolerance for oddity and obviousness. Without meter, current poetry is often doomed to triteness or incomprehensibility. Perhaps there are two kinds of thinking: the rational kind, which can deal only with small amounts of high-probability information and arrange them in a narrow repertoire of ways, which arrangements remain stable once formed; and the intuitive, which deals with vast quantities of half-apprehended, low-probability information, arranging it in a shifting variety of configurations according to whatever laws the material itself seems to suggest. Meter helps us pass through the gates of horn from the first to the second, and convinces us that we are not hearing nonsense, but oracles.

Not that I am advocating a return to strict meter. Rather, meter should be at least the norm of poetry, which we keep in mind as we write, rather as a ship's compass guides the ship even when it is not bound for the North Pole itself. With meter a poet can explode into all those selves and fictions he yearns for, and which, in our age, he often lacks so badly that he murders himself out of starvation for them.

Of course there were many poets (Berryman, Plath, Ransom, Thomas, and others) who used meter or at least referred to it. Not all Augustans stuck to the heroic couplet. Our metrical problems are as much a symptom as a cause of our poetic malaise, and I use them as a focus and surrogate of other ills.

Up to this point I have used the comparison of Augustan poetic expectations in order to demonstrate the narrowness of our own. However, there is one area where we are even more restricted that they: in the "image" of the poet. Augustan poets came in all shapes and sizes, and in several shades of political-moral-religious opinion. With us, a poet must fit an iron mold.

He or she must have inherited a large dose of the romantic image; however, in our besetting fear of embarrassment, this image has been understated and reunderstated until it is almost impossible for a human being to sustain. Even the flamboyance of a Dylan Thomas or an Allen Ginsburg is just one more twist of self-deprecation. Next, all contemporary poets of note are out of sympathy with the dominant movement and themes of middle-class culture; the majority from the point of view of the political left, with a scattering of the equally malcontent on the right. Furthermore all contemporary poets are required to be able to demonstrate some credentials of anti-intellectualism: at least a contempt for technology and the exact sciences, and an ignorance of contemporary philosophy; at best, and especially in America, a complete oblivion to cultural and intellectual history, the fine arts, and literature before 1920. Generally speaking contemporary poets are supposed to regard the enterprise of at least *western*, if not *all* high culture, as a disastrous failure. It is as if through a sort of cultural and social nonconformity a poet can achieve that genuine artistic nonconformity called originality; but too often the former is a *substitute* for the latter.

II

At this point it would be well to clarify the purpose and explain the method of this polemic. It is a polemic, first of all; that is, it is concerned to take one side of the issue and is not intended as a balanced view. Secondly, it is a polemic that is directed not at an individual or group of individuals but at a climate of taste. A climate of taste is the sort of cultural-metaphysical entity that need possess no actual foundation: take, for instance, the case of a roomful of people, each of whom individually wishes to drop into an informal tone with the others, but at the same time feels that the others wish to preserve formal decorum. Nobody wishes to be formal, yet everybody is so because they think the others wish it. The collective opinion of what others think has taken on an active reality of its own. Such an entity, though it has no ground, can be tremendously powerful. Thirdly, this polemic is actuated by a profound sense of indignation on behalf of the dead poets who could no longer put up a fight against this powerful metaphysical entity and who took their own lives as a result; and is intended to suggest to the survivors that there are still great and challenging poetic possibilities, if we are not afraid of those first moments of embarrassment and shame when we confront each other with our real creative powers for the first time. This polemic is even an attempt to persuade those poets who may already have concluded that suicide is the only aesthetically honorable course for a poet to take, that they may be wrong, that there are virtues in survival.

It may have been noticed that I have given hardly any specific living examples of the attitudes I describe, and that I have not noted the exceptions. I am not concerned, as I have said before, to attack individual poets or even critics, but to defend them against an enemy that has already got partly within their walls; and the exceptions know themselves and need no help of mine. It is enough for me if the condition I describe is *recognized*; it needs in itself no argument by example, any more than does the recognition of the pattern in the carpet. I am presenting not a set of cases but a point of vantage; and my attitude towards contemporary poets is not contempt but admiration for having achieved so much in the teeth of so huge a misapprehension as one under which we suffer.

What is this misapprehension? Part of it is, of course, the old Romantic predicament. Let me paraphrase from Coleridge in Frost at Midnight: if the eave-drops of dynamic process fall, they are lost; but if the secret ministry of poetry hangs them up in silent icicles, they are no longer dynamic or processual. If the matter of poetry is experience, the poet has used himself up both as poet and as human being as soon as that experience is exhausted. Wordsworth in *The Leech-Gatherer* contemplates the "mighty poets in their misery dead"— he fears for himself the fate of Chatterton, the marvellous boy. Unfortunately he did not have the resolution and independence to declare himself as a challenger to nature, and therefore his creative powers could never take on the inexhaustibleness of nature's. Passion that is "recollected in tranquillity" rather than invented for, and in, the work of art itself, will run out eventually. Many poets in our century "ran out" too—Eliot and Ransom are major examples. Ransom had the grace to admit it.

But the great twentieth-century paradigm of truth is not process but relationship, field, structure. Philosophically this change was necessary: but poetically it was very dangerous, for we never really discarded the basic conception of the work of the poet as mimesis. Instead of imitating process, a poet must now imitate relationship, structure, field.

To imitate, for the poet who believes in concrete imagery, is essentially to reify, to translate back into a language whose essential philosophic premise is that the world is made of things, a perception that is now not of things or even processes but sheer pattern. This is what "no ideas but in things" means. It is a recipe for poetic impotence; it is also absolutely reactionary in aesthetic terms. Our notion of what we reason about is Einsteinian, but our notion of how we reason is Aristotelian. T. S. Eliot in his last major poem, *Four Quartets*, said that every poem is an epitaph: the poem freezes into thingness a great swathe of the field of his life. The problem is something like that of the early quantum physicists who were constrained to render into objective Daltonian atomic terms a phenomenon that was not safely objective and which contradicted entirely the language in which it was expressed. To "split the atom" is literally a contradiction in terms: etymologically it is not simply impossible, but nonsense. It is only when we realize that all science is also partly technology, that is, that there is no pure knowing, for all knowing involves doing, that the contradiction ceases to paralyze us. The atom becomes splittable when we split it. Scientists do not just imitate nature, they create it. Scio, ergo ago. Epistemology is not just ontology, but also creation. We cannot be passive receivers of information, for we cannot render information received in that fashion into any form we already know. However, there is one way of avoiding the scientific problem of the nature of reality: by resorting to a purely mathematical description of reality. This is to attempt to substitute the method of representation for the understanding which is the purpose of representation: roughly equivalent to eating pieces of paper with the word "food" written on them.

And it is precisely this predicament that faces contemporary poetry and poets. On one hand, the nature of the reality is such that to represent it in terms of "things" is to make nonsense of it; on the other, to represent it in pure verbal patterns—the equivalent of mathematics—is to violate the essential character of language and understanding. Broadly speaking these two alternatives describe the two main streams of contemporary poetry: one which by sheer force of "concrete" imagery attempts to break through the endless webs of relation and appearance; and another which, by attempting to reproduce those webs in the intricacies of language , loses touch with the comprehension of the reader—and also, perhaps, of the poet himself.

A catalogue of the ways in which contemporary poets have attempted to cope with this dilemma would usefully illustrate the nature of the dilemma itself.

One way is by writing poems like crossword-puzzles; attempting by a finite complexity of interconnections to suggest the infinite interconnectedness of the real world. Almost all postwar, and most twentieth-century, poets have tried something of the kind. The noblest effort in this mode is surely Pound's *Cantos* which, like the greatest Augustan and Romantic poems, almost escapes the stranglehold of its own theory. On a smaller scale, the bread-and-butter poem of the magazine or anthology is of this kind. Their problem is that New Critical or Structuralist methods of exegesis have kept pace with, and, indeed, outstripped the ingenuity of such poems: if they *have* a logic, professional academic explicators, supported by huge sums of government and private money, organized in a concerted effort, and with much more time to spend on it than the poet himself, will uncover that logic; and will often uncover more than was consciously put in in the first place. The complication of the poem, once exhausted, no longer reminds us of the complication of the world and is useful only as an object of interest, like a pretty bit of broken machinery on the mantel—a conversation piece. William Carlos Williams' description of a poem as a machine made of words dooms poems to the fate of machinery—obsolescence. In any case, if the poem is complicated enough to please the critic, it will be too complicated for the patience of the general reader; and if it is simple enough for the reader, he will feel ashamed for liking what the critic finds inadequate grist for his exegetical mill. Perhaps the whole myth of poet, reader and critic that the "crossword-puzzle" poem implies needs to be replaced if these problems are to be overcome. A poet cannot simply be a constructor of clever toys for critics.

Another recourse of the contemporary poet, embedded in a medium or vocabulary that is fundamentally contaminated with "modern mimetic" theory, is to attempt to *be* the primitive myth-maker that is demanded by one strain of contemporary theory. Myths, if they are to be truly "mythical," must be unselfconscious, static, humorless, conservative, devoted to mapping the conceptual world of their culture in a single structure that warns us of its boundaries and neutralizes its conflicts. Myth has now been shown to embody a pure structure of determinate transformations; crudely by Fraser and his followers, more rigorously by the structuralists. It is no coincidence that myth has always been of the profoundest interest to contemporary critics, for in this conjunction the apostles of the purified mimesis of form discovered the original maps that made sense of the world by closing it off.

Thus when the contemporary poet tries to be a myth-maker, he attempts to imitate the shamans or spirit-doctors of more "primitive" phases of human culture. He achieves mystical states by the use of mescal and peyote, he pretends to be a man of the earth, or he tries to find roots in a place or class, or with the original dwellers of the place he lives in—Celts or Indians—or with some contemporary popular cult or craze. Some of them, potentially the most creative, *invent* cults and crazes to become part of—like the Beats, for instance. Such poets compare their own impotence unfavorably with the vigor of folk art and music, "primitive" chants, and so on.

However, it is fairly obvious that for an educated bourgeois (which is what more contemporary poets are) such a course of behavior can only ever be a sort of emotional tourism, a pleasant but finally unproductive nostalgia. He is attempting to do the impossible, like trying *not* to think about something, for instance— that is, to become naive, a bricolleur, responding to obscure and unconscious psycho-socio-cultural forces to which he has, as a poet, a peculiar sensitivity. He is trying to be unconscious of what he comes to know in the region of consciousness. It is an attempt at a kind of intellectual suicide (often accompanied by an ostentatious anti-intellectualism); but intellectual suicide can never be entirely successful unless accompanied by its physical counterpart.

A sub-class of these poets is composed of those who try to attain the "insight" of children, animals, the insane; and therefore to justify the critic's amused condescension to the poet which the theory demands. For since poetry is the mimesis of the forms of the world, the exegete is a sort of super-poet who develops the subtle structures of exegesis out of the cruder ones of poetry.

Like these, but actuated by different motives, are those contemporary poets who, dimly recognizing the ignominy of the poet's position (despite the superficial adulation of him), have rejected the Western intellectual-aesthetic tradition altogether. The anti-intellectualism of this group is more genuine than that of those

I have discussed earlier, since it is an attempt to not play the intellectuals' game, rather than to adopt the position of the non-intellectual *within* their game. But together with the greater personal integrity of the latter group goes a corresponding alienation from their intellectual and artistic heritage, a consequent impoverishment of their art, and a greater logical inconsistency of position. For to be consistent they must reject *all* theories; yet this rejection is itself based on and constitutes the enactment of a theory. Moreover, later generations of poets trained by these rebels do not possess the unconscious structures, which their elders still found meaning in rebelling against, and are often simply boorish, ignorant, and more or less random in their poetic practice. Only one generation of iconoclasts is possible at a time.

Another way of coping with the subtle double-binds of our contemporary notion of art is a retreat to a polite, small poetry which recapitulates and defuses current aesthetic perceptual and psychic fashions. Much contemporary British poetry is of this stripe; it is the most dignified, if among the least adventurous of responses, and it protects the poet's human personality from the potentially ravaging effects of our aesthetics. It produces nice poems (and there is no irony in "nice") whose effect is pleasurable in much the same way as a salad *aux fines herbes* can be. Indeed, if it has the effect of reconciling the bourgeoisie to itself, it will be performing a valuable service. But that greatest of all social classes, the middle class, needs more than an apology; it needs a sense of its own splendor, a mission, an ideal of itself as heroic in its own way as the one Homer provided for his Akhaian aristocrats with flowing hair.

III

It is now time for an excursion into the aesthetics of class. I am not going to *argue* what follows; if the reader recognizes its truth, argument is unnecessary, and if he doesn't, I believe the ideological commitments on this question are so strong that mere argument will have little effect. What I propose is that the aristocracy never had time or inclination for the creation of important enduring art—the artistic geniuses among them tended, because they were economically able to do so, to make *themselves* into works of art, and they are dead. The more radical side of my proposal is that the working classes are also more or less artistically sterile. For a member of the proletariat to become an artist is for him to cease being a member of the proletariat. Given our contemporary aesthetic theory, in which the middle class, the self-conscious class, is prevented by its own nature from creating great art, the following pattern tends to occur with those artistic geniuses who survive a working-class background: they express, at the moment of saying farewell to it, the rigors of their prior inarticulate experience; are acclaimed by bourgeois critics and readers; find themselves incapable of further work; attempt by self-pastiche to regain their artistic innocence; fail; and are then accused of being corrupted by their success.

The great writers of the past were all members of the middle classes. The middle classes, by which I mean that portion of society ranging from skilled artisans to professional people and owners of small business concerns, have produced almost all the noteworthy achievements of mankind. They are like the modest mammals of the natural world, whose destiny it was to supersede the much more impressive dinosaurs, with their splendid scales and feathers, and give birth to the masterpiece of the animal kingdom, man; who is justified in his claim to be nature's masterpiece by the simple fact that no other species is even capable of knowing what a masterpiece *is*. If this remark seems ethnocentric (or rather genocentric?), it can be justified by appealing to nature itself; all species are concerned solely with their own survival and aggrandizement, and it would be unnatural for us to be different. And as with our species, so with our class.

I feel here the resistance of an immensely solid and unconscious habit of thought: that habit which is peculiar to our half-century, a fear of cultural and even genotypical hubris; a fear of putting too much importance on one's own viewpoint, a fear deriving from that kind of relativism which does not recognize that it denies itself, for the statement "everything is relative" is, by its own admission, also relative. The "habit of thought" to which I refer is a broader social version of the aesthetic theory I have described, that theory which sees the world as so complete that the artist can only imitate it. What do I, as poet, have to say that nobody else can say? All statements have structure; structure is everything, then why is my statement better or more interesting than any other? What does my class have to say, since the most significant utterances are those of which I have no analytic consciousness, and my class is the analytic class? What does my society have to say, since there are other societies and everything is relative? What does my species have to say, the ecology-destroying species, the species that breaks the natural relationships of the world, those relationships which must be the substance of my saying?

To ask these questions is indeed an act of courage for a poet; but there is a last act of courage that even the most adventurous poets of our time do not seem able to attain: the courage to go ahead with the personal, cultural, human enterprise despite the realization of its arbitrariness, its absurdity: the courage to accept that all our utterances must be self-validating, must vouch for themselves, must insist of the truth of their view of the world without appeal to any absolute standard or ground. Only a true *poetic* conception of the nature of art can offer justification for such courage; without it the courage is arrogance or foolishness.

Thus a poetry which *glorifies* (and glorification, the according of values to the previously undervalued, is one of the great purposes of poetry)—which glorifies itself, its writer, the class whose consciousness gave it birth, the culture, the species of its begetting—is what we lack, and what, I argue, we desperately need.

This question also has political dimensions. Many bourgeois artists feel that the values of their culture and class were demonstrated to be monstrously evil by the phenomena of Nazism and capitalist imperialism. Actually Nazism was in part a reaction *by* the bourgeoisie *against* the values of the bourgeoisie: it invoked racial passions and focused its hatred on the Jews, who made up the most prominently bourgeois and traditionally self-conscious elements of German society, a scapegoat for all the bourgeois sins. Those who despise the liberal hardworking educated family man with a small business or profession find themselves with strange bedfellows. Communism, like its more native counterpart, National Socialism, similarly sees the bourgeoisie as its enemy; and where Communism has taken root, poetry has usually died out, except where the occasional nonconformist earned the notoriety of survival. Communism and Nazism seek for grounds and justification in inchoate, sub-personal forces (racial or class loyalty), desiring the certainty that they perhaps imagine "primitives" to possess.

As for Capitalism, it is highly doubtful that it exists at all in any sense in which it can be distinguished from any other form of economic organization. In its broad form it seems to be synonymous with "economic organization"; in its narrow sense it involves a curious reduction. If capitalism is "the private control of the means of production," and if production means, presumably, "creation," and if creation means "the conferring of value," and if the chief "means" of conferring value is, as we know it to be, the human mind, then all societies, to the extent that people own their own minds, are capitalist. The word "Capitalism" is really just the most successful way yet devised to make creativity a sin. Self-proclaimed "anti-capitalists" are really trying to stamp it out altogether.

Of *course* creativity is a threat. It changes the world, it is the hardest (perhaps the only) work imaginable, and it creates new ratios of value. "Capitalists" tame it by making it despise itself; and communists try to replace it with a purely abstract, and therefore predictable, notion of historical progress, which is something like chopping down all the growing things in order to make room for Growth.

I would not have entered the weary debate between political left and political right (which will one day appear as quaint as the religious differences that divided the protagonists of the Thirty Years' War), but that its real danger to poetry needs to be re-emphasized. For poets, with their exquisite moral sensibilities, have found it incumbent on them not to do precisely what poetry must do: create value. To create value is to create desire; poetry, advertising, and propaganda are modes of production. For a highly gifted poet to export his productions to others is a form of imperialism. In a sense all interactions are economic; anyone who is moved by another to see the world in a different way is the victim of exploitation. Exploitation is the terrible gift of a *desire* from the exploiter to the exploited, that gives the giver power over the recipient. Of course, all gifts do this. And all exploitation takes place with the implicit consent of the exploited.

One solution for the poet is to create an art that *destroys* value, as "revolutionary" poets try to do. Instead of killing themselves they try to kill their society. But were they successful, they would also dry up the milieu of their own validity. Validity and success are mutually exclusive. Revolutionary poets are by definition failures. Furthermore, an art that destroys value is logically impossible, for value is a relative context, negative value is also value, and the destruction of values in one place creates unexpected values in another; but the latter may be even less to the liking of the artist than what he destroys. "Anti-art" tends to be all too successful; it creates a positive love of schlock.

Because of their creative, that is, their exploitative energies, however, poets have gone on writing, sometimes marvellous poetry; but many have felt the need to pay for their crime by the self-punishment of suicide.

Others, trusting that there is one form of forgivable exploitation, that is, self-exploitation, have cannibalistically fed their lives to their poems, ripping apart their own motives and laying bare level after level of subconsciousness, until in exhaustion they end their lives to escape their insatiable enemy. Less gifted literary people applaud as they do so, for a poet's suicide proves the dangers of the creative enterprise, as those who fear love welcome the spectacle of those who destroy themselves for love.

Others again, aware of the logical contradictions of their art, have unburdened themselves, by death, of a stymied and hopeless consciousness.

But the shifts of the poets are all ways of evading the central problem of our age, which is *time*. Suicide is only the most radical. The middle class is the class of self-consciousness, for which time is super-cyclic growth or progress; we can never return to the state of the child, the dream, the animal, the unconsciousness of simply being a member of a species; so middle-class art is the only possible art of our time.

The "modern mimetic" theory is a convenient translation of the psycho-economic problems I have described. Perhaps the foregoing also explains why the really great poets writing in English in our century have been political conservatives: Stevens, Pound, Eliot, Yeats. Since inequality did not disturb them morally, they were able to evade much of the force of our contemporary double bind. However, with the exception of Stevens and Yeats, even these poets did not emerge unscathed. Pound, in a singlehanded attempt to recreate out of the fragments of past heroic cultures a coherent sense of a modern cultural enterprise, fell for the fascist interpretation of history, which is essentially atavistic; his bugbear was usury, which is the economic foundation for the middle class. The *Cantos* do finally tail off into chaos. Eliot, perhaps realizing earlier than did Pound the fact that the old world had broken up—"these fragments I have shored against my ruin"—resorted to the certainties of religion, and, like Wordsworth, paid the price of a personal salvation that does not include an aesthetic renewal: artistic impotence.

Only Stevens and Yeats survived the deadly effects

of modern mimetic theory. Superficially Yeats, too, suscribed to several of the available accommodations to it, that I have described earlier: the vision of the poet as a naif, the anti-intellectualism (as in his very popular poem "The Scholars"), the turning with disgust from the modern affairs of men to the world of the primitive, the child, the insane, and brute nature itself.

But Yeats was never taken in by these attitudes: they were the materials his time offered him, and he used them. What is important is that throughout his life he held to the conviction that the art of poetry is an act of poiesis, that the goal of the poet was not truth but the glorious fiction, that, far from penetrating to the naked reality of things, he was giving the poor bare forked animal splendid clothes whose beauty he might put on with their power. The golden bird is an artifice, a handiwork, that scorns common bird or petal. And if one cited, say, "The Circus Animals' Desertion" as an example of his coming down from his high horse and admitting the truth, even here he has the hauteur to recognize how trashy the mere truth is. Yeats never ceased telling stories, putting on masks, inventing fictions; Eliot, on the other hand, abandoned them in his poetry after the marvellous Sweeney poems. *Prufrock* is a paralyzed story. Perhaps *Practical Cats* and the plays were an attempt to return to the vitality of fiction; but the former are clearly not serious, the invention is hedged and apologized for by its format; and the latter are so heavily loaded with *moral* truth that they can barely carry themselves. But Yeats to his dying day went on inventing; and even his great cosmologies and historical schemata were recognized by him as fictions. Fictions are nascent facts, however; when one tries to tell the truth, it eludes one, but when, as Yeats did, one spins fables with sufficient conviction, they become the truth.

In one respect, however, Yeats did not need to face the problems of the twentieth-century poet. Yeats was brought up amid a still-vital peasant culture, was later accepted by the traditional aristocracy, and because of the peculiar circumstances of Ireland's colonial status, the mediocrity of its middle class could be blamed on the demoralizing effects of British rule. Moreover, this middle class was ennobled by revolution:

> I write it out in verse—
> MacDonagh and MacBride
> And Connolly and Pearse
> Now and in time to be,
> Wherever green is worn,
> Are changed, changed utterly:
> A terrible beauty is born.

Although the equation of the Irish revolution with the siege of Troy did not work, it could at least be made.

We are still faced with the poetic paradox of needing to write for a class that is demoralized and which wallows in its demoralization, while owning up to the fact that we belong to that class. Perhaps one avenue of hope is the poetry of Wallace Stevens: an insurance man, maker of fictions, committed to his species, his class, and his personal consciousness, prepared to deal with scientific, religious and philosophical questions in his poetry; a master of metre. Nevertheless Stevens had his work cut out clearing a space for poetry and initiating the rudiments of a poetic program: the flowering of the new Renaissance that we need is yet to come.

Dick Allen is the author of four books of poetry including *Flight and Pursuit* and *Overnight in the Guest House of the Mystic*, a National Book Critics Circle Award nominee. The recipient of a National Endowment for the Arts Fellowship and an Ingram-Merrill Fellowship in poetry, his poems and essays appear regularly in such magazines as *The New Yorker, Poetry, The New Criterion*, and *The Hudson Review*. In 1989 he guest-edited the special issue of *Crosscurrents* on Expansive Poetry.

Bruce Bawer is the author of three books, the most recent of which is *Diminishing Fictions* (Graywolf, 1988), a collection of criticism about the modern American novel. A regular contributor to *The New Criterion*, he has published essays and reviews in such places as *The American Scholar, Commentary, The Nation,* and *Connoisseur;* his poems have appeared in *Poetry, Boulevard,* and *The Hudson Review*, as well as in a chapbook entitled *Innocence* (Aralia Press, 1989). His critical study *The Middle Generation* was selected by *Choice* magazine as one of the Outstanding Academic Books of 1987.

Lynn Emanuel is an Associate Professor at the University of Pittsburgh. She is the author of *Hotel Fiesta*. She has received an NEA Fellowship and has been a member of the Literature Panel for the National Endowment for the Arts. Her poems have appeared in *The Hudson Review, Ploughshares,* and *The Kenyon Review*. A native of New York City, she is currently a member of the Pennsylvania Council on the Arts' Literature Panel, from which she has received three Fellowships.

Rita Dove grew up in Akron, Ohio. A presidential scholar in 1970, she attended Miami University, received a Fulbright Fellowship to study modern European literature at the University of Tübingen, Germany, and earned an M.F.A. at the University of Iowa. Currectly teaching at the University of Virginia, she has received fellowships from the Guggenheim Foundation and the National Endowment for the Arts, among other honors. Her books include *Fifth Sunday* (short stories), *The Yellow House on the Corner, Museum, Thomas and Beulah*, which won the 1987 Pulitzer Prize, and *Grace Notes*.

Frederick Feirstein is a psychoanalyst in New York City. The first of his four books of poetry, *Survivors*, was selected as an

Outstanding Book of 1975 by the American Library Association. His fifth, *City Life*, a collection of narrative and dramatic poems, will be published by Story Line Press in 1991. He has been the recipient of a Guggenheim Fellowship in poetry, a CAPS Fellowship, the John Masefield Prize from the Poetry Society of America, and a Quarterly Review of Literature Colladay Award for his book-lenth poem *Family History*.

Dana Gioia is a businessman in New York. He is the author of *Daily Horoscope*, the editor of *The Ceremony and Other Stories by Weldon Kees*, co-editor (with William Jay Smith) of *Poems from Italy: A Comprehensive Bilingual Anthology of Italian Verse.*, and co-editor (with Michael Palma) of *New Italian Poets* (1991 Story Line Press). He has recently edited *Formal Introductions*, an anthology of New Formalist poems. In 1984 *Esquire* chose Gioia for their first register as "One of the Best of the New Generation: Men and Women Under 40 Who Are Changing America." With Robert McDowell, he is currently editing an anthology of new narrative poems to be published by Story Line Press.

Mark Jarman's fourth book of poetry, *The Black Riviera*, was published in 1990 by Wesleyan University Press. He has received numerous awards in poetry, including two National Endowment for the Arts Fellowships, the Joseph Henry Jackson Award, a Sotheby's International Award, and a Pushcart Prize. Since 1980, he has been the co-editor of *The Reaper*, a magazine devoted to the resurgence of narrative in contemporary poetry. He currently teaches at Vanderbilt University.

Robert McDowell is the author of *Quiet Money*. His criticism, fiction and poetry have appeared in such magazines as *The Hudson Review*, *The American Scholar*, *Poets & Writers*, *London Magazine*, and *Crosscurrents*. Since 1980 he has co-edited *The Reaper* and since 1985 has been the publisher of Story Line Press.

Robert McPhillips writes frequently on contemporary literature for such publications as *The Sewanee Review*, *The Washington Post*, *The Nation*, *Prairie Schooner*, *Crosscurrents*, and *American Literature*. He is a graduate of Colgate University where he was elected to Phi Beta Kappa and received his Ph.D. in English from the University of Minnesota. He currently teaches English at Iona College.

Carole Oles is the author of three books of poetry including *Night Watches: Inventions on the Life of Maria Mitchell, Quarry,* and *The Loneliness Factor.* Her poems and reviews have appeared in such magazines as *The Nation, Poetry, The Christian Science Monitor* and *The Georgia Review.* She has received Fellowships in poetry from the National Endowment for the Arts, The MacDowell Colony, Massachusetts Artists Foundation, and the Bread Loaf Writers Conference. She is the recipient of a Pushcart Prize and a Writer's Choice Award.

Frederick Pollack is the author of *The Adventure,* a book-length poem published by Story Line Press in 1986. A native of Chicago, he received his undergraduate degree from Yale University in 1967 and his M.A. from San Francisco State University in 1986. His essays and poems have appeared in such magazines as *The Hudson Review, New England Review/Breadloaf Quarterly,* and *Salmagundi.* He currently lives in Los Angeles, California, where he is working on a long poem, and a book-length essay entitled "The Intellectual in the 21st Century."

Hilda Raz has published *What Is Good* (Thorntree Press), a collection of poems, and *The Bone Dish* (State Street Press), a chapbook. Her essays and poems have been in *North American Review, American Book Review, Pennsylvania Review, The Literary Review, The Women's Review of Books, Earth's Daughters, Denver Quarterly, Poetry Miscellany* and elsewhere. An essay will appear in 1991 in *Women Who Write* from Longstreet Press. She is Editor-in-Chief of *Prairie Schooner.*

Frederick Turner is the author of twelve books, among them five books of poetry. His essay, (with Ernst Pöppel), "The Neural Lyre," won *Poetry's* Levinson prize. He is a former editor of *The Kenyon Review* and a regular contributor to *Harper's Magazine.* He is the Founders Professor of Arts & Humanities at the University of Texas at Dallas.

Marilyn Waniek teaches at the University of Connecticut and has received a Pushcart Prize, a National Endowment for the Arts Fellowship, and the Connecticut Artists Medal for her work in poetry. Her first three volumes of poetry were published by Louisiana State University Press.

ABOUT THE EDITOR

Robert McDowell is the author of a book of poetry, *Quiet Money* (Holt, 1987), and co-translator (with Jindriska Badal) of Ota Pavel's *How I Came to Know Fish* (Story Line, 1990). With Mark Jarman, he is the founder and editor of *The Reaper* magazine. His poetry, essays, reviews, and fiction appear regularly in magazines in the United States, England, and Australia.